Gentleman of Japan

NOTES

FROM

A JOURNAL OF RESEARCH

INTO THE

NATURAL HISTORY

OF THE

COUNTRIES VISITED

DURING THE

VOYAGE OF H.M.S. SAMARANG,

UNDER THE COMMAND OF

CAPTAIN SIR EDWARD BELCHER, C.B., F.R.A.S.

BY

ARTHUR ADAMS, R.N., F.L.S.,

Member of the Royal College of Surgeons of London, and
of the Entomological Society of Stettin.

Rediscovery Books

Reproduced by kind permission of the
Royal Geographical Society

Published by
Rediscovery Books Ltd
Unit 10, Ridgewood Industrial Park,
Uckfield, East Sussex,
TN22 5QE England
Tel: +44 (0) 1825 749494
Fax: +44 (0) 1825 765701
www.rediscoverybooks.com

This edition © Rediscovery Books Ltd 2006

Published in association with

Royal Geographical Society with IBG

Advancing geography and geographical learning

In reprinting in facsimile from the original, any imperfections are inevitably reproduced and the quality may fall short of modern type and cartographic standards.

"look who list thy gazeful eyes to feed
With sight of that is fair, look on the frame
Of this wyde universe, and therein read
The endless kind of creatures which by name
Thou canst not count, much less their natures aime,
All which are made with wondrous wise respect,
And all with admirable beauty deckt."

SPENCER; *Hymn on Heavenly Beauty.*

CHAPTER I.

CAPE DE VERDS.—CAPE OF GOOD HOPE.—JAVA.

Porto-Praya—A Rainbow—Aspect of the Village—Negro Children—The Lion-ant—Vegetation of Santiago—The Bird of Pharaoh—The Fishing Eagle of Africa—The Gecko—Splendid Sun-set—Leave Porto-Praya—The Petrels—The Dolphin—Jelly-fish—Beautiful Physalia—Double the Cape—*Simon's Bay*—Scenery—Vegetation—The Honey-suckers—The Fishing Cormorant—Reptiles—The Sand-mole—The Long-eared Fox—Singular habits of a Beetle—Insects fertilizing Flowers—Leave Simon's Bay—Eve on the Indian Ocean—Habits of the Pteropods—The *Straits of Sunda*—Transparent Crustaceans—Fecundity of the Ocean—Remarkable Crabs—*Welcome Bay*, Java—Scenery—Natives—Habits of the Plantain Squirrel—The Walking-leaf Insect—The Carrier-Trochus—Animal of Marginella.

AFTER a somewhat tedious and protracted voyage across the Atlantic, we anchored at Porto Praya, in the island of St. Jago, on the 3rd of March, 1843. The first incident that occurred to me on landing, was getting stung in the hand by a large hymenopterous insect, a species of *Pepsis*. A splendid double rainbow which just then made its appearance, soon, however, diverted my attention from that painful circumstance, for, with a high and noble arc, this "airy child of vapour and the sun" spanned the firmament, one end buried in the ocean, and the other lost behind the rugged mountains of St. Jago. On strolling through the village, nothing, at first sight, amused me so much as the astonishing number of little, pot-bellied, naked children, sprawling about the sandy thoroughfares; groups of young, black girls, dressed up in gaudy shawls, and, in many cases, smoking short pipes, contributed materially to the strangeness of the scene; while itinerant fruit-venders, ugly negroes "things of shreds and patches", shouting their unintelligible jargon, put the finishing touch to the picture. The doctrines of Malthus appear here to be utterly disregarded, and the place literally swarms with children. The negro-mother bears her living burden on her hip, supported by a broad and padded band, one of the urchins' legs being before and one behind. The countenance of these young Ethiops is most amusing and grotesque; they are always very solemn in their look, and their sloe-black eyes gleam keenly all around, save when you notice or caress them, when they hide their tiny heads in apprehension and alarm. Before they well can hobble on their legs, the heavens form their only roof and God their only safeguard. Often have I seen them sprawling on the ground, licked by dogs, pawed by playful cats, kicked by careless goats, and sometimes sorely pecked by saucy fowls; covered with dust, and scrambling on its belly, the little creature strains and giggles, striving to approach its mute companions,—poor thing, as mute itself and helpless as the worst of them!

Strolling along the beach I noticed the large, hideous Sea-slug (*Aplysia*), and the cunning *Octopus*, the manners of which are described in such a very amusing vein by Darwin.

Some parts of the sandy plains of St. Jago are covered with the ingenious pit-falls of the Lion-ant (*Myrmecleon formicarius*), and I observed that the crowd of little, naked negro-children who were collecting for me, always repeated a peculiar humming kind of song as they scratched the larvæ of this cruel tiger of the insect-world from the sand with their fingers; no doubt a kind of ditty similar to that repeated by English children, when they watch the Lady-bird take flight from their finger.

Mr. Darwin, whose delightful narrative must always be read with interest and pleasure, has justly described the usual desolate appearance of this island, but I think he has hardly done justice to its yet remaining vegetation. In the course of my rambles, even in the vicinity of Porto Praya, I was much struck by the aspect of many plants, although my eye, not then being accustomed to tropical forms, might have viewed them with an interest too earnest and partial. For, although the island of St. Jago, of a volcanic origin, is covered with a dry and barren soil, yet there may be seen plantations of Coco-Nuts, Plantains, and Tamarinds, with the Pandanus and Palmyra Palms, besides Orange, Fig, and Lemon trees, and Pine-apple plants. Near the village of Ribeira-Grande, I noticed the beautiful and elegant *Melia Azederach*, with its lively panicles of lilac flowers, and small olive-like fruit.

The *Aloes*, growing here in large masses, have a very pretty effect when their blossoms are expanded, and, among their large yellow spikes of bell-shaped corollas, many singular small species of *Coleoptera* were found. The *Batatas edulis* is met with nearly wild, and, as it trails along the ground, its large, red, infundibuliform flowers relieve the sterile aspect of the landscape, the sombre effect of which is further enlivened by the gaudy yellow petals of the Cotton plant (*Gossypium herbaceum*). A splendid species of *Asclepias* rewarded our research, though it appeared to be very uncommon, and a pretty little labiate flower, the *Ajuga Iva*, was found in considerable numbers, which yielded, when pressed, a very agreeable odour of musk, and was hence formerly named *Tencrium Moschatum*. The *Datura Tatula*, though originally a native of Portugal, grows wild, and is a violent narcotic poison, and might be substituted for Strammonium in the practice of medicine; another species, *Datura Metel*, with a very large and splendid white corolla, is also very common. The Castor-oil plant (*Ricinus communis*) with its glaucous spikes and prickly capsules, seems to thrive here, as in most other barren places in the tropics, although the oil is not valued by the natives; the negro children, however, seem very fond of the kernels, which are agreeable to the taste and not purgative.* The *Cucumis Colocynthis* is a very common weed in St. Jago; the ripe fruit is as large as a small orange, and in the green state is intensely bitter and powerfully cathartic.

* According to Crawford the same neglect of this useful purgative is evinced throughout the Oriental Archipelago; he says, "The Castor-oil is never, I think, used medicinally by the Indian Islanders, but is the principal material used in lamps."

At St. Jago the Bird of Pharoah (*Percnopteris leucocephalus*) not only consumes offal and excrement, but preys on lizards and locusts, eternally hovering about in a vile ignoble way, after the manner of the Carrion-Crows. Its flight is very heavy, nor does it ever soar like the Eagle or the Kite. It performs the part of an useful scavenger in a country where putrefaction is so rapid. The natives of the Cape de Verds, however, do not appear to hold it in the same veneration and respect as we are told the Egyptians did of yore. Another great destroyer of the innumerable Grylli that swarm here is the pretty *Dacelo Iagoensis*, a species of Kingfisher, a very pretty slim species of *Sylvia*, and a small Hawk, very much resembling in plumage the Sparrow-Hawk.

The Fishing Eagle of Africa (*Haliæetus vocifer*) may occasionally be seen hovering about these islands. Elastic and buoyant, this agile dweller in the air mounts to soaring heights, scanning, with sharp and piercing eye, the motions of his prey below. Energetic in his movements, impetuous in his appetites, he pounces with the velocity of a meteor on the object of his wishes, and, with a wild and savage joy, tears it to pieces. His whole sense of existence is the procuring of food, and for this he is ever on the alert, ever ready to combat, to ravage, and destroy.

Numbers of a small, black, land Salamander are found concealed under the stones among the sand, and huge Locusts swarm by myriads.

The *Tarentola Delalandii*, a singular grey-coloured Gecko, is common on Quail Island, near the anchorage of Porta Praya. It is a dull, sluggish, and retiring animal, shrouding its uncouth form in dark holes and obscure corners of the rocks. It is nocturnal in its habits, shunning the garish light of day, and creeping forth at eve to seek its insect food. Although repulsive in its aspect, it is perfectly harmless, and, like all its tribe, has the power of climbing perpendicular surfaces by its broad and plaited toes.

On the 7th of March we left the Cape de Verds; a sluggish mist covered the distant mountains, and the sun, which looks very large in these latitudes, as he sank below the horizon, appeared to have burst, and, like some gigantic meteor, to have poured forth all its fire in one stupendous flame-coloured fan, or gold and crimson tail of some unheard-of bird. The great comet was visible during the night. During our passage across the Indian Ocean, I was much amused in observing the mode of flight of the Petrels. These wild and free-born denizens of the deep, seem to sport in all the consciousness of liberty. They cleave the atmosphere of their boundless home on rapid wing, soaring aloft with the lightness of a feathery cloud; they skim the surface of the deep, they float upon its bosom, and I have seen the storm-loving Petrel (*Thalassidroma pelagica*), that "wanderer of the sea", dive beneath the waters to secure its prey. They always love the troubled ocean, for then their food is more easily procured, and when the sky is lowering and the scud begins to rise, when the wind blows high and the billows are crested with foam, the Petrels are abroad.

The species differ in their modes of flight: the Giant Petrel (*Procellaria gigantea*) flies in a wild and sweeping manner, poising himself, and often remaining motionless in the air like an Eagle. The flight of the Cape Pigeon (*P. Capensis*) is erratic, and neither powerful nor rapid. There is one species as large as a Kestrel, and entirely of a sooty black; it has long powerful wings, and a rapid steady flight, like the wide sweep of some gigantic Swift; these hunt in couples, and are very wild and shy. Another, called the "Whale-bird" by the seamen, is solitary in his habits, and his sweep across the ocean is more extensive than that of other species. This, as well as *P. turtur* and *Forsteri*, describe vast circles in the air, and dart suddenly on their prey. Another wild and sprightly species is not much larger than a Lark; erratic, wavering, and rapid in its flight, it always keeps aloof from the ship, and, even more than any of the others, appears to delight in stormy weather.

During our passage the sailors were fortunate enough to catch some Dolphins, and, although the beauties of this fish when dying have been so often expatiated on, perhaps the following note, made at the time, may not be uninteresting, for I fancy that in no two Dolphins do the dying colour-changes follow precisely in the same order. The one I observed, from a grass-green, covered with round ultramarine spots, became silvery, and the green faded, while the deep blue of the dorsal fin, and golden green of the back, remained. From this, it changed to a burnished brass colour, the blue spots vanished, and were succeeded by an azure tinge on a silvery ground, followed by a dull, opaque, leaden grey. One poet has said,

> " parting day
> Dies like the Dolphin, whom each pang imbues
> With a new colour as it gasps away,
> The last still loveliest, till—'tis gone and all is grey."

There are many other fish that change colour several times before they die; I have seen species of *Pimelodus* or Cat-fish, change from a warm and glowing smalt, during the last few pangs, to a dull leaden hue, losing, at the same time, the delicate pinky tinge of the sides and abdomen. The common Sucking-fish (*Echineis Remora*) from a brown, bright, shining, blackish colour, changes, even in the water, to a leaden hue, and, as it dies, assumes a tancolour, which grows paler by degrees until it fades into a dirty white.

In calms, the South Atlantic abounds in *Acalephæ*, and much amusement may be derived, in a long sea voyage, from the observation of these beautiful organisms; for endless are the moulds in which prolific Nature has cast them. Some are shaped like a mushroom, others assume the form of a riband, others are globular, while some are circular, flat, or bell-shaped, and others again resemble a bunch of berries. Their motions are generally tardy, their sensations dull, and directed entirely to the procuring of food. They often float without any apparent animation, trusting to the winds and waves to waft them about, and to carry them their food. Some keep a little beneath the surface, and propel themselves by contracting and dilating their pellucid discs, while others, as the *Beroe*, have a rapid rotatory motion. They have been termed the "living jellies of the deep", and are endowed, in many cases, with an acrid secretion, which, irritating the skin, has also caused them to be called "Sea-nettles." There is one large species common in the Straits of Singapore, dreaded by the Malays, on account of the violence of this power. Dr. Oxley informed me that he was obliged to amputate the thumb on account of the violent inflammation, induced by this poison, in the person of a Malay fisherman.* In colour, perhaps, the most delicate is the lovely *Velella*, with its pellucid crest, its green transparent body, and fringe of purple tentacles. Specific distinctions have been taken from the form of the crest, as in *V. pyramidalis*, but I have noticed this part rounded, more or less pointed, and, in some cases, even lobed, in what I have considered the same species.

The *Velella* has been seen as far north as 40°, covering a large surface of the Pacific Ocean, and tinging the water for many miles. I have seen them covering the coasts of some of the Islands of the Meia-co-shima Group by myriads, strewing the beach for miles with their delicate, pellucid skeletons.† Sir Edward Belcher

* I have seen *Rhizostomata* off the Peninsula of Malacca swimming by in large troops, comprising many thousands of individuals, many of which measure as much as three feet in diameter. They have been found to weigh, according to Peron and Lesueur, as much as from fifty to sixty pounds. The same naturalist, speaking of these animals, observes, that "they seem extremely feeble, but fishes of large size are daily their prey."

† Professor Owen, in his nineth Hunterian Lecture, for 1843, observes that occasionally some of the singular forms of *Acalephæ* of the tropical seas are stranded on the south-western shores of England. "I have picked up on the coast of Cornwall the little *Velella*, which had

informs me that he has attempted to reduce them to isinglass, by boiling, but that they appear to be quite worthless in a commercial point of view.

The *Physalia*, or "Portuguese man-of-war", is very delicately tinted, sometimes white and pink, and sometimes of a lovely lilac, with a pale crimson crest. Byron has termed the Nautilus " the Ocean Mab, the Fairy of the Sea "; modern science has, however, dispelled the poetic illusion of " oars and aerial sails ", and altered its mode of progression altogether. The phrase of the poet will more particularly apply to the above-mentioned *Acalepha*, which rears its fragile crest above the waves in the calm regions of the tropics, and allows the gentle breeze to waft it on its course.*

Among the numerous varieties of *Physalia pelagica* found by us floating on the surface of the Indian Ocean, was one taken in trawl, of a form so peculiar, and of a colour so distinct, as to warrant its being called by a different specific name, although the form of the bladder alone is not sufficient to characterize these animals. The body of this specimen was of a delicate transparent blue, and the crest, twisted slightly on itself, was lilac, blending

been wafted thither, unable to strike its characteristic lateen sail. There also I have seen wrecked a fleet of the Portuguese men-of-war (*Physalia*), which had been buoyed by their air-bladders to that iron-bound coast."

* I observe by his Hunterian Lectures that the same idea occurred to the mind of Professor Owen. Alluding to *Velella*, he says, "one of the genera, *Velella*, has a process of the firm internal skeleton, arising from the upper surface of the body-disc, to which it is set at the same angle as the lateen-sail of the Malay coast; it is wafted along by the action of the wind upon this process, and may have been mistaken for the fabled Cephalopodic paper-sailor (*Argonauta*)."

into pink towards the summit. The vesicle was, moreover, provided with three horn-like appendages, one curved like an Ammonite, of deep Prussian-blue, with another of a smaller size projecting from it, and a third, of a green colour, situated at the opposite extremity of the vesicle. The tentacles and ovaries were of dark-indigo colour.

On the 25th of April, 1843, we were anchored in Simon's Bay. As you double the Cape, the scenery looks very uninviting to the eye of the naturalist, who views it for the first time, but as you draw nearer, the mountains grow more and more interesting. The wild and naked aspect of the almost savage scenery is much improved by woody gorges or chasms, and even on the brown sides of the mountains, coloured patches soon appear on your nearer approach, as the numerous species of heaths and composite flowers begin to be recognized, and now and then some picturesque knoll, crowned with a fantastic tree, will interpose its form, and break the monotonous outline of the landscape.

During our stay there, the deep water of the offing appeared to swarm with endless varieties of the "finny drove", and the hollows in the rocks, and the shallow ponds along the sandy shores, were full of interesting Mollusks, and curious Crustaceans. If you climb the mountains, in some of the woody thickets you may chance to hear the beautiful golden Cuckoo, uttering at intervals its short, sharp note, or you may observe large showy-looking Shrikes, darting about, busily intent on prey, lively Creepers, clinging, in sportive attitudes, to the over-hanging boughs, and the pretty Wood-pecker *(Dendrobates griseocephalus)*, climbing up and down the boughs, sounding, with his bill, the rotten portions of the tree, for there he knows he is sure to find choice morsels. For the botanist, there are many objects to attract the eye, even immediately after landing.

The *Plumbago Capensis* ornaments every cultivated patch of land at Simon's Town, relieving, by its lively blue corollas, the sombre hue of the dry and arid soil; and numerous feathery *Acacias* spring up in the centre of the town, delicate, graceful, and refreshing. The *Mesembryanthemum edule* covers the sterile grounds, and adorns the parched and sandy earth with verdure, where no other plant will grow; and the bare rocks are ornamented with moss, and variegated with a thousand different Lichens. The Ferns I gathered were most beautiful. Not very far from Simon's Town, there is a wild and rugged chasm, with a stream tumbling down the middle, rolling hurriedly in its headlong course, and scattering a refreshing moisture on everything around, where these delicate and lovely *Cryptogamia* grow in great profusion. Here the minute and fragile fronds of the *Hymenophyllum*, the curious foliage of the *Pteris*, the narrow-leaved *Blechnum*, the elegant *Adiantum*, and a rare and singular species of *Asplenium*, either with the fronds laden with sporules, or with the fructification pretty far advanced, are seen springing from the damp surface of the rocks, or waving gracefully from the fissures, like so many emerald plumes. In the immediate vicinity of the town, the silvery catkins of *Cunonia Capensis* glitter in the sunbeams, and the huge downy blossoms of the Silver tree (*Protea argentea*) attract numerous sun-birds and honey-suckers. The rich orange bells of the *Leonotus Leonora*, the showy flowers of a hundred *Ericaceæ* (the pride of the colony) and the diversified forms of the ever-changing *Proteas*, mingled with extraordinary looking *Staphelias, Myrtles, Diosmæ, Gladioli,* and *Salvias,* form together a rich and varied feast for the florist, and to the botanist, a collection of a mixed and most singularly beautiful description. In the neighbourhood of the Table Mountain, and for some considerable distance up its flanks, the character of the vegetation is very analogous to that already noticed. Magnificent *Acacias,* and majestic *Aloes,* grow at the foot of the mountain in splendid condition, elevating their showy forms far above the prickly shrubs, and lowlier plants that grow around them. The aromatic *Diosma,* the juice of which the aboriginal Hottentots mingle with the grease with which they anoint their bodies, here grows in rich abundance, scenting the very sod beneath the feet; and many a gay *Lobelia* gems the earth around.* Whole tracts are covered with luxuriant Proteaceous plants, *Apocynums, Asclepiadaceæ, Stapeleæ, Pelargoniums,* in full flower, mixed with fantastic *Euphorbias,* gay *Heaths,* succulent *Crassulaceous* plants, *Arums,* and *Lilies,* giving the dry heathy nature of the scenery a peculiar charm, quite unexpected in such an apparent waste and desolate expanse. Nor must nume-

* Among the botanical curiosities of the Cape is the long-spined *Euphorbia heptagona*, with the milk of which the Kaffirs poison their arrows; the Dill (*Anethum graveolens*) is not uncommon; and the pretty-looking Marigold (*Calendula pluvialis*), which indicates fine weather, by opening its flowers like the 'Shepherd's weather-glass', or scarlet Pimpernel (*Anagallis arvensis*) of Europe, may also be mentioned, although volumes have been written on the vegetation of the Cape.

rous delicate and ornamental *Iridaceæ*, and the fantastic blossoms of the *Orchis* tribe be passed over in silence, for various are the singular shapes that cross the path in traversing these barren plains of Africa.

The sandy parts from Simon's Town to the Table Mountain, are covered with the succulent leaves of the Fig-Marigold, which gaily disports its yellow blossoms in every direction, while *Euphorbias*, of anomalous forms, spring up around, startling the eye with the strange fantastic shapes they almost invariably assume. In short, the way of the traveller is cheered at every step by strange and brilliant flowers, and curious plants that give an air of pleasing variety to the otherwise rude wilderness of the Cape.

Among the most interesting objects that attract the eye of the naturalist, during his excursions in the vicinity of the Cape, none are more likely to interest him than the Honey-suckers and the Cormorants.

The *Nectariniæ*, or Honey-suckers, do not differ materially in their habits from the Fairy-like Sun-birds, except in clinging to boughs and stems, more after the manner of the *Certhiæ*. They stoop their heads, and insert their long and narrow beaks into the tubular corollas, to search for the honey and insects of the nectaries. From analyses of the contents of their stomachs, I ascertained that their food is always insects and honey. They are more homely and unpretending in their feathery garb, and want the vivacity and dazzling aspect of their fellow-plunderers, the *Cinnyrides*.

The Cormorant forms quite a peculiar feature in the scenery of the Cape coast. Seated on the rocks, with sundry Divers and Penguins, upright, motionless, and solemn, they remind you of some magisterial assembly in their sable robes, met together in grave and earnest conclave. The Cormorant of the Cape lays its eggs in holes, among the rocks, and the insatiate young ones, although constantly gorged by their industrious fisher-parents, yet are never satisfied, but with open beak, eager eye, and out-stretched neck, they flap their formless wings, and appear to be continually crying out "more, more"!

The Fishing Cormorants of the Cape (*Phalacrocorax Africanus*) usually unite to form large fishing parties. They wind their way, in single file, starting from the rocks along the shore, then swimming in the tranquil waters of the bays, invariably led on by some experienced and sagacious old admiral, they commence their fishing. When their pilot spies a shoal of fish he suddenly makes a vault out of the water, arching his neck, bending his body, and drawing up his legs, when diving headlong down, he is followed immediately by all his anxious adherents, who perform their somersets in precisely the same manner. The flotilla remains submerged some little time, when it rises once more to the surface, and the feathered fishers again renew their diving and plunging piscatory evolutions. During short rambles in the vicinity of the Cape, many interesting forms may be obtained by the naturalist. Among others collected by us was the *Agama hispida*, a hideously ugly Lizard, sluggish in its habits, and having a very broad body, covered with spines, a very short tail, and, as customary more or less with African animals, coloured with that tint which Schlegel emphatically calls the "colour of the desert." I have seen a variety of this *Agama* with the skin perfectly smooth, and even the tail almost entirely devoid of spines. A friend succeeded in killing a very large specimen of the *Naja nivea*, the bite of which is considered very deadly by the inhabitants of the Cape; Tortoises (I believe *Testuda geometrica* and *T. angulata*) may be procured, at certain seasons, in any numbers, by taking the trouble to climb the mountains. I have frequently picked them up in my walks, and our Surgeon, Dr. Mahon, on the roadside from Simon's Town to Cape Town, made captive a very large flat-backed Water-Tortoise (*Emys galeata*) which was fishing in a pool. It is rather remarkable that this same Tortoise is the only one, out of several dozens of Tortoises brought from the Cape, now alive in England, although from the date of his capture to the present, it has been kept almost entirely from the water.

Notwithstanding the apparently revolting smell and disgusting nature of Cockroaches, many animals, besides the little *Otocyon Lalandii*, are passionately fond of them. Several *Graculi religiosi* on board our ship were in the habit of hopping about the lower deck, greedily pursuing and devouring them. A small monkey took, likewise, great delight in seizing and masticating them, with much gusto; to say nothing of our peacocks, which were passionately addicted to their consumption. In England, as is well known, the Hedge-hog is kept for the purpose of thinning their numbers.

The Sandmole (*Bathyergus maritimus*) causes great havock in the gardens, in the vicinity of Simon's Town, undermining the parterres, and consuming the roots of the flowers. I saw several unfortunates just dug out of their burrows by a little negro boy, who informed me that he was employed by a certain old gentleman, owner of a garden in the neighbourhood, to destroy these depredators at so much per head. Although called *Zandmoll* by the colonists, it is a true Rodent, but lives under ground, and raises hillocks like the Mole of Europe, or the Tucotuco (*Ctenomys Brasiliensis*) of South America. Like that little animal, also, it renders the ground in some parts, unsafe for horses, owing to the long loose subterranean galleries it forms in the sand. Although furnished with very minute eyes, the Tucotuco is not absolutely blind, as Darwin affirms it to be. They very soon die in captivity, like the common Mole, which I could never succeed in keeping alive for any length of time. The skeleton of the *Bathyergus* reminds one somewhat of that gigantic extinct quadruped the *Megatherium*, but of course on a diminutive scale.

A large species of *Ateuchus*, a kind of Beetle, is common in the sandy roads about the Cape. You will see it, frequently, like Sisyphus, rolling a huge round ball of dung up a bank, by placing its hind legs against it, and moving backwards. It frequently happens, that the ball which contains the eggs rolls to the bottom, when the poor patient Beetle begins its toilsome labour over again.

―――――"adverso nixantem trudere monte
Saxum; quod tamen à summo jam vertice rursùm
Volvitur, et plani raptim petit æquora campi." *

* Lucret. lib. iii. ver. 1013.

The *Ateuchus Ægyptiorum*, the Beetle held sacred, and so often seen depicted in the hieroglyphics, and carved on the monuments, of the ancient Egyptians, has the same habit of enclosing its eggs in large round masses of excrement, and rolling them along with its hinder legs for the purpose of burying them in the ground.

The Cape, although very well explored by travellers, yet appeared to me to offer fine opportunities to the Entomologist, so great seemed the variety of insect-forms everywhere encountered. The large white spathas of the *Arum*, which grows abundantly in the vicinity of Simon's Town, usually have specimens of *Anisonyx*, and other *Glaphyridæ*, feeding on the spadix, and assisting the process of impregnation by throwing about the pollen as they move their bodies, which, for this purpose, are covered with long hairs. Feeding on the *Protea argentea*, or Wittlebroom, the splendid plant which is commonly used as fire-wood at the Cape, I have found species of *Hopliæ*, *Dicheli*, and other *Melolonthidæ*, which apparently seem to perform the same kind office of disseminating the pollen from flower to flower. Smaller species are found imbedded, by dozens, in the heads of the composite flowers, in company with a single *Cetonia pubescens*.

On the 6th of May we left Simon's Town for Singapore, and after a somewhat tempestuous passage across the Indian Ocean, arrived at Welcome Bay, in the Straits of Sunda, on the 10th of June. There are certain phenomena to be observed, and animals to be studied, however, even when traversing the high seas, with no land in sight. As, for example, when the wide ocean heaves languidly in its mighty bed, and, lost in gorgeous hues, the dull red disc of the setting sun sinks slowly down beneath the horizon, the Noddy and the Frigate Pelican, those "feathered fishers", seek a resting-place for the night; the "Tropic bird wheels rockward to his nest"; the Petrels are no longer seen, the ghost-like Albatross comes sweeping by, the Dolphins cease to bound, and the *Acalephæ*, and other fragile beings of the deep, return to unknown solitudes. But the lovely *Ianthina*, and the fairy-like *Physalia*, do not gather in their floats, but, in company with the giddy *Hyalæa*, now sport upon the surface; the *Creseis* and *Cleodora*, those living hairs of glass, that glitter in the moon-beam, are more numerous than in the day, and the *Argonauta, Carinaria*, and *Atlanta*, take their pleasure on the surface of the sea.

The *Pteropods* are little active and energetic Mollusks, common in almost every sea. They are the very butterflies of the deep, and, from their extreme vivacity, would appear to be possessed of acute sensibilities. Insatiate and greedy, they are ever on the move, spinning, diving, and whirling in every direction. The *Hyalæa tridentata* reminds one forcibly of the erratic diving and plunging evolutions of the *Dyticus*, and *Hydrophilus* of the ponds of Europe. The *Pneumodermon*, when touched by a foreign body, feigns death, rolling itself up in a ball, like an Armadillo, or *Glomeris*. The *Cleodora Balantium*, one of the handsomest of the tribe, is much steadier in its mode of progression, than *Hyalæa, Creseis*, or even *Cuvieria*, owing, probably, to the comparative weakness and small size of the alar membranous expansions. This species, as well as the *Cleodora cuspidata*, when alive in the water, is perfectly pellucid, although it almost invariably becomes semi-opaque when dry. Among the species, most numerous in individuals, that commence their lively evolutions towards the decline of day, on the calm bosom of the ocean, may be mentioned *Hyalæa longirostra*, of Leseur, and the beautiful and delicate *Hyalæa trispinosa*, of the same naturalist.

On the 10th of June, 1843, we slowly sailed through the Sunda Straits, the tranquil waters of which were crowded with myriads of diaphanous Crustacea, of the genera *Erichthus, Phronima, Stenosoma, Alima, Nerocila, Idotea, Spheroma*, and others, creatures ever sparkling beneath the wave, and glittering, as their glassy shields reflect the rays of the sun. They swim leisurely in dense strata near the surface, sinking, however, when the sea is at all ruffled. M. Risso says, " they empty the pellucid discs of certain *Acalephæ* to serve them as canoes," which curious circumstance I have been several times able to confirm. These small isopodous, horny, and generally-transparent Crustaceans, do not swim like the *Crangon*, with the belly upwards, and by sudden jerks backwards, but propel themselves steadily onwards by repeated contractions of the post-abdomen, and natatory caudal appendages. They are exceedingly predatory and voracious, occasionally seizing *Medusæ* of greater bulk than themselves, holding them in their prehensile jaw-feet, and tearing them in pieces with their mandibles.

On these occasions, one must naturally be impressed with the astonishing fecundity and diversity of form exhibited throughout creation. Each portion of the large masses of floating weed consists, when carefully examined, of a little densely-populated world, being crowded with living beings, all active and full of bustling animation; strange-shaped little fishes, bright sea-slugs, tiny shells of the Nautilus tribe, grotesque sea-spiders, and whole gangs of odd crabs, *Medusæ*, and transparent shrimps. The Podosomatous forms of spider-like Crustaceans are very slow and languid in their progression, moving their slender articulations but feebly, seemingly as if encumbered by their inordinate length. They hide in hollow sponges, or the anfractuosities of madrepores and corallines, and some I have seen take up their abode among the spines of large *Cidares* and *Echini*. Their habits, are slow, sly, cautious and predatory. We found them in large numbers in the sea of Mindoro in twenty fathoms, and sandy bottom, entangled in huge bunches of pinnatiferous *Keratophytes*.

In the Straits of Sunda, we obtained by the dredge several fine specimens of the beautiful *Galathea elegans* of White. It is very active in its movements, darting backwards by sudden powerful jerks, snapping its chelæ quickly together, and producing a clicking noise. When swimming, the post-abdomen is first bent under the body, and again violently forced backwards. In the recent state, the body of the common variety is yellow, with three dark-red bands. The post-abdomen is pink. The chelæ are bright pink, and finely marked with two series of dark-brown irregular spots. The legs are pink, with a dark stripe on the femur, and a brown transverse band on the penultimate joint. The under surface is flesh colour with two longitudinal stripes on the breast; frontal spine orange. Near the same spot a specimen of that very rare and remarkable Crustacean, the *Ilos muriger*, of White, was dredged at a depth of ten fathoms, associated with specimens of other crabs, chiefly of the genera *Leucosia* and *Philyra*. It is as inert and feeble in its progressive movements as *Calappa* or *Cryptopodia*.

While lying in Welcome Bay, in Java, I obtained from one of the Javanese, who thronged about us in their canoes, a very pretty specimen of Squirrel, and as I had it some time in my possession, for the purpose of observing its habits, a brief account of this little quadruped may not prove uninteresting.

The *Sciurus bilineatus*, or Plantain Squirrel, is constantly kept by the Javanese as a pet. One I had in my possession was an amusing little animal, full of frolic, and playful as a kitten. He never carried his tail over his back, like the greater number of his consimilars, but would trail it gracefully along the ground. When angry, he would dilate this ornamental appendage, and bristle up the hairs, like an irritated cat. His natural cry was a weak chirping sound, but when teased beyond his powers of endurance, he would make a sharp, low, and passionate noise. He seemed to court caresses, and received them with pleasure. His food consisted of Bananas and Cocoa-nuts, which he would usually nibble like a rat, though sometimes he would place it between his paws. He was a remarkably cleanly little creature, continually dressing his fur in the manner of the *Felinæ*. When he slept, he rolled himself up in a ball like the Dormouse, with his tail encircling his body. Always active and blithe, he would sometimes perform feats of extraordinary agility, bounding to great distances, and clinging to every object within his reach.

The only specimen of *Phyllium*, or Walking-leaf insect, whose habits I have had an opportunity of observing, was given me by the Resident of Anjer, together with some young Guava plants, on the foliage of which it subsists. It was very inactive during the day, hanging suspended by its fore-feet to the leaves of the Guava, but on the approach of night, it would walk about with an undulating motion of the body, or hanging suspended, as during the day, would rapidly vibrate its leaf-like wings, in a tremulous manner. On two occasions it took short flights, but soon fell to the ground as if exhausted. It feeds voraciously as evening approaches, biting out large semi-circular bits from the edges of the leaves. This insect, which was a female, dropped an egg every night for some time. The egg is in the form of an elongated, pentagonal cylinder, with the angles winged, and, like the eggs of other *Phasmidæ*, provided with an operculum at one end. The eggs are white on their first emission from the body of the mother, but afterwards become darker and darker until they eventually assume a brownish-black colour. The ova were retained in the ovipositor sometimes for half a day, as are those of the large *Blatta*, that common nuisance on board ship. The *Phyllium*, whose habits are alluded to above, is most probably a new species, and is in the possession of Sir Edward Belcher.

At Anjer I had an opportunity of examining the animal of a very large and handsome species of *Marginella*. The *Marginellæ* are quicker and more lively in their movements than *Cypræa*, crawling pretty briskly, and moving their tentacles in various directions. They travel much faster than a snail. The two dilated anterior angles of the foot appear to be endowed with acute sensation, the animal making use of them as feelers. Many are of the most beautiful, and brilliant colours; a pale, semi-transparent, pinkish-yellow mantle, with a range of semi-elliptic crimson spots around the thin free edge, and the remainder covered with vertically radiating, linear spots, and short waved lines of the same colour; the foot, also of a yellowish delicate pink, is marbled all over with the deepest and richest crimson, and the same with the siphon. The tentacles are yellowish, with a row of marbled crimson spots. The eyes are black, and very minute. The animal of the species above described, when roughly handled, retracted itself entirely into the shell. It was dredged up in three fathoms water, sandy bottom, not far from Anjer, in Java.

Another species of *Marginella*, from the east coast of Africa, is similar to the former, but the foot is rather more expanded and more rounded behind. The left side of the mantle is rather more produced over the body of the shell than the right. The ends of the tentacula, and siphon, in this species, are yellow, and the basal parts streaked with carmine. A third species from Unsang, east coast of Borneo, also taken with the dredge, was of a light-brown colour, with burnt sienna around the margin of the mantle.

I may, here, perhaps, introduce a brief notice of the habits of the Carrier-Trochus, or *Phorus*, whose history, at present, is so little known; on our passage from Singapore to Java, numerous specimens were obtained every time the dredge was used.

The *Phori* are very numerous in the China and Java Seas, living in from fifteeen to thirty fathoms water, and generally preferring a bottom composed of the detritus of dead shells and sand, mixed with mud. I have described the animal, for the first time, in the 'Annals and Magazine of Natural History.' As a curious adaptation of means to answer a certain purpose, the mode of progression of these singular Mollusks is peculiar, and deserving of notice. They crawl like a tortoise, by lifting and throwing forward the shell, with the tentacles stretched out, the proboscis bent down and the operculum trailing behind. As they invariably inhabit places where the surface is rough, and would not admit of a gliding motion, nature has ordained that they should progress by a succession of small jumps, or tumbling evolutions. In the shortness of the foot, long annulated proboscis, and cylindrical body, these Mollusks resemble somewhat those of *Imperator*, but the sessile eyes, divided foot, and nature of the operculum, render them a perfectly distinct family. In the operculum being partially free, they approximate to *Solarium*, whilst the short divided foot, cylindric body, and long extensile trunk, reminds one of the animal of *Ianthina*. They are small for the size of the shell, and have much the general appearance of the animal of *Strombus*, like which they appear to walk, but their eyes are sessile. In order to enable them to escape from their enemies, nature has instructed them to cover their shells with the same materials as those of the banks which they inhabit. Sometimes for this purpose they select sand, often small stones, and more frequently the debris of dead shells, belonging to other genera. The *Thelidomus*, which might be considered as the fresh-water analogue of *Phorus*, has, I believe, been ascertained to be formed by the larvæ of an insect, thus depriving Mr. Swainson of a favourite type among Mollusca. The animals of *Phorus* are of a dull, opaque-white colour, the eyes large, and black, and the proboscis pinkish. In *P. onustus* of Reeve, the end of the proboscis is yellow, and the inferior surface pink. The operculum is horny, soft, and flexible, with concentric and radiating fibres covered with ridges, formed by the fibres being elevated, one above the other, in succession.

Among other peculiarities in the habits of Mollusca, perhaps one of the most striking is the case of *Stilifer*, a little parasite that lives upon the juices of, and takes up its abode in, the coriaceous integument of Star-fishes. Having, by means of its long, narrow, and slender foot, insinuated itself among the sutures of the armour the Asterias is provided with, it forms a snug nest in the soft parts, where it remains imbedded, with the apex of the spire just protuding. When placed in a watch-glass, under the microscope, I observed that it does not appear to be possessed of the power of locomotion, but that it extrudes its foot to its greatest extent, and makes use of it as an exploring organ, moving it about in all directions.

CHAPTER II.

BORNEO.

Arrive at Sarawak — Gigantic Orthoptera — Remarkable Insects — Curious habit of a Beetle—Prevalence of certain tribes of Insects—Butterflies—Insects used as Ornaments—A splendid Glowworm—Instincts of Spiders—Singular Forms of—Habits of—The Close-eyed Gudgeon — The Fighting-fish of Siam — The Organ-fish—Curious Blenny—Thunder Storm—Tree struck by Lightning—A Man killed—The Crocodile—Nondescript Plant—Habits of the Musang—The Slow-paced Lemur—The Wou-Wou The Flying Fox—The Pitcher Plant—Forest Scenery—Exuberant Vegetation—Aspect of the Woods by Day—Their appearance at Eve—Nocturnal chorus of Animals — Night Alarms—Gigantic Lizard—Beautiful Tree-Snake—Enormous Cobra—Capture of a Python—Adventure with a Snake — Changeable Lizard — The 'Tokè'—The Chichak—The Grass Lizard—The Bingkarou—The Fringed Gecko—The Flying Dragon.

FROM the 19th to the 26th of June we remained at Singapore, but as we made that busy Emporium of the East a recruiting port on four separate occasions, I shall, at present, refrain from offering any remarks on the natural history of that important little island, nor need I here detail our proceedings in Borneo, nor expatiate on the disaster that there awaited our good ship, as all that has already received ample justice in the Narrative of Sir Edward Belcher. The following remarks are the result of my impressions of scenery, and observation of various forms of animated nature, with which I became acquainted during the period of the detention of the ship at Sarāwak.

In the vast forests of the interior of Borneo, there are found enormous Orthopterous insects, huge Grasshoppers, as large or larger than sparrows, of inert and somewhat inactive habits, which hop feebly among the undergrowth, in damp, dark, shady places. A specimen, presented to Sir Edward Belcher by Mr. Brooke, at Sarāwak, was of this nature. A giant in size, it measured more than four inches in length; the leaping members not being well developed, the antennæ filiform and of great length, and the colour entirely of a beautiful delicate grass-green. Unfortunately, this magnificent insect was lost, with very many other interesting specimens, during the disaster of the ship in the river. A drawing, which I made before the occurrence of the accident, shows it to belong to an apparently new genus, placed somewhere between *Steirodon* and *Phylloptera*, and, should it eventually prove such, I would suggest to its fortunate re-discoverer, that it should be named *Megalacris Brookei*, in honour of the philanthropic and talented Rajah of Sarāwak, who first procured it from Dyaks, who brought it from the interior of the island. Orthopterous insects swarm in many parts of Borneo, and among others which I have observed may be mentioned, as being of especial interest, a *Gryllacris* with dark chesnut bands on the elytra, and an orange body; a new and singular *Gryllacris* covered all over with a velvety coat, like the Mole-cricket; an elegant *Phylloptera*, with bright, yellowish-green, semi-pellucid wings, and the head and thorax covered with small, raised pustules; a golden-brown *Acheta*, a very pretty, lively insect which takes prodigious leaps; a singular *Cyphocrania*, with the back of the head produced into a horn, and long reticulated, semi-opaque, brown wings; and a new species of *Blepharis*, an insect apparently made up of so many withered leaves, which crawls very slowly among the foliage of the low trees, and takes short feeble flights like an *Empusa*. The chief use of the *Geotrupidæ*, and other coprophagous Beetles, in tropical countries, would seem to be not so much to remove excrementitious matter from the surface of the earth, as to spread it abroad for the purpose of manuring the soil. This they effect by first collecting it in convenient round balls, or masses, in which they deposit their eggs, and then, rolling them along with their hind legs, they bury them in different places in the ground. Such was the useful occupation in which I found a species of *Gymnopleurus* engaged, under the shade of a grove of Casuarina trees, where the ground was covered in many places with large quantities of the dung of wild boars and of deer, which dozens of these indefatigable black-coated gentry were carefully spreading over the soil.

From the chrysalis of the only species of the *Sphynx* Moth I had observed in Borneo, and treasured by me with great care, emerged, after the lapse of a considerable time, two individuals of that odd-shaped, cosmopolite, hymenopterous insect, the *Evania appendigaster*! The coprophagous Beetles, and the scavenger *Staphylinidæ*,

Silphidæ, and carnivorous *Carabidæ*, are by no means numerous in Borneo, their place being more than occupied by the myriad *Termites*, Ants, and other insects that keep the surface free from putrefying objects. The Lamellicorns and other vegetable feeders are, on the contrary, very common forms, and, in conjunction with innumerable species of *Orthoptera*, feed upon the plentiful supply Nature has provided for their use, in the vast forests that everywhere clothe the surface of this fine island.

Enormous diurnal *Lepidoptera*, the handsome, great *Ornithopteri*, are generally noticed flapping lazily their large, broad wings in the dark mazes of the forests, sweeping above the low trees, and avoiding the climbers and branches of the taller trees, with a singular bat-like dexterity; although tolerably numerous, the Butterflies, however, cannot vie with those of Tropical America. In a ramble through the woods, near Santubon, I procured specimens of a rare and splendid species of *Pycanum*, allied to *P. amethystinum* of Fabricius, having bright, burnished, emerald-green elytra, and the body ornamented on each side with alternate bands of black and orange. The *P. amethystinum* is sometimes set in a brooch, as among certain Indian tribes are the *Buprestis chrysis* and the Diamond Beetle. In the Philippines, the beautiful, polished, green species of *Stephanorhina*, and the handsome *Caryphocera*, with large black blotches on the elytra, are also held in much estimation, and are preserved in a dry state as ornaments. One of the most common Hemipterous insects (which, taken as a class, not only appear to be very numerous in Borneo, but also very curious in form and brilliant in colour) is a species of *Catacanthus* allied to *C. aurantius* of Fabricius, with a bright yellow thorax, two black spots on the elytra, and the margin of the abdomen marked with alternate bands of light, clear, semi-transparent yellow and deep shining black; a very pretty species of *Callidea*, a genus belonging to the *Scutelleridæ*, of a burnished golden green, with large, round, black spots, is also very common in the woods throughout the territory of Sarăwak. But, perhaps, one of the most beautiful insects observed by me while staying in this part of Borneo, was a Glow-worm, two females of which were in my possession. In this splendid *Lampyris*, each segment of the body is illuminated with three lines of tiny lamps, the luminous spots on the back being situated at the posterior part of the segmentary rings in the median line, while those along the sides of the animal are placed immediately below the stomates or spiracula, each spiraculum having one bright spot. This very beautiful insect was found shining as the darkness was coming on, crawling on the narrow pathway, and glowing among the dead, damp wood, and rotten leaves. When placed around the finger, it resembles, in beauty and brilliancy, a superb diamond ring. The Spiders constitute another highly amusing study for the entomologist in these regions, so dismissing for the present, our tiny friends the *Ptilota*, or winged insects, let us regard a few of these Apterous forms, usually considered so repulsive, the Spiders.

In consideration of their apparently helpless condition, and the soft nature of their integuments, Nature, always inclined to protect the weak and helpless, has given the

Spiders a multitude of wonderful instincts, by means of which they are enabled to defend themselves from injury, provide themselves with food, and furnish safe retreats for their tender progeny. They spin their toils of cunning device, and even powerful insects, armed with formidable stings, are made captive with impunity, despite their struggles to escape the captor. These Spiders' webs generally attract the attention of travellers, and, certainly in some parts of the forests of Mindanao, Borneo, and Celebes, there is great and wonderful diversity in the form and construction of these ingenious and delicately-woven nets. Many have black webs, some have white, others brown, and in Mindanao I have observed toils formed of perfectly yellow threads. The nets of the great species of *Nephila*, which abound in equatorial regions, frequently stretch across the path, from bush to bush, and prove very troublesome to the naturalist while threading the thickets where they are numerous.

The imagination can scarcely conceive the bizarre, and fantastic shapes with which it has pleased Nature to invest those hard-bodied Spiders, called by naturalists *Acrosoma*. They have large, angular spines sticking out of their bodies, in every kind of fashion, perhaps intended as some sort of defence against the soft-billed birds, which doubtless would otherwise make dainty meals of these Arachnidans, exposed as they are, temptingly suspended in mid air, on their transparent webs in the forest glades. Some are protected by these long spines to such a degree, that their bodies resemble a miniature "cheveux de frise", and could not, by any possibility be swallowed by a bird without producing a very unpleasant sensation in his throat. One very remarkable species (*Gasteracantha arcuata*, Koch) has two enormous, recurved, conical spines, proceeding upwards from the posterior part of the body, several times longer than the entire Spider. The *Drassi* are gloomy Spiders, haunting obscure places, and their garb is dark coloured and dingy in accordance with their habits. They are mostly pale brown, black, dull red, or grey. The *Thomisi* are varied in their colour, in harmony with their usual abiding places. Thus, those that spend their lives among the flowers and foliage of the trees, are delicately and beautifully marked with green, orange, black, and yellow. One species, which I have named *T. virescens*, simulates the vegetation among which it lives, is not agile in its movements, but drops, when alarmed, among the foliage; it is of a pale delicate semi-transparent sap-green, with the eyes and chelicera red; there is a large mark on the surface of the abdomen, beautifully variegated with yellow, pink, and black, and margined with dead-white spots; the under surface is green in the middle and opaque white on either side; the spinneret is pink.

A few observations on the *Periophthalmus*, or Close-eyed Gudgeon, and some other remarkable ichthyological forms which I have noticed in this part of Borneo, may not, perhaps, be altogether uninteresting to some of my readers.

About every group of rocks large numbers of handsomely-coloured fishes play, and dart among the Corallines and Algæ, some with rays of black and orange; some azure with transparent fins; some yellow, others resembling in brilliancy of tint the parrots, the loris, and sun-birds of the forests. Those that live in shallow water are brightly coloured, whilst those dwelling in the high seas, out of soundings, are generally of a dull or sombre hue.

One of the greatest ichthyological oddities one meets with in the tropics, is the close-eyed Gudgeon (*Periophthalmus*). On every slimy bank, among the Mangrove swamps, and on the muddy borders of ditches, the curious eye will detect the shiny, uncouth form of this grotesque, amphibious fish, jumping about like a frog, or sliding awkwardly along on its belly, with a gliding motion. It is equally at home on the " beached margent of the sea," where it is seen skimming along the surface of the water, or jumping and leaping from stone to stone. By means of its pectoral fins it is enabled to climb, with great facility, among the tangled roots of the Mangroves, where it finds a goodly harvest of minute *Crustacea*. Crabs and worms do not, however, constitute its only food, for I have found in the stomachs of some I examined, insects in both the imago and larval state.

The sailors call the *Periophthalmus* " Jumping Johnny ", and appear very much amused at its wary cunning, and surprising efforts to escape capture. I have, however, seen parties of Dyaks pursuing the larger species over the wide mud-flats, and capture them with the greatest dexterity. Many other fish, besides the *Periophthalmus*, have the same power of living for a time out of their native element, among which may be mentioned *Ophiocephalus*, *Macropodus*, *Helostoma*, *Anabas*, and *Calyacanthus*. Pliny was aware of this fact, which he thus alludes to, " Quin et in

Indiæ fluminibus certum genus piscium, ac deinde resilit."*

Another very singular little fish is the Fighting-fish, which is kept in vessels of water for the amusement of the Malays. If irritated, it immediately changes colour, passing through shades of the most varied and brilliant tints. When two of them meet, they fight with the bitterest animosity, darting at each other with the swiftness of thought, the victor frequently killing his adversary. They feed on small flies and worms, and are easily preserved in glass vessels. A curious species of *Blenny* is very common on the coast, hiding in the deep cylindrical holes in the shallow pools left at low water, at the orifices of which they may be observed protuding their obtuse noses, and tentacular filaments, using them as a decoy or bait like that famous angler the Fishing Frog (*Lophius piscatorius*). The small fry swimming past these tempting lures, are attracted towards them, when the hidden *Blenny* suddenly darts upon them with the greatest velocity, and drags them into its den, there to consume them. So excessively cunning, active, and wary, is this little *Blenny*, that all my endeavours to procure a specimen proved unavailing. On the 31st of August, 1843, while on board the Brig 'Ariel', then lying off the mouth of the river of Borneo, I had the good fortune to hear that solemn aquatic concert of the far-famed Organ-fish, or "Drum", a species of *Pogonias*. These singular fishes produce a loud, monotonous, singing sound, which rises and falls, and sometimes dies away, or assumes a very low drumming character, and the noise appears to

* Hist. Nat. Lib. ix, C. 35.

proceed mysteriously from the bottom of the vessel. This strange sub-marine chorus of fishes continued to amuse us for about a quarter of an hour, when the music, if so it might be called, suddenly ceased, probably on the dispersion of the band of performers.

The peaceful avocations of the student of nature, when engaged in active service, may sometimes be interrupted by disastrous events, an example of which I shall here relate; nor is it the only instance in which, in my capacity of Assistant Surgeon, I have been a party concerned. The incident I allude to, occurred one night during one of the most tremendous storms I have witnessed in Borneo, while the 'Samarang' was anchored off the Santubong entrance of the Saräwak river. The horizon was overcast long before the storm burst forth, and a portentous lowering gloom gathered in every direction, but when the rain came down in torrents, and as it does only in the tropics, the sky was like an universal pall, spread out over nature, or a hugh black curtain, shutting out the stars of heaven, illumined only now and then by vivid and continuous flashes of forked lightning, followed by terrific peals of thunder, which seemed to shake the earth.

The surface of the ocean was violently disturbed, and lashed into foam by the driving gale, and on the shore the lightning had struck a huge Casuarina tree, under which our carpenters, who were cutting wood here, had erected their tent, and had fallen and crushed a poor Dutchman, as he lay on the sand at its root. On my proceeding in the barge to his assistance, the fury of the sweeping blast throwing the spray about, contrasting with the tossing of the dark forest trees, formed a wild and most magnificent scene. The poor man was so dreadfully mangled as to be beyond the aid of surgery, and expired shortly after my arrival at the spot.

Many of the rivers of Borneo have low, swampy banks, over-hung sometimes by the dark foliage, twisted branches, and snake-like roots of the Mangrove, or fringed on either side by dense clustering masses of the elegant and useful Nipa Palm (*Nypa fruticans*). On the ebbing of the tide there is, moreover, a margin of soft and slimy mud, abounding with various Crustaceans, some of a beautiful blue colour, which live in holes, and, hopping about on their pectoral fins, are the *Periophthalmi*. *Neritina crepidularia* adheres to the petioles of the Nipa leaves, *Cerithium truncatum* to the foliage, and now and then the plunge of a *Hydrosaurus* may startle the observer. On one occasion I observed a Crocodile extended quietly on his belly in the soft mud; I stood still, watching him as he lay extended in listless ease, with his long, lank jaws, and dusky-brown, scaly skin, in bold relief against the mud, and as he turned his head slowly and espied me with his dull lurid eye, he bent his nose close to the surface of the ground, lashed his compressed tail from side to side, and wallowing, retired into the dark still waters. One of these reptiles was in my possession alive, but as the Dyaks had firmly secured his jaws with a rattan muzzle, there was little to fear from his ferocity. He was very soon, however, offered up as a victim on the altar of science.

The novelty of Mr. Waterton's exploit, of riding upon

a Cayman's back, is not quite so great as many people imagine. Pliny relates that the *Tentyritæ* were in the habit of jumping into the river Nile, and riding on the backs of the Crocodiles, and when, moreover, these savage *Saurians* turned their heads for the purpose of biting their unwelcome burden, the ingenious riders placed a stick in the mouth and held the ends with their hands, thus bringing the vanquished reptile to the shore, as if with bit and bridle.

In the course of an excursion up the Sarăwak river, in company with Sir Edward Belcher and Mr. Brooke, I found a large and very singular flower, growing in a dark damp forest, on the side of a hill, not far from the mountain of Serambo, in Borneo. It sprung from the exposed root of a tall tree with large light green leaves, in the manner of some gigantic epiphyte or rhizanth. The flower was about sixteen inches in length, of a hard, dense consistence, and of a light reddish-brown colour, deepening towards the summit. The buds were like the full-blown flower in appearance, of the same dirty red colour, but closed at the upper extremity. Travelling through the forest on foot, and requiring to undergo considerable fatigue, I was enabled to preserve or more minutely examine this vegetable wonder. I carried it to the village, where it did not appear to excite much interest, and after making a rough sketch of it, I abandoned it to its fate; I simply allude to the fact here in the hope that another botanist, more fortunate, may fall in with the plant again, and make it better known.

My opportunities of observing the habits of the mammiferous animals of Borneo, were neither very numerous or favourable. I may, however, mention a few peculiarities in the economy of some whose acquaintance I cultivated, which may, perhaps, serve to amuse the reader. A Musang, as the Malays term it, (*Viverra musanga*) during the time it was in my possession, afforded much amusement, and deserves honourable mention at my hands. In many of his manners he resembled the *Mangusta*, or Indian Ichneumon, placing his nose low, and trailing his tail along the ground. When annoyed, however, he arched his back, bristled his hairs, and dilated his tail in the manner of an angry cat, and would spit and bite very severely. He would also gambol like a kitten, and bite the fingers gently with his sharp white teeth. He climbed with great facility, and was perfectly at home among the rigging of the ship. He was an inquisitive and cunning little animal, ferreting out everything edible, rifling the messes of the seamen, especially their sugar, and sucking the eggs belonging to the stewards. For these petty thefts he has been flung over-board several times, but swimming with ease and rapidity, he ascended by the rudder-chains, shook himself, and resumed his ordinary peculations. On one occasion an enemy having thrown him into the sea, a friendly cook gave him a rope, when he climbed nimbly inboard, and was saved. One ill-fated day he ventured into the holy precincts of the Captain's cabin, in pursuit of a rat, overthrew some bottles, and shortly afterwards, being detected in the yet more heinous offence of stealing the Captain's Pigeons, his death-warrant was signed, and he was accordingly executed by the sentry of the galley.

As an instance of the poor Musang's cunning, I may

mention that he was observed to descend into a boat, purloin a Banana, quietly stow it among the booms, and repeat the process till he had accumulated a pretty large store, when he leisurely commenced consuming the grateful fruit till not one remained.

On my last visit to Sarãwak, my friend Ruppell presented me with two live specimens of the slow-paced Lemur (*Stenops tardigradus*). They are stupid, quiet, gentle, little quadrumanes, with beautiful, soft, woolly fur, and enormous black eyes. Their common cry is a peculiar, faint, wailing sound, but when angry, they make a chattering noise. They are quite torpid during the day, but tolerably active after nightfall. The female gave birth to two young ones, very helpless little creatures, which clung tenaciously to their mother's soft fur, in any position, sometimes on the sides, and often under the belly. Both the parents and young ones, however, soon went the way of all pets, and their dried skins are the only evidence of their former existence.

I have often observed the Wou-wou (*Hylobates leucisus*) in its sylvan haunts, and unlike the *Hylobates agilis*, which M. Dauvaucel says is shy in its habits, it will hang suspended by its long arms, and swinging to and fro in the air, allow you to approach within fifty yards, and then suddenly drop upon a lower branch, and climb again leisurely to the top of the tree. It is a quiet, solitary creature, of a melancholy, peaceful nature, pursuing a harmless life, feeding upon fruits in the vast untrodden recesses of the forest, and its peculiar noise is in harmony with the sombre stillness of these dim regions; it commences like the gurgling of water, when a bottle is being filled, and ends with a loud, long, wailing cry, which resounds throughout the leafy solitude to a great distance, and is sometimes responded to from the depths of the forest by another note as wild and melancholy.

I saw the Galugo (*Galeopithecus*) both in Borneo and Basilan in a wild state. It is crepuscular, and hangs suspended during the day to the under surface of boughs in the tops of high trees. When it moves, it seems to shuffle and scramble among the leaves, and sometimes drops suddenly from its elevated position. It feeds on leaves, and the stomach of one I examined was filled with remains of the foliage of *Artocarpus*, and other trees. The Spanish Officers at Basilan shoot large numbers of *Galeopitheci* for the sake of their beautiful skins, though in an excursion I made with them we were not able to procure a single specimen. At Sarāwak I had a living *Galeopithecus*, or Fying Fox, in my possession, which was procured on the occasion of felling some trees, in the top of one of which the animal was suspended. It was very inactive on the ground, and did not attempt to bite or resist. Having probably received some internal injury, it shortly died. On examining the body, I found it was a female with young; the embryos, two in number, appeared to have the lateral expansion of the skin, as in the adult.

Among the numerous rare and interesting vegetable productions to be found in Borneo, is the "*Daum gundi*," or Monkey-cup of the Malays, the Pitcher plant of the English (*Nepenthes destillatoria*, and other species,). It is a very common plant in the Sarāwak territory, where it may be seen, with its curiously-formed leaves, clinging to the trunks and foliage of the trees that fringe the banks of the rivers, or in the interior of the forest. The *Nepenthes* has been frequently and well described, but as I have seen it growing in dense masses, in every stage of developement, a short notice of this very remarkable plant may not be found uninteresting. Besides the *N. destillatoria* I have observed another species, particularly common on the Island of Moarra, near the mouth of the river of Borneo. This kind has narrower leaves, is a smaller plant, but climbs in the same manner, and has small, long, narrow pitchers. Both species are slender twining plants, chiefly supported by the shrubs that grow around by the twisting of the stalks of the pitchers. The flowers are simple perianths, consisting of four sepals, of a brick-red colour, with a yellow stigma, arranged in terminal spikes, which grow upright and crown the summit of the plant. The young plants have only the round, gibbose, and fringed pitchers. There are two kinds of pitchers in each species, one growing at some distance from the ground, which is long, slender, and usually green, or marbled, spotted at the mouth only, and furnished with a very long foot-stalk; the other kind is formed of the lower leaves, and is generally placed upon or near the surface of the ground. These latter Monkey-cups, as the Malays term them, are most generally half-full of insects, chiefly ants. The pitchers, when full-grown, almost invariably contain fluid, in different proportions. In some cups there is nearly an ounce in others only a few drachms. Many of them contain insects, which if not killed, find it difficult to escape out of the limpid and musilaginous liquid. In one pitcher I found five crickets, hundreds of small ants, mostly dead, and numerous larvæ of mosquitoes and other gnats. The cups near the ground frequently contain living larvæ of dipterous insects; while the young and elevated cups are free from them, and contain pure limpid water. The appearance of these beautiful and delicately-formed vegetable vases is extremely interesting and singular as they hang suspended by their fragile handles, offering a cooling draft to the different animals that frequent the neighbourhood. By pouring the water of several dozens of pitchers into one of large size, I have several times succeeded in quenching my thirst with a good half-pint. Many of the full-sized cups will hold *considerably more than a pint.*

In an account of Balambangan, by Lieut. James Barton ('Oriental Repertory,' vol. ii.) there is a very amusing statement respecting this plant. He observes, "The northern part is over-run with various species of the *Nepenthes*; but whether the abundance of water is derived from thence, or whether they be the consequence of the abundance of water, must be left to the decision of naturalists! some caution", he adds, "may be prudent in rooting them up, lest the former should be the case." Many other plants are furnished with pitcher-shaped leaves besides the *Nepenthes*, as the *Cephalotus*, of New Holland, the *Sarracenias*, or Side-saddle flowers, and the *Dischidia Rafflesiana*, which I have found growing in the forests of Celebes, climbing about the trees, with its singular leathery pitchers partly filled with a limpid fluid, and surrounded with fibrous roots. In the 'Oriental Repertory' (vol. ii.) a kind of cane, called "Tugal" by the natives of the Sooloo Islands, is alluded to, which when cut through, will, it is said, furnish an abundance of clear water, and in the same paper is mentioned a certain creeping plant, termed "Bahaùmpùl", which, on being divided, yields a quantity of slightly gummy water.

Although forest-scenery, with its luxuriant vegetation has been so often, and so well described, I cannot resist the inclination to give my own impression of those vast and solemn temples "not made with hands", which will, moreover, tend to show the great similarity which exists with respect to the grander and more important features between all primeval forests, whether in the Eastern Archipelago or in the Western Hemisphere.

In the forests of Celebes, Mindanao, and Borneo, besides the eternal ringing song of the shrill *Cicada*, a solitary note is sometimes heard from some high tree-top, or a loud, long whine, from the depths of the dark and sombre forest. The aged trunks are hung with Orchideous epiphytes, and variegated with *Lichens*, while on the humid soil, dark fetid *Fungi*, nauseous, and mis-shapen, spread their dingy forms. A shy Lizard, scaling a naked trunk, or huge *Blattæ*, running among the dead leaves, will startle you for a moment. The Honey-Bee secures its hoard high in the summit of some leafy bough; the White-Ant builds its cumbrous nest about the knotted roots; and, in among the tangled maze, huge Spiders spin their subtle toils. Here and there, the ground is furrowed by the Wild Boar's snout, or, where the Mangroves spread their roots, painted *Gelasimi*, or Land-Crabs, holding up their one huge pincer, in a manner perfectly ludicrous, though meant to be threatening, are scampering about in all directions. Occasionally you notice one of those silent over-growings of vegetation, where the form of some Titanic tree is strangely distorted, "with knots and knares deformed and old," or some trunk embraced in the python folds of an enormous Creeper. I remember seeing, at Tanjong Datu, a tree, of large dimensions, growing on the top of an enormous granitic boulder, the roots of which, descending in the form of long ropes, buried themselves in the ground, thus supporting the tree in a perpendicular position.

These aberrations of growth, are frequently met with in the tropical forests, where great heat prevails, and the ground is always moist. Although usually dim, and often nearly dark, these woods are sometimes illumined by a transient streak of light "fair vistas shooting beams of day", and on the leaves, where the sunbeams play, showy *Diptera* are to be captured, and, numbers of *Buprestidæ*, with glittering metallic wings. Generally, however, with the exception of the loud song of our merry friend, the *Cicada*, an unbroken silence reigns throughout the forest, which is very solemn and impressive. But as the evening breeze sets in, this silent majesty of the woods is disturbed by the harsh notes of the Horn-bill (*Buceros Rhinoceros* and *Astracius*), the screaming of Loris, and the chattering of Monkeys in the trees. The wood-paths are become instinct with life, and now is heard the whistle and the song, the shrilly cry, and gurgling, mellow sound, the loud shriek, and all the varied notes of the "plumy people of the grove."

More particularly during the period of the immersion of our good ship, had I an opportunity of examining some of the peculiarities of tropic scenes and scenery, and what particularly reminded me of our novel position, were certain remarkable differences in the natural phenomena at the close of day, between Sarãwak in Borneo, and Hampshire in England. In England, for example, the bats are on the move, dashing wildly under the foliage of the trees, but here we see enormous *Pteropi* or Flying-Foxes, soaring high above our heads, with steady, flapping fright; the Mosquitoes begin to sound their shrilly trumpets; the "Chichak" chirps as he darts across the ceiling; the Glow-worms shine; the Fire-flies glitter on the trees; the warty Toad unveils his form, and the *Polydesmus* and *Zephronia* venture forth to feed.* I remember, on one occasion, while out on an anti-piratical expedition, about sixty miles up the river Linga, being particularly struck with the appearance of a tropical forest by night. On every side, the dim and shadowy trees stood out like ghosts, perfectly still, and lighted up occasionally by dense clouds of Fire-flies; the ground on every side, for many hundred yards, was a watery swamp, giving birth to myriads of Mosquitoes, and slime-bred animals of every description. Occasionally, we were awoke from our deepest slumbers, by the shrieks of wild animals, and the croaking din of innumerable frogs, but more frequently than all, by certain "grey-coated trumpeters", as Milton calls the gnats. I had

* A new species of *Polydesmus* from Borneo in the British Museum, I have named *P. Newporti* after Mr. Newport, who has particuliarly devoted himself to the study of the Myriapoda. A new and large species of *Zephronia* in the same collection, and from the same island, I have named *Zephronia gigas*. I may here inform the less scientific reader, that the first named insect resembles a Centipede, and the latter a Wood-louse more than an inch in length.

heard of the body-louse and chigger, the red acarus, and the Sand-fly, but what are they compared with the Mosquito? I remember well on the present occasion exclaiming in a rage, "Ah! infernal Mosquito! when 'thy shrill horn its fearful larum flings', driving all sleep from weary eyes, and making the night pass away as a long and feverish, fitful dream, surely thou art a demon of the Insect-world". I have seen the faces of myself and some of my messmates, appear in the morning, as if they had the small-pox, their countenances being inflamed, swollen, and covered with white tubercles, and that during a single night! In England, when the sun declines, scarcely a sound echoes to the "dull ear of the night-cradled earth", but in Borneo, as soon as daylight begins to wane, a strange nocturnal chorus fills the air, which continues, without intermission, until the morning. The performers in this chorus of "beings of the night's shadows" are very numerous, and each has a distinct part assigned to him. A subterranean Beetle "opens the ball" from the dark bosom of the earth, producing a loud, continuous, singing noise, made mellow and booming by the winding of his cavern. The Frogs follow up closely this first musical indication, making the swamps resound with their harsh croakings. The mournful note of the Goat-sucker crying out monotonously at intervals, echoes dismally around; the Cicadæ not yet tired with their long day's work make the dim shades resound with their long loud song; the Grass-hoppers, long-legged Choristers, in their merry way, chirp with all their might; one monotonous continued wailing cry uttered by some unknown songster continues the live-long night; now you will hear an interrupted hissing whirring sound from some huge locust; now a loud and silvery chirp; then a soft and gentle sibillant sound; anon a harsh croak, a distant yell, or a low gurgling gutteral cry.

The entire symphony, if so it may be called, this "requiem to the day's decline" heard at a distance reminds one of that peculiar sensation termed a "ringing in the ears"; there is no cessation, no rest, no respite; still the noise continues, sometimes growing louder, then drooping and dying away, then bursting forth again as if with renewed enegy; in fact, I believe each performer tries to emulate the others, giving out great impulsive strains at intervals.

Twice was the midnight tranquility of "Cockpit Hall" disturbed by the visits of a Porcupine, that was accustomed to wander in a half-tame condition about the jungle in the neighbourhood, and as these night alarms afforded us some amusement, I shall relate them to my readers. Our house, like other Malay and Dyak dwellings, was, of course, raised on posts from the ground, the space below being occupied by pigs and poultry. Now it happened, as we slept one night on the floor above, dreadful whirring noises, attended by loud gruntings, and hurrey-skurreyings were heard all about the enclosure beneath the house. Anticipating a hunt, I descended our rude ladder, and, followed by a little volunteer with a lantern, crept through the wicket, but instead of fronting a wild Boar or Cat-of-the-woods, my knife encountered merely the quills of the Porcupine, which having entered our premises to forage, could not easily find his way out again. On another occasion, we were awoke by strange, unearthly noises, somewhat resembling the grunt of a hog, mingled with sundry guttural and wheezing notes, gradually approaching our quarters from the jungle at the back. A small hunting party was soon organized, and sallied out in chase. The sounds grew nearer and nearer, when suddenly, a rustling noise was heard, the bushes shook, and out rushed the object of our alarm, in the shape of a Porcupine! These animals, like Hedgehogs, appear to be almost entirely nocturnal in their habits, and I had no idea that the quiet creatures one sees in Menageries, were in the practice in a wild state, of making such hideous noises, and of trotting about with so much animation. On another occasion, a reptile, described as a gigantic *Iguana*, having been seen in the neighbourhood of our dwelling at Sarāwak, I was anxious to procure it, as I conceived it must be a large species of *Hydrosaurus*, or Lace-lizard. For this purpose, I watched two days by the side of a spring, which I fancied the reptile would select as his head-quarters during his stay in our neighbourhood, this being a peculiarity of these creatures, and on the third day, sure enough, he came, trotting leisurely along, and stretched himself at full length on the brink:

"Nunc etiam in gelida sede lacerta latet".

Throwing myself on him, I wounded him with a clasp-knife in the tail, but he managed to elude my grasp, and made for the woods. I succeeded, however, in tracking his retreating form, on hands and knees, through a low, covered labyrinth, in the dense undergrowth, until I saw him extended on a log, when leaving the jungle, I called my servant, a Marine, who was shooting specimens for me, and, pointing out the couchant animal, desired him to shoot him in the neck, as I did not wish the head to be injured, which he accordingly did. Entering the jungle, I then closed with the wounded Saurian, and, seizing him by the throat, bore him in triumph to our quarters. Here he soon recovered, and hoping to preserve him alive, to study his habits, I placed him in a Malay wicker hen-coop. As we were sitting, however, at dinner, the black cook, with great alarm depicted in his features, reported that "Alligata get out his cage." Seizing the carving knife, I rushed down, and was just in time to cut off his retreat into the adjoining swamp. Turning sharply round, he made a snap at my leg, and received in return a "Rowland for his Oliver," in the shape of an inch or so of cold steel. After wrestling on the ground, and struggling through the deserted fire of our sable cook, I at length secured the runaway, tied him up to a post, and to prevent further mischief, ended his career by dividing the jugular. The length of this Lizard, from actual measurement, was five feet ten inches and a half.

These gigantic Lizards (*Hydrosaurus giganteus*) are rather shy and reserved in their habits, and not very agile in their movements. They affect a swampy habitat, frequenting the low river banks, or the margins of springs, and although I have seen them basking on rocks, or on the dead trunk of some prostrate tree, in the heat of the sun, yet they appear more partial to the damp weeds and undergrowth in the vicinity of water. Many, indeed, are pre-eminently aquatic, as I have noticed in the rivers of Celebes and Mindanao. Their gait has somewhat more of the awkward lateral motion of the

Crocodile, than of the lively action of the smaller Saurians. When attacked, they lash violently with their tail, swaying it side-ways with great force, like the Cayman. These modern types of the *Mososaurus* and *Iguanodon* have a graceful habit of extending the neck and raising the head to look about them, and as you follow them leisurely over the rocks or through the jungle, they frequently stop, turn their heads round, and take a deliberate survey of the intruder. They are by no means vicious, though they bite with severity when provoked, acting, however, always on the defensive. On examining their stomachs, Crabs, Locusts, Beetles, and the remains of the *Periophthalmus*, or Jumping-Fish, the scales of Snakes, and bones of Frogs and other small animals were discovered. Like that of the *Iguanæ* of the New World, the flesh of these Saurians is delicate eating; I can compare it to nothing better than that of a very young sucking-pig.

At the island of Mayo we landed amid the surf, upon a group of high, bare rocks covered with *Chitons*, *Littorinæ* and *Nerites*, with large painted *Grapsi* running about in all directions. As I climbed the rugged acclivity, a huge Monitor Lizard, upwards of five feet in length, disturbed in his noonday siesta, made off to a swampy ravine on the other side, climbing the perpendicular ascent with awkward activity, and stopping now and then to look round and examine his pursuer. The romantic chine in which he finally disappeared was abundantly supplied with trickling rivulets, that came tumbling down among enormous boulders, from their sources in green clumps of tall *Pandanus* trees, springing from the height above. The specimen of *Hydrosaurus giganteus*, from the north coast of New Holland, in the British Museum, is seventy-eight inches in length. Many African species, as, for example, the white-throated *Regenia* (*R. albogularis*) and the Nilotic Monitor (*M. Niloticus*), also attain a great size. How admirably adapted are these semi-aquatic, dingy-hued Saurians to the hot, moist swamps and shallow log-laden lagoons that fringe the rivers of this densely-wooded island! The imagination is carried back, while contemplating the dark forms of these *Hydrosauri* plunging and wallowing in the water, or trotting along deliberately over the soft and slimy mud, to that "Age of Reptiles" in the world's infancy, when the vast muddy shores of the primeval ocean were peopled by those lazy lizard-like monsters, and slow-moving giant Efts, the *Mososaurus*, which must have been between the *Monitor* and *Iguana*, twenty-five feet long with a laterally compressed tail; the *Saurodon* with its lizard-like teeth; and the *Dinosauria* and *Megalosaurus*, large carnivorous Crocodile-Lizards. Along the banks of the fresh-water rivulets of Mindanao, numbers of these great water-loving Lizards are seen, plunging and diving in the dark, still streams, basking on the banks, trotting among the foliage, or lying flat on their bellies upon the treees thrown across the rivers and stagnant ponds Among these I think I recognised the two-streaked Lace-Lizard (*Hydrosaurus Salvator*) and another smaller species, entirely of a dull-brown, In the stream that runs through the village of Anjer, in Java, I noticed also numerous Saurians of this group, of somewhat more sluggish movements, most probably *Uranus heraldicus*, and other species closely allied. When wounded, these large Lizards bite very severely, but unless provoked are perfectly harmless. They are easily shot, but it is not without some difficulty they are caught alive.

Among the most active and graceful of the Tree-Snakes to be found in Borneo is the *Dryiophis nasuta*, a slender, grass-green reptile, with a yellow line extending along the sides, and with the muzzle prolonged into a sharp-pointed snout. I had two of these beautiful creatures in my possession, at different times, one from Borneo, and the other from Celebes. The Dyaks, when they presented me with the Bornean variety, carefully secured in a joint of bamboo, with a cork made of rolled up leaves, considered it to be highly venomous, and were greatly surprised at observing me playing with, and teazing it, most probably confounding it with a green species of *Megæra*, which is poisonous, and which I have also seen in Borneo. The *Dryiophis*, however, is perfectly innocuous, and is, to boot, one of the most graceful reptiles that glide upon the ground; Satan might have assumed its form when he courted the notice and admiration of our common mother. It is a very active and playful Serpent, and feeds on Grass-hoppers, Ants, and other insects, which it seizes, with the velocity of lightning, frequently darting out its long, black, forked tongue, before making the final spring. A party in one of our boats, proceeding up the Sarāwak river, encountered a large black-coloured Cobra (*Naja Tripudians*), seven feet long, making his way through the water with his head slightly raised, and his tongue protruding. He was immediately attacked, wounded, and, after much struggling, hissing, and many contortions of the body, finally secured, and brought up for my inspection.

During our residence at Sarãwak, a very handsomely variegated *Python*, about fourteen feet in length, was detected in the act of devouring a chicken, beneath the boards of Mr. Brooke's house. A party, headed by the gunner, armed with boarding-pikes, soon wounded the reptile, and secured him. When brought to me, he was apparently in a dying condition, so, after admiring the beauty of his spotted skin, I fastened him to a post in my friend Ruppell's room. During the dinner-hour, however, he had recovered himself, slipped the noose over his head, and escaped, no one knew whither, and all our searching after the beautiful snake was unavailing. During a visit to Sarãwak, in September, 1844, Ruppell informed me that many months afterwards, on some stores having been removed, the same Python was discovered, comfortably coiled up under some bags of rice. No half-measures were pursued this time by his merciless captors; he was transfixed with spears, his head cut off, and his skin preserved as a trophy. He measured, after death, fourteen feet in length. Before the search was made, several fowls and pigeons were found lacerated, and half-dragged under the house. A party of Songi Dyaks, from Serambo, having occasion to make a journey to Sarãwak, encountered a *Python* on the banks of the river, thirty feet long; they succeeded in killing it, and tied its head to a tree on the river's brink. The day before our trip to the Antimony and Gold Mines, it was seen extended across the river, secured to the trunk of a tree, but when we passed the spot, it had unluckily been washed away by the freshes that rush impetuously from the mountains, at certain times, and overflow the banks. *Pythons*, or Boa-Constrictors as they are commonly called, of an enormous size, are reported to have been seen in the interior by the Dyaks. On one occasion, a large dark-coloured snake was observed by the natives swimming down the river, when they gave chase. They soon overtook the reptile, and killed it by repeated blows on the head with their paddles. This serpent, which was presented to me, measured seven feet long, was innocuous, and had a compressed form and a dorsal crest, extending the whole length of the body. I pursued a similar serpent, that surprised us when bathing, but did not succeed in capturing him. A curious circumstance occurred at Siniavin, showing the dread entertained by the Malays against the serpent race. Taking a stroll before breakfast, behind the village, I perceived a very prettily-marked snake, at the bottom of a small, shallow pool of water, and stooping quietly down, impaled the reptile between my finger and thumb, and thus succeeded in making him my prisoner. On my return, after showing my prize to the party, in order to elicit proper admiration of its black and red mottled skin, I proceeded to the river's brink, for the purpose of securing the animal in an empty stoppered bottle, which, according to custom, I had brought with me for zoological contingencies, like the present. The serpent being safely lodged in " durance vile," I was rather surprised, some little time afterwards, at seeing a great commotion among the " Tambang-boys," and my curiosity prompting me to investigate the cause of their leaping precipitately into the water, and evincing other signs of excitement and alarm, I soon ascertained that the awkward movements of Sooboo, Mr. Brooke's coxwain, as he was engaged in clearing out the boat, had broken the bottle, containing the captive snake, and that no sooner had the men caught a glimpse of his gliding form, than they, one and all, rushed tumultuously over the side of the Tambang into the river, while the serpent, soon following their example, swam peacefully to the opposite bank, and found a safe retreat among the dense, weedy mass that fringed the river. Sooboo afterwards informed me, that the species of snake I had captured in the morning, was considered by the natives, one of the most venomous in the country.

The *Polychrus virescens*, like the Chamelion, changes its colour, assuming various hues, which are dependent on rage or fear. When first captured, and trembling in the hand, it throws off its bright green mantle, and assumes a coat of sober russet-brown, which is sometimes varied with lighter spots; frequently it remains of a fine emerald green on the belly. It is the "Gruning" of the Malays, and probably the "Chameleon" that Marsden mentions, as being common in Sumatra. It hunts for insects among the foliage of the trees, and is fond of travelling out to the end of a slender branch, to watch the Diptera, as they wheel in circles by. I always found their stomachs loaded with insects. The Gruning bites very severely.

The "Tokè" of the Malays, is a very common lizard among the "attap" dwellings of the Dyaks. It feeds on beetles, and other insect-forms that find a home in holes of rotten wood. It emits a peculiar chirping sound. The eggs are somewhat smaller than a wren's, and are concealed in damp and rotten logs. The young, when first excluded, are of a bluer tinge than the mother-reptile, and begin to crawl immediately on their expulsion from the ovum.

The House-Lizard, or "Chichak", of the Malays, (*Plyadactylus Gecko*) is common. During the day it conceals itself from view, and towards evening, runs across the rafters, emitting its sharp, chirping note. On one occasion, I was much amused with a struggle between one of these domestic reptiles, and a large tarantula spider. The Chichak proved victorious, and succeeded in swallowing the insect, whose enormous legs, protruding from the lizard's mouth, gave the compound animal the aspect of some wondrous Octopod.* The natives are fond of the "Chichak," permitting it to harbour in security, for it clears their bamboo-dwellings of Spiders, Scorpions, Centipedes, and other vermin.

The Grass-Lizard (*Tachysaurus Japonicus*) is a slender, graceful reptile, of the most brilliant green, with a yellowish stripe on either side, and a tapering tail, four times the length of the body. It is found among the high grass, and in dense brakes, where the flowers are thickest. Here light, elegant, and sprightly, it preys on flies, and Orthopterous insects, which it captures in a most expert and dexterous manner. I have met with it also among the Korean Islands, the Meia-co-shimahs, and at Sama-Sana Island, in the China Sea.

---

* Pliny records the fact, however, that spiders are in the habit of capturing small Lizards, first entangling them in their webs, afterwards destroying them with their jaws, a spectacle, he observes, worthy of the amphitheatre!

The large Brown Lizard is common in Hong-Kong, Korea, and in Borneo. When caught, it bites severely. It is a ground Lizard, and is very active, preying on insects of various kinds. The Malays call it "Biṅgkarong." I have seen, while lazily reclining under the cool shade of the trees on the small Island of Burong, this large brown Lizard very attentively watching by the side of a populous Ant-hill, and, as the unsuspecting inhabitants came forth, in regular columns, as is their wont, he would lick them up, with a complacent shake of the head; looking about him, at the same time, in a knowing manner, with the fore part of the body raised high upon the legs, and his long tail undulating gently from side to side. Many thousands of the population of their city were, doubtless, consumed, in the course of an hour, by this fearful dragon without their walls.

I have observed the Fringed Tree-Gecko (*Ptychozoon homalocephala*) ascend the stems of trees with considerable agility, feeding greedily on the *Termites* that march in swarms up and down the trunks, but I fancy the observation of Boie, that "they use the expansions on their sides as a parachute," to be incorrect. I have seen them cling to the smooth stem of a Palm, and remain for a long time perfectly motionless. They appear to court the shade, and owing to their assimilating in colour to the bark, they are not easily to be perceived, even by the eye of the naturalist. They are certainly not aquatic, as M. Cuvier once imagined. In the young animal, the membrane is corrugated, and as if shrivelled up, although it is not rudimental, and, in some specimens, the free margin of the mouth is entire, while in others, it is scalloped, and irregular.

The *Uroplates fimbriatus*, another curious little Lizard, with the tail edged with a thin membrane, is also found in Borneo. I have caught it as it was running up and down the stems of the *Areca* palm, and I have seen it, also on the *Papyia*. This fimbriated *Gecko* is about the same size and colour as the common varieties of the *Ptyodactylus* that frequent houses, and is likewise a native of the island of Madagascar. One of the most beautiful Lizards I have met with in Borneo, is the *Tachydromus sexlineatus*, which is elegantly marked with white and black streaks and spots. It is generally found in sunny places, among dead leaves, and is astonishingly active. Before I take leave of the Bornean Reptiles, I must say a few words about the *Dracunculus quinque-fasciatus*. This tiny, painted Dragon of the East, the Flying Lizard of the Woods, is fond of clinging with its wings to the smooth trunks of trees, and there remaining immoveable, basking in the sun. When disturbed, it leaps, and shuffles away in an awkward manner. One I had in my possession, reminded me of a Bat, when placed on the ground. Sometimes he would feign death, and remain perfectly motionless, drooping his head, and doubling his limbs, until he fancied the danger over, then cautiously raising his crouching form, he would look stealthily around, and be off in a moment. It consumes flies in a slow and deliberate manner, swallowing them gradually. The eggs of the Lined Flying-Dragon (*Dracunculus lineatus*), which I have examined in Borneo, are white, and much smaller than those of the Golden-crested Wren. They are joined together in the manner of those of a Snake. The inclosed young have the lateral membrane fully formed. The eggs are found among decayed vegetable matter, and under the loose bark of trees.

The Banded-Head Dragon (*Dracunculus ornatus*) is a native of the Bashees, as well as of the Philippines, but I do not remember having seen it in Borneo.

CHAPTER III.

BASHEE AND MEIA-CO-SHIMAH GROUPS.

Macao—Its appearance from the Roads—*Batan*—A Marriage Feast—Rejoicings over the Dead—Exhibition of the Magic-Lanthorn—Appearance and Dress of the Women—Vegetation—Insects—Anecdote of a Spider—Pirate-Crabs—Story about a Land-Crab—Beautiful Molluscous Animal—Singular Crustacean—Sea-Eggs Star-Fish—Red-blooded Worms—Sharks—*Meia-co-shimahs*—Lost in the Woods—Scenery—A natural Amphitheatre—Proposed scheme of abduction—Gratitude of the Natives—Mountain Scenery The Screw-Pine—The Hibiscus, Banyan, Camelia, and other plants—Combination of Temperate and Tropical Forms—Palms—Bamboo—Torches—Edible Cryptogamic Plant—Vegetables—Reptiles—Blue-tailed Lizard—The Diodon—Enormous Octopi—The Kraken—Habits of Cephalopoda—Mollusca used as food—Modes of defence of Mollusks—Enemies of Mollusks—New Genus of Dorididæ—Habits of Crustaceans—Insects—Glow-Worm—The Centipede—The Scorpion—Spiders—Aspect of the Coral-reefs—Zoophytes.

On the 14th of September, 1843, we arrived at Hong-Kong, where we remained till the 29th of October, when we again made sail, and, on the 30th, anchored in Macao roads. Our short stay at this place did not, however, offer much to the notice of the naturalist, and I have already, in the body of the work, alluded to the busy appearance of the streets, and paid my humble tribute to the famous Cave of Camoens. I shall therefore, after briefly alluding to its appearance, from the water, proceed on to the Bashee Group. Macao offers a somewhat interesting sight when seen from the anchorage in the roads; the heights of the mountains, Charil, and Nillan, are crowded with forts and hermitages, and stretching along the water, the broad quay, or landing-place, (Praya grande,) shows a row of neat and airy houses. Two churches, and numerous monasteries of Capuchin, Augustin, and Dominican Monks, and one female convent, that of St. Clare, (rather curiously dedicated to the Conception of the Mother of God) ornament the city, and relieve the monotony of Chinese Bazaars, &c. The greater part of the population consists of "Mesticos," or a mixture of Chinese, Malay, and Portuguese.

On the 2nd of November, 1843, we left Macao roads, and on the 12th, arrived at Batan, where we remained till the 27th, and partially surveyed the group. Since that, several other visits, in February, 1844, in March, 1845, and in May and November of the same year, have enabled me to make a few observations, which may not be unacceptable or uninteresting. I remember on one occasion, being very much amused at a wedding-feast at which I was present, and as it exhibits a few peculiarities of the habits of these Islanders, I shall shortly describe it. The marriage-feast consisted of raw pork, finely chopped up, Yams, and Sweet-Potatoes, not omitting large quantities of their national beverage, the abominable Bashee. The ground was their table, their plates were torn from the Arum and Banana, "cujus folia instar patinæ natura formavit," as Rumphius would observe, and their fingers the knives and forks. After cramming their bodies with this, to us, indigestible collation, they adjourned to the dancing-room, a large shed-like building, where, to the sound of a fiddle, the only one in the island, they achieved a variety of extraordinary dances, not generally known among the "*Corps de ballet*," or others learned in the Terpsichorean mysteries. I had the honour of leading off the first set with the bride, and our performance appeared to give universal satisfaction; and soon the noise, chattering, and merriment would have done honour to a Christmas party in the rural parts of our own dear "Merrie England."

When a person is dangerously sick, and not likely to recover, his friends all leave him, and the house is carefully closed; the same custom prevails when a woman is in the pains of labour. Should the person die, a large pig is killed, and placed by the side of the deceased, and eating and drinking take place among the friends and neighbours, who assemble together for the express purpose; the whole proceeding reminding one exactly of an Irish wake, with the exception, perhaps, that the "Keeners" are not quite so accomplished and noisy.*

At the village of St. Carlo, in Batan, the evening exhibition of the magic-lanthorn gave great satisfaction to

* Marsden, in his 'History of Sumatra', alludes to a similar practice among the natives of that island. Referring to their funeral rites, he observes: "On this occasion, they kill, and feast on a Buffalo, and leave the head to decay on the spot, as a token of the honour they have done to the deceased, in eating to his memory;" and again, "the women who attend the funeral make a hideous noise not unlike the Irish howl."

the native Indians, who came attired for the occasion in their best habiliments, and even those spectators of the fairer sex were more decently covered than is their wont, and all assumed the most modest and well behaved deportment. Bursts of unrestrained merriment occasionally uprose, as some ridiculous phantasm, more fantastic than ordinary, met their wondering eyes. The short lace jackets, partially veiling, but not quite concealing the bosom, the sarong, tightly fitting about the hips, and the small bare feet, with the tips of the toes resting in little embroidered slippers, set off the well-made, symmetrical forms of the young girls, many of whom were really pretty.

Among the plants that grow wild in these islands, is the *Datura tatula*, an aromatic *Absinthium*, much valued as an anthelmintic and stomachic by the natives; an aromatic plant, very much like the *Teucrium Scorodonia*; a species of *Lamium*, with large showy purple flowers; the red and yellow-flowered *Canna*; the *Spondias dulcis*, and *Ebony* (*Diospyrus melanoxylon*); the Sweet-scented Violet (*Viola odorata*), a very palatable mountain Raspberry, the Castor-oil plant, and *Convolvulus*.

The insects which appear to be most common among the Bashees belong to the *Rhynochophora* and *Chrysomelidæ*. Small jumping beetles, *Halticæ*, commonly known by the name of "Garden Fleas", are very numerous, as are several *Scutelleridæ*; one *Callidea*, in particular, with a purple thorax, and light-green elytra, with black spots, is a very common insect. In some parts, the leaves are covered with innumerable larvæ of a handsomely-marked species of *Cassida*, all of them being concealed under little tents, formed out of their own excrement. A *Cereopis*, with an orange head and thorax, and black elytra, covered with orange spots, is common among the leaves in sunny places, and a velvety *Laguria*, with metallic-looking, green, punctulated wing-covers, is frequently seen pitching for an instant on the surface of the leaves, and taking flight again with the greatest velocity, having more the habits of some active dipterous insect than of a beetle. A small green *Mantis* is not uncommon, crawling among the culms of the long, rank grass.

In these islands I have noticed a large species of *Nephila*, which appears undescribed. The thorax is covered with a silvery pubescence, the abdomen has nine bright-yellow spots; the shanks of the first pair of tibiæ have a broad yellow band, and those of the posterior tibiæ, and penultimate joints, at their proximate ends, have a similar band. The rest of the body and legs is black. It forms a large, strong geometrical web. I have named the species *N. xanthospilota*.

The larvæ of the *Cryptocephali*, which abound here, form hollow, flattened cases of the comminuted cuticle of the leaves of the Sea-Convolvulus, and may be seen crawling about by hundreds, like the larvæ of *Cassidæ*. When, however, they are about to undergo their metamorphosis, they adhere firmly to the upper surface of the leaves, by means of a glutinous secretion, which is insoluble in water, and thus prevents their being washed away by the rains.

Under the decayed bark of trees I noticed, near Santa Ivanna, numbers of a species of *Chelifer*, running up and down the trunk, like so many pigmy Scorpions.

Among the Bashees, Spiders, of the genera *Nephila*

and *Acrosoma*, are numerous. There is one very large and handsome species of the latter genus, which has a strange habit, when alarmed, of suddenly erecting the second pair of legs, with a rapid, jerking motion; while, at the same time, he gathers together all the other legs, and shakes his web violently, in order, apparently, to intimidate his adversary, or, perhaps, to ascertain the strength of his position. If, however, the cause of alarm be continued, he coils himself up, while all his members become rigid, as in death, and then falling to the ground he remains like a small, inanimate, brown ball, until the enemy has departed. His cunning never forsakes him, even in his greatest emergency, for he continues all this while actually to maintain a communication between himself and his web, by means of a fine thread, fixed at one end to the centre of his toil, and at the other attached to the spinneret at the end of his abdomen. By means of this attenuated and invisible cord, he will climb up again when the danger is over, and resume his old pastime of rapine and blood-sucking.

The dry rocks swarm with Robber-Crabs, in their borrowed houses, all very busy and vivacious. These *Paguri*, or "Pirate Crabs," are very numerous throughout the Indian Islands, taking refuge, some in the prostrate bodies of decayed trees, some in the dead leaves and underwood, and some penetrating the verge of the forest, and ascending the *Hibiscus*, and other trees that border upon the sea. Many, again, are littoral in their habits, and others live at great depths. One species was obtained off the Cape, at 230 fathoms, having fabricated for itself a most ingenious dwelling, in the form of a univalve turbinated shell, from an *Ancillaria*, incrusted with an alcyonoid sponge. Others, again, like the *Birgus latro*, live high up the mountains, in holes of rocks, and in hollow trees. Regarding this Pirate, the natives of Batan tell very remarkable stories. They say it utters a sharp cry when caught, that it bites most severely, and defends itself with desperation, that it carries its eyes in its tail, runs with surprising celerity, feigning death when alarmed, and cuts down with its chelæ the young Cocoa-nut trees. From observation, I can say they run swiftly backwards, feign death when disturbed, feed on fruits, and are of immense strength. They are numerous at the Meïaco-shimah Group, where they inhabit holes in the banks among the pine woods. At Cocos Island, they are said to be destructive to the young Cocoa-nut trees. Sir E. Belcher informs me they attain to an enormous size in Pitcairns Island, and that there is a tradition of a woman, after having been cast ashore senseless, from a wreck, being deprived of her babe, by one of these giant Land-Crabs, and who was rescued only by the death of the captor.

The Hermit-Crabs form three large divisions, the *Birgus*, entirely terrestrial, and unprovided with a borrowed protective shell; one (*Cenobita*) which lives in shallow bays, fresh-water pools, or on the borders of woods, near the sea, and which closes the aperture of its dwelling with its left chela, and second left ambulatory foot; and a third-class (*Paguri*), which live at the bottom of the sea, at greater depths, which have foot-claws, elongated and feeble, extending straight forwards, and never closing the aperture of their stolen habitaculum. On being captured, they always retreat to the further end of the shell.

On the little Island of Ibugos, one of the Bashee Group, I had the pleasure of observing the large and handsome *Pleurobranchus testudinarius*, figured in Philippi's 'Enumeratio Molluscorum Siciliæ' (Tab. XX. Fig. 1.), in its native element. It was gliding quietly along, at the bottom of a shallow salt-water pool, near the shore. The cheloniform back of the animal is splendidly variegated with various rich and glowing colours, chiefly ruddy browns, Vandyke, Sienna, and Bistre, with Lake and Indian yellow, relieved by numerous dead white specks. The integument is covered with hexagonal markings, which each rise to a central nucleus, giving to the creature, when in motion, very much the appearance of a diminutive Tortoise. The branchial organs, beautifully lamellated, are arranged in two rows; they are placed in the body-groove of the right side, just above the foot, and are slightly protruded beyond the margin of the mantle. The belly is of a dark slate colour, the gills are purplish, and the appendages of the head of a rich red-brown. In its movements, this Mollusk is slow and deliberate, crawling in a slug-like manner, at the bottom of the water. The chromatogenous vesicles, or cytoblasts of colouring matter, when examined microscopically, were found very large, and well-developed in the soft, coloured skin of this beautiful Mollusk.

On the same flat, weedy beach, there is a peculiar species of *Callianassa*, which digs pits in the sand, in the manner of the Ant-Lion. It is a long, red-coloured powerful Crustacean, and allows the antennæ to be protruded some way from the mouth of its snare, and when the *Ophiuri*, or other animals, come unwarily by, his foot-claws are immediately darted forth, and the victim is dragged forcibly down to be devoured at leisure. The *Thalassina Scorpionoides* lives in holes, in a similar manner on the dry land, but is a weak, inactive creature, and does not seem possessed of the same ingenuity.

Among the numerous interesting marine forms of organic life to be met with among the Islands of the Bashee Group, not the least worthy of note are those Echinodermatous animals, the *Ophiuri, Asteriades, Holothuriæ*, and *Echini*. Eccentric in appearance, disgusting in their habits, they crawl languidly at the bottom of the sea, always intent on procuring food, consuming voraciously whatever comes in their way, so that they have appropriately been termed the "Scavengers of the deep." The *Ophiuri* affect the shallow weedy sands, which the water never leaves perfectly dry. They are fond of concealing themselves under flat stones, creeping into the anfractuosities of Corallines, or wrapping their bodies in the Algæ that lie around them. They sometimes bury their central discs in the semi-fluid sand, gently vibrating their snake-like arms, and protruding their tubular feet, which latter seem to serve them also as breathing organs. When pursued by an enemy, they move with considerable dispatch, dragging their bodies sideways, by seizing upon the irregularities of the ground with their long, flexible brachia.

A superb *Asterias*, upwards of a foot in diameter, beautifully marked with crimson, and covered with small dark spots, was obtained from the same locality. In deeper water along the coasts of these islands, the dredge furnished us with numerous *Spatangi*, the spines of which, when the animals are alive, have a slow oscillating movement, but they do not serve as such important organs of locomotion, as they do in the *Cidaris* and *Echinus*. The flattened forms of *Echinodermata* are very numerous all over the China Sea, strewing the muddy and sandy floor, and every time the dredge was examined, numbers of *Scutella*, *Lobophora*, and other forms, were procured; they appear to have less vivacity and perception than even the *Spatangi*. Among the *Echini* procured in this way, was a very handsome species, having bright ultramarine spots in the radial grooves, extending from the mouth to the anus, with spines long, slender, and marked with alternate light and dark rings; others were procured of a delicate rose-colour, and large and splendid *Cidares*, with tuberculated, compound spines, having other flattened spines and narrow calcareous plates in the sulci between the segments, were also noticed among other beauties brought to light by the dredge. The tubular processes which issue from the ambulacral pores in this *Cidaris*, are capable of enormous dilatation, and the sucking discs at their extremities, are possessed of considerable powers of tenacity. I observed the animal after rolling itself along, by means of its spines, assisted by its tubular appendages, the so-called feet, commence leisurely to ascend the sides of the wash-deck bucket, in which I held it captive, nor did it cease its persevering endeavours until it had arrived at the very edge, when, on touching it, the tubular tentacles were withdrawn, the suckers became detached, and the creature fell to the bottom of the vessel. The fact of this locomotion of *Echinoderms* was well known to Pliny, who observes, "sunt echini, quibus spinae pro pedibus."

The *Comatulæ* are very large and of splendid colours, in the Indian Seas. I have figured one gigantic species, the pinnate arms of which are of the most beautiful green, the oval disc being of a bright yellow. The *Comatula*, which is merely a detached *Pentacrinus*, and possibly only an adult form of those pedunculated *Echinoderms*, enjoys a very considerable latitude of motion, and can even raise itself from the bottom, and propel its body through the water by a series of successive jerks, employing the long flexible arms in the same manner as the *Argonaut* and *Octopus*. Both *Comatulæ* and *Gorgonocephali* are very difficult to preserve properly, even if they are first steeped in fresh water.

A species of *Holothuria* is common on the shores of these islands, of a dark black colour, being covered with a thick stratum of pigment, which stains the fingers purple, when the animal is touched. The original aspect of this "biche de mer" is concealed by granules of sand, which entirely cover the large cylindrical body. Its branchiæ are very beautifully fimbriated, and are of a deep purple colour. There is another species of *Holothuria* with a soft brown, tesselated, integument, which, on being touched, after suddenly ejecting the entire contents of its sacciform body, including the whole of the viscera and appendages, through the anal orifice, shrivels up, and immediately dies. Another species is of a brilliant crimson colour, with several rows of bright yellow pedicelli, an ultramarine coloured ring round the oral aperture, and beautiful compound branchiæ, of a pink rose colour. In another species, I noticed that the branchiæ were composed of numerous isolated trunks, beautifully ramified, and all radiating from the crown-shaped anal aperture so as to form, in appearance, a lovely violet star.

The *Sternaspis* inhabits deep water, and was procured by us on two occasions from a muddy floor. It is very inactive in its habits, and when alive moves the spines at one end of the body in an oscillatory manner. It appears to be an animal of delicate constitution, dying and shrivelling up very shortly after being taken. The worm-like *Sipunculus*, which inhabits the loose moist sand, in which it forms rather deep burrows, resembles a gigantic *Arenicola*, to which it also approximates in its habits.

A small species of spotted Shark is rather common along the shore, and appears to be a very active depredator among the shoals of fish that here abound. I made a capture of one of these fish-tigers, which, unluckily for him, had run aground upon a shallow sandbank. After making surprising efforts to bite his assailant, and regain his native element, he finally became my lawful prize.

Speaking of Sharks, I may here mention a curious circumstance, showing the extreme voracity of these fish, which occurred at Unsang, on the East coast of Borneo. A large species of *Zygæna* sprang from the water, seized a bullock's hide which was drying at the bows of the ship, and succeeded in tearing a portion of it off. One hundred miles from Batan, a shark was caught with a partially digested pig in his stomach, which had been thrown overboard at the anchorage of San Domingo, in that island. Sharks are always, and justly so, detested by the sailors, and they ever experience a certain savage delight in hacking them to pieces with their knives, before life is extinct; and there really is something very unpleasant in the quiet splashings of these voracious monsters, when they are numerous round a ship, and something very revolting in the greedy pertinacity with which they seek the filthy garbage and offal thrown overboard.

Annelides are observed in great numbers along the flat shores of some of these islands. Vermiform, and slow-moving, they mostly exist blindfold, and buried in the sand; while a few are provided with articulated members and move freely about. The *Eunice tubicola* lives in a long horny, transparent tube, within which, strange to say, it can readily turn end for end. The tube is furnished at one extremity with a delicate valvular apparatus, which allows the water to flow but in one direction. The skin of some of these *Annelides* is soft, and covered with a slimy secretion, and I have seen one species cover itself with loose calcareous grains, like the huge dark-coloured *Holothuriæ* of the coast of Ibugos. They, however, appear to be, for the most part, helpless and indolent beings, not possessed of much activity, but vegetating in their dark abodes, leading lives insignificant and obscure. Some few, however, as the *Nais* and *Scyllis*, would seem to repudiate such an accusation, seeing that they enjoy a greater latitude of locomotion, with the possession of senses much more developed. They are very difficult to preserve entire, owing to the facility with which their segments separate when the animals are captured. Although apparently so inert and helpless, in many instances they are provided with means of aggression and defence by no means despicable, consisting in long, sharp, arrow-headed bristles. Many of these setigerous forms, as *Aphrodite*, *Euphrosone*, and some others, prove most troublesome to the zoologist, when examining the contents of the dredge, penetrating the skin by means of their fasciculi of small sharp spicula, and producing the same unpleasant irritating effects as the spicula of some sponges, the hairs of certain caterpillars, and the *Dolichos pruriens*, and many other plants.

On the 27th of November we left the pleasant Batani Islands, and on the 1st of December, arrived at Patchung-san, one of the Meïa-co-shimah Group, and I shall now proceed to offer a few observations connected with the natural productions of these islands, merely premising that the scientific details will be published in another work.

Every one of the party seemed to enjoy himself on the occasion of our survey of this island, and each one had some little adventure to relate which had happened to himself. In one trip, as I was astride a wretched apology for a horse, a most miserable "Rosinante," furnished with heavy uncouth stirrups, a wooden saddle, a preposterous bit, and grass-rope bridle, in hot pursuit after a curious Land-Crab, a most cunning and active species of *Birgus*, I unfortunately lost my way, and wandered about the woods, perfectly "at fault." Trusting, however, to the intelligence of my beast, and thinking he must be better acquainted with the intricacy of the forest-paths than myself, I gave him the reins, such as they were, and allowed him to exercise his own discretion, when, after conducting me through numerous dense thickets; walking with me up rugged, stony, precipitous steps, nearly perpendicular; now stumbling over loose stones, and now half-hanging me, like Absalom, on the branches of the trees; after traversing the beds of shallow, running rivulets, and threading marshes, almost knee-deep in mud, I found, to my great vexation, and regret for equine sagacity, that the foolish animal had, after all, mistaken his road, and had conducted me to the margin of the sea, in a beautiful, wild and desolate spot, with enormous rocks, clothed with verdure, towering around and above me, and huge masses of broken coral strewing the strand beneath. I had not much time, however, allowed me to contemplate the beauties of the scene, or the novelty of my situation, for the jealous vigilance, or polite hospitality as they wished it to be considered, of our friends, the poor islanders, interrupted my reverie, and prevented my being altogether food for the crows. They kindly urged me forward in the right road, and persuading me to quicken my pace, before long, I was comfortably lodged in a temporary house built in a few minutes, for the accomodation of the Captain, on the summit of a hill, surrounded, on every side, with beautiful woods. Here we bivouacked for the night on beds of dry grass, the natives crowding round large fires in the open air, and the mandarins seated on mats, under a shed, smoking their pipes, drinking innumerable small cups of tea, and talking together nearly the whole of the night. Sometimes our path lay along a grassy plain, varied at intervals by huge piles of rocks and stones, overgrown with Vines, and other climbing plants, or masses of dark Pine trees, covering and surmounting the wooded knolls, and furnishing deep shady glades between them. At other times, we would wend our way through miles of sable forest, dark, shadowy, and silent, and filled with nothing but lofty Pines; in our course, ascending precipitous and rocky paths, crossing narrow causeways, or rude bridges over waterfalls; and then again our road would be in open daylight, across broad fields of Sweet-Potatoes, or by the side of "padi" swamps. In Koo-kien-san, we came, on one occasion, suddenly upon a most magnificent natural amphitheatre. From a verdurous plain, covered with the Palmetto Palm, and prickly *Pandanus*, gigantic *Hibiscus* trees, and long coarse grass, huge hills uprose in every direction, their sides densely and beautifully wooded with trees of varied foliage, while here and there a patch of bare red rock, or yellow stratified acclivity would relieve the sameness of the universal green. In many places were ravines with running water trickling down the sides.

To such an extent did I ingratiate myself with these good people, by giving them medicines, and adopting their habits, that, in this same island of Koo-kien-san, a plot was actually laid to carry me off into the mountains, in a rude kind of sedan, with tempting offers of a wife and house, and as much tobacco as I pleased. My services as a Surgeon might have had some influence in bringing them to this determination. Finding, however, all their pressing tenders, and what they conceived tempting offers, of no avail, their chagrin was very manifest, and they contented themselves with dressing my hair in their peculiar fashion, investing me with the silver "Kami-saschi," and placing around me an "eschaw," or robe, then sitting in silence, deplored the resolution I had thought proper to adopt. At one of the villages, an old Chief brought down his infant daughter in his arms, and besought my assistance, as she was afflicted with a tumor in the neck. On my pointing out the course he should pursue, he joyfully returned to the village, and shortly afterwards returned, begging my acceptance of a small present, which consisted of some ground-nuts, a couple of fowls, a flask of "saki," and some Sweet-Potatoes.

In some of the mountain scenes, among the still quiet glens, apart from the villages, there is an air of rude grandeur and magnificence, hardly to be looked for on an island of such comparatively small dimensions as Koo-kien-san. In one part of the island a stream of water falls from a great height, producing one of the highest waterfalls, perhaps, hitherto known; and towering above this, are several tapering peaks, which, seen glittering in the splendour of the setting sun, produce as fine a picture as any Salvator Rosa could have desired. In other precipitous parts, vast masses of rocks, lichen-stained, and overgrown with a wild and tangled vegetation, lie crowded and jumbled together in the utmost confusion, rendering it very rough and difficult work for our small-footed ponies. Although both myself and pony came rolling down one of these precipitous passes, with high banks on either side, yet I would rather trust my neck to the sagacity of these hill-bred animals than to my own pedestrian exertions. In some of these romantic, and beautifully-wooded valleys, a large white-flowered *Convolvulus*, or rather *Calystegia*, climbs among the tangled thickets in the wildest luxuriance, and, mingling its pure blossoms with those of a yellow-flowered *Hibiscus*, produces quite a pleasing effect.

Among the Meïa-co-shimah Islands, I first had the curiosity to taste the fruit of the *Pandanus*, or Screw-Pine, and found it refreshing and juicy, but very insipid. When perfectly mature, however, they certainly look very tempting, and resemble large rich-coloured Pine-Apples. In several instances I found the interior of half-decayed fruits filled with a fermented, subacid liquor, and have no doubt that a decent wine might be manufactured from the pulp. The stones, though very hard, contain a pleasant kernel.

A large yellow-flowered *Hibiscus* grows in vast quantities, offering a most beautiful spectacle in the deep woody gorges of Koo-kien-san. In the young shoots, the spiral vessels resembling spider-webs, could be distinctly seen with the naked eye, on breaking through the green stems. On the open plains, a small *Campanula* with a very flat blue corolla, and a curious flower, with white tufts on the petals, are very common.

In some parts of Pa-tchung-san we passed through large masses of the *Canna Indica*, with red and yellow flowers, sometimes inclining to a deep orange, producing a very beautiful and brilliant effect, and near the villages the *Camelia Japonica* attains the dimensions of a large tree, frequently several feet in diameter, and loaded as it was, at the time of our visit, with handsome red wax-like blossoms, it imparts a very gay aspect to the scenery. Groves of Guava (*Psidium pyriferum*) and a small species of Orange, contribute materially to the same end. In the quiet spots, selected for the interment of the dead, the Banyan

> spreads her arms
> Branching so broad and long, that in the ground
> The bended twigs take root, and daughters grow
> About the mother tree, a pillar'd shade
> High overarch'd, and echoing walks between.
> *Paradise Lost.*

The sugar-cane grows sparingly, and is accounted a luxury rather than a necessary of life. Altogether, there is a strange mingling of temperate and tropical forms, both in the Animal and Vegetable Kingdoms, among these islands. You will find the Violet and the Rose the *Polygala* and the Marygold growing side by side with the Plantain, the Pepper and *Pandanus*; you will see the Fire-fly, and the Painted-Lady Butterfly occupying the same trees, and the Centipede, *Theliphonus*, Scorpion, *Opatrum*, and *Hister* under the same stones. The Palms gradually decrease in numerical importance and diversity of species, as you recede from the equatorial line. The Cocoa-nut does not grow much beyond the twentieth degree of latitude; but the *Pandanus*, or Screw-Pine, is apparently the most hardy of them all, and is the last to disappear. At the Island of Pa-tchung-san I found the *Musa paradisaica*, but very poor and small, and rarely producing fruit; the Palmetto, or Fan-Palm, (*Borassus flabelliformis*) however, seemed to thrive very well in the same island, and is used by the natives for a variety of purposes, particularly in the manufacture of hats. Among these islands I found the long Pepper (*Piper longum*) creeping among the loose stones of tombs, in wild uncultivated places, and the red globular berries of the half-ripe fruit, formed a pleasing contrast to the green foliage of the trailing Vines.

The Bamboo (*Arundo Bambos*) grows wild in large dense brakes, and in many parts the plains and mountain-flanks are covered with Pine forests, the trunks, in several cases, being chipped away by the natives for the sake of the resinous wood, which is here employed as candles, and which produces a bright, strong, clear light. They use, likewise, a kind of light, dry wood, as slow-matches, binding bundles of it together with grass, never allowing it once to be extinguished during many days. In numerous localities, more particularly on the summits of the hills, there is a kind of Cryptogamic plant, with a soft green, and somewhat gelatinous *thallus*, crumpled and irregular in appearance, which is eaten by the poorer sorts of the people. A kind of wild Celery, apparently the same as our *Apium graveolens*, is likewise employed by them as an agreeable anthelmintic and stomachic. Yams do not appear to be known, but Sweet-Potatoes, Peas, Turnips, Carrots, and Radishes, are met with in large quantities. The Cotton plant (*Gossypium herbaceum*) is cultivated in fields in many parts of the Meïa-co-shimah Group.

You will see darting among the grass, in the Islands of the Meïa-co-shimahs, a very elegant and beautiful little Lizard, with the throat and sides tinged with a delicate red, and five bright yellow lines running along the back, the central line dividing at the junction of the head and neck, and again uniting at the apex of the muzzle. The dorsal surface is black, and the sides are reddish-brown, with minute dark spots; the belly is of a light dull yellow, the legs are dark brown above, and light coloured on their under surface, and the tail, long and tapering, is of a lively and brilliant ultramarine blue. This pretty little *Saurian* is very active in its movements, frequenting the long grass and undergrowth, feeding on Flies, Locusts, and Caterpillars, and, in its turn, very frequently falling a prey to the small species of Viper peculiar to these islands.

The Green Turtle (*Chelonia mydas*), notwithstanding the inclemency of the season, was seen swimming in the tranquil bays, and a handsome yellow *Hydrophis*, banded with black, was also met with, frequenting the rocky coasts, hiding in holes of Corallines, and basking on the exposed rocks. It swims with great elegance, and dives with facility.

A species of *Trigonocephalus*, with the poison-fangs enormously developed, attains here to a very large size. A small *Coluber* is very common; and a handsome spotted *Tropidonotus* was procured, very similar to the *T. natrix*, or Ringed Snake, of Europe.

A brilliant green Tree-Frog (*Hyla*), with a bright orange abdomen, is found on the margins of the rivers, and among the four species of Lizards I noticed, including the blue-tailed *Zootica* and the *Tachysaurus Japonicus*, was a large brown species, remarkable for its black eyes, the golden iris being very narrow, and entirely concealed by the eyelids. The Toad, the Tree-Frog, the Viper, the Lizard, and the Snake, assume nearly the same form, size, and colour, that we observe in Europe; but here also occur forms, like the *Chelonia* and *Trigonocephalus*, which remind you that these regions are connected in their natural productions, with the Islands of the Archipelago of Malayan Asia.

Among Fish, a species of *Diodon* is common in the bays of Pa-tchung-san and the adjacent islands. The eye of this singular Fish is large, with a black pupil and splendid golden iris; when first caught it bites severely with its trenchant teeth, and spits at those who approach it. The *Diodon* swims heavily, and at the bottom, feeding on small *Crustacea*, Shell-Fish, and *Annelida*; when irritated, it distends its mis-shapen ugly body, and when puffed up in this manner, can, with difficulty, make progress through the water. I have seen seamen practise a rather cruel experiment on the poor *Diodon*, which they term "sprit-sail-yarding." This consists in passing a thin piece of wood across the skin of the back, which prevents the Fish from sinking, and at the same time enables it to make use of its fins; in this condition the unfortunate animal progresses through the water, to the great edification of Jack, who laughs, and calls it his "little steamer!"

Octopi, of enormous size, are occasionally met with among the Islands of the Meïa-co-shimah Group. I measured one, which two men were bearing on their shoulders across a pole, and found each brachium rather more than two feet long, giving the creature the power of exploring a space of about twelve feet, without moving, taking the mouth for a central point, and the ends of the arms for the periphery. Dorsal plates of *Sepiæ*, moreover, are found strewing the beaches, a foot and a half in length. These are not quite so monstrous, however, as those of a certain species which Trebius Niger, quoted by Pliny, mentions, the head of which was of the size of a cask, the brachia each thirty feet long, and the death of which was so difficult to achieve.* Pliny, himself, however, allows that in the Mediterranean *Loligines* may be found five cubits in length, and *Sepiæ* two! Sir Edward Belcher informs me that the fishermen of Newfoundland have a legend among themselves, that the backbone of a Cuttle-Fish was once found lying on the northern shores, as large as a whale! Surely the living owner of that dorsal plate must have been the famous "Kraken" that we remember to have read about! On moonlight nights among these islands, I have frequently observed the *Sepiæ* and *Octopi* in full predatory activity, and have had considerable trouble and difficulty in securing them, so great is their restless vivacity at this time, and so vigorous their endeavours to escape. They dart from side to side of the pools, or fix themselves so tenaciously to the surface of the stones, by means of their sucker-like *acetabula*, that it requires great force and strength to detach them. Even when removed, and thrown upon the sand, they progress rapidly, in a sidelong shuffling manner, throwing about their long arms, ejecting their ink-like fluid in sudden violent jets, and staring about with their big, shining eyes (which at night appear luminous, like a cat's,) in a very grotesque and hideous manner. The natives of most of the islands in the China Seas dry these Mollusks; as likewise the soft parts of *Haliotis, Turbo, Hippopus, Tridacna*, &c., and make use of them as articles of food. But from my little experience of this kind of diet, notwithstanding the

* Vide Pliny, Cap. xxx. Lib. 9.

assertion of the learned Bacon, in his 'Experiment solitary touching Cuttle-ink,' that the "Cuttle is accounted a delicate meat, and is much in request,"* I should say that it is as indigestible and innutritious, as it is certainly tough and uninviting. Cephalopods, however, are eaten at the present day on some parts of the Mediterranean coast; and in Hampshire I have seen the poor people collect assiduously the *Sepiæ*, and employ them as food. Besides using a small kind of salted beans, the natives of the Meïa-co-shimahs flavour the balls of Rice and of Sweet-Potatoes, which constitute the principal articles in their system of dietetics, with a peculiar composition, very similar in taste to "Blachong," the universal sauce of the inhabitants of the Oriental Archipelago, a substance made out of decomposed Shrimps and small Fish, fermented, and dried in the sun. Notwithstanding the proverbial partiality of the Japanese for *Soy*, I never saw that condiment employed at any of the entertainments of the Meïa-co-shimites.

The common Snail of the Meïa-co-shimahs is eaten by the natives, as the *Helix aspersa* and *pomatia* are occasionally in Europe. The Malays are fond of the *Cerithium telescopium* and *palustre*, found in the Mangrove swamps. They throw them on their wood fires, and, when sufficiently cooked, break off the sharp end of the spire, and suck the tail of the animal through the opening. The *Haliotis* is taken from the shell, dried in the sun, strung together on rattan, and is eaten raw by the same people.

The poorer people of the Philippines are fond of the *Arca inequivalvis*, boiling them as we do Cockles and

* Works. Nat. Hist. p. 167. Bohn's Ed.

Muscles; the flesh, however, is red, and very bad-flavoured. Some *Monodonta*, which I have eaten among the Korean Islands, are quite peppery, and bite the tongue, producing the same unpleasant effects upon that organ, as the root of the *Arum maculatum*, or leaves of the Taro, but in a much less intense degree; and a species of *Mytilus*, found in the same locality, has very similar unpalatable qualities.

The *Paludina*, common in the Padi fields, in these islands, escapes detection, by covering itself over with small hard masses of mud, in which state it resembles those turbinated habitacula of the larvæ of some freshwater insect, to which Swainson has applied the name *Thelidomus*, conceiving them to be true shells, representing, I believe, in his quinary system, the genus *Phorus*. This peculiarity of the *Paludinas* did not appear to me to be accidental, as I have seen shells of the same genus in England, Java, and elsewhere, which entirely wanted the very peculiar appearance above alluded to, and the *Lymnæas*, in the same ponds, were not muddier than is usual with those shells. All Mollusks have certain means of avoiding threatened dangers. The Gasteropods withdraw their bodies within their shells,

> As the snail, whose tender horns being hit,
> Shrinks backward in his shelly cave with pain,
> And there, all smother'd up, in shade doth sit,
> Long after fearing to creep forth again.—*Shakspeare*.

The *Pteropods* contract their bodies when alarmed, and sink suddenly to the bottom; the Bivalves close their shells, and bid defiance to the enemy; the *Pholas* and *Solen*, like many of the Cephalopods, including the

Cuttle-Fish and *Loligo*, eject, as is well known, a coloured fluid, and so escape in the midst of the clouded water they have produced. The *Ianthina* and *Aplysiæ* have the same powers, especially the large *Dolabella Rumphii*; and the *Actiniæ* squirt water in the face of the intruder, as they shrink back into their burrows.

When we consider how very numerous the enemies of Molluscous animals are, we must allow they have much need for such ingenious modes of defence. On the high seas they constitute the prey of Dolphins, Cachelots, and of a thousand voracious fishes, besides insatiate Albatrosses and industrious Petrels, which are ever on the alert to capture them. Along the shores they are snapped up by patient Turnstones, and enterprising Oyster-catchers; and in fresh-water ponds they become the lawful prey of Plovers, and all those other birds that love oozy watery haunts. Terrestrial Mollusca find enemies, even among insects, many *Silphidæ* attacking and destroying them in the same manner as the *Hydrophili* and other *Philhydrida* prey upon and devour the *Paludinas* and *Lymnæas*, among aquatic genera.

The list of genera of fresh-water shells in these islands is limited, as far as my experience goes, to *Paludina*, *Lymnæa*, and *Assiminæa*; no *Succineæ*, *Neritinæ*, *Planorbes*, *Ampullariæ* or *Melaniæ* were observed by us. The land-shells were *Helix*, *Pupa*, *Clausilia*, *Truncatella*, *Carocolla*, and *Cyclostoma*.

In the shallow pools left by the receding tide on the shore of Koo-kien-san, one of these islands, I discovered a large species of *Dorididæ*, which appears to be the type of a new genus, differing from all the other genera of the family, in having the vent and the gills, which are extruded from it, situated beneath the edge of the mantle, which latter is extended beyond the circumference of the foot, while in all the other genera, as far as I am aware of, the vent and gills are situated on the mantle itself. This genus may be called *Hypobranchæa*, and will be figured in the 'Zoology of the Samarang,' now in course of publication. The species (*H. fusca*, Adams,) resembles in appearance a large, flat, sandy-coloured Slug, and crawls along in a slow and languid manner over the sandy surface. Owing to its exact resemblance in colour and appearance to the floor on which it lives, it is well calculated to escape the notice of many of its enemies. My specimen was mutilated by a spade in the hands of a seaman, owing to this circumstance, and although a considerable portion of the foot and mantle was removed, such was the tenacity of the life of the animal that it crawled away apparently as if uninjured.

Two of the most remarkable Crustaceans to be met with in this Group, are the *Scopimera globosa* of De Haan, and the *Mycteris deflexifrons*, of the same naturalist. The *Scopimera globosa* forms burrows in the muddy banks and sandflats, just above low-water mark, perforating the surface in every direction. In some parts of Koo-kien-san, these Crabs are so numerous that they impart a peculiar colour to the shores when seen at a little distance. They walk but slowly, and are very inactive in their habits. When disturbed, they make awkward efforts to get out of sight, by quickly burying themselves in the sandy mud like some *Macrophthalmi*.

The *Mycteris deflexifrons*, although somewhat resembling

Ocypodes in many particulars, yet differ materially from them in vivacity of movement. Like their swift-footed consimilars, however, they form superficial burrows in the sandy mudflats, into which they retreat in a clumsy, scrambling manner, on the approach of danger. In many parts of the Meïa-co-shimahs I have ridden over many acres of sandy mud, covered with these bright blue Crabs, and on looking behind could perceive a dark straight line, made by the passage of the horse, as he caused them to burrow in the mud, in his progress onwards. They seem to enjoy themselves just after the water has left the flats dry, and appear then to be most on the alert in procuring food.

There is a species of *Gelasimus* allied to *G. Chlorophthalmus* (Edwards), with a bright orange foot-claw bigger than its body, which inhabits burrows, formed among the grass, in muddy places near the sea, and among the poorer classes the *Ocypode ceratophthalma* is collected as food. They dig them out of their deep sandy burrows with great eagerness and diligence, by means simply of their hands. I have seen them sometimes drive them out by insinuating a long pliant twig into the winding labyrinth of the crab, and so forcing its inmate to make its appearance. I have known them also, where the ground was hard, pour water into the holes, and so inundate the poor *Ocypode*. These people, by examining certain marks, can tell whether the swift-footed inhabitant is at home or abroad, and conduct their operations accordingly.

On the flat sandy beaches of this group of islands, if you take the trouble to turn over the stones which the tide has left dry, you will perceive hundreds of *Porcellanæ*, flattened Crabs, shuffling along the surface of the upturned stones in a very ludicrous manner. They are very active and bustling in their habits. This observation, however, applies more particularly to *P. pulchripes* (Adams and White) and the species allied to it; for another species, *P. versimana*, (Adams and White) is found among the coral reefs of Koo-kien-san, and is apathetic and indolent, and *P. obesula* (Adams and White) was dredged from twenty-four fathoms in the Sooloo Sea, and was very sluggish in its movements. A very rare and delicate little Crab was ascertained by me to belong to the fauna of this group, namely, the *Elamena unguiformis* of De Haan. It is spider-like in its appearance, slow in its movements, and lurks concealed in holes of the under-surface of stones immediately below high-water mark. I discovered, also, a species of *Calappa*, allied to *C. spinocissima*, under stones, in the shallow sandy bays, which covers itself with sand, and when captured feigns death, remaining perfectly motionless with all its members snugly tucked under the carapace, and the chelæ folded on the front of the shell. It is a timid and slow-moving creature.

A new species of *Alphæus*, a curious looking shrimp-like animal, which inhabits pools under stones on sandy beaches, and when disturbed makes a sharp loud clicking noise, by snapping the foot-claws, likewise rewarded our research. In the Padi fields, a species of *Gecarcinus*, allied to *G. lateralis*, is very common, running about in all directions, feeding on the larvæ of Dragon-flies and other insects, and becoming, in its turn, the prey of the large Herons that are always to be seen fishing for Frogs in those localities. To these may be added new species of *Hippa, Remipes, Trapezia, Macrophthalmus, Pilumnus* and others, which will be described in another place.

In many parts, these islands are over-run with various kinds of *Sesarma*, the species of which differ very much in their habits. Among those I detected as belonging to the Fauna of the Meïa-co-shimah Group, one was found under stones, on sandy flats just below high-water mark; another inhabited the coral reefs; a third, fresh-water rivulets and pools, hiding under stones and logs, and climbing the roots of trees with great facility. Another, allied to *S. affinis*, De Haan, has the same habits; another species, with the same love of climbing and hiding under stones, runs more upon the dry land, among the roots of grass, &c., and is very agile. One, of a marbled, light sandy colour, with pale grey blotches, lives in the holes of the sand, in brackish pools; another, with a hairy carapace, dark brown and purple, inhabits holes in the sandy beach above high-water mark; while in another part of the world, I found a species living in fresh-water rivulets among weeds; and in the forest of Celebes another under damp stones and logs, at some considerable distance from fresh-water ponds.

Most of the *Dorippe* inhabit deep water, from twenty to thirty fathoms, living on a muddy bottom. They are very numerous in the China Sea. The Chinese fishermen often bring them up in their nets, and among large numbers which I have observed in their boats, I have found nearly every individual with an adventitious body (I believe an alcyonoid sponge) attached to the carapace, and retained in its position by the hooks of the two small posterior dorsal pairs of legs. This body is divisible into a thin brown layer, with concentric fibres, and an external, white lamina, with radiating fibres, and a dark central nucleus. I have frequently noticed precisely the same peculiarity in *Dromia verrucosipes*, in the Meïa-co-shimah Group, and I believe naturalists have perceived the same habit among other genera. Many of the specimens both of *Dorippe* and of *Dromia* which I examined in this condition, had perfectly soft carapaces, and this body may serve them as a protection during the season of their moulting The *Caphyra pectenicola* (White) bears a small pecten shell, in a similar manner. This curious little Crustacean, which was dredged by us in the Sunda Straits from thirteen fathoms, takes up its abode in the deepest valve of the deserted *Pecten*, locking itself on by the claws of its posterior legs to the ears of the shell, its tender back being secured from harm by this adventitious covering. Sir E. Belcher informs me that he discovered another species in the Gulf of Papagaya, inhabiting the single valve of a *Terebratula*, which was in a partially softened condition.

Many other genera, as *Hyas*, *Maia*, *Arctopsis*, *Mithrax* and *Pericera*, are well known to have similar propensities, loading their backs with foreign bodies, Sponges, Algæ, and other Phytozooic and vegetable productions.

On the summits of the hills near the sea-coast of many of these islands, and particularly on those of Koo-kien-san, I procured numerous *Talitri* and *Gammari* from among the roots of the long damp grass; rather a remarkable circumstance, as these Crustaceans are usually found close to the margin of the sea, concealing themselves under stones and sea-weed. They were jumping about in all directions, and appeared to wage a continual war, not only with hundreds of *Tropidinoti* and other *Orthopterous* insects, but with a bark brown *Carabideous* insect, which was found running with great rapidity among them, evidently bent on destruction.

The *Charybdis miles* of De Haan was swimming and shuffling about in the shallow water of the flat, sandy beach, proving a very troublesome companion to those seamen who were bare-footed, on account of the very long, large, sharp spiny powerful claws, with which they are furnished; for although they fold the chelæ on the forepart of the carapace, and contract their legs when caught, they would dart among the legs of the boat's crew, and inflict rather severe scratches. As, however, they were large, and fit for the pot, this was considered a mere trifle by honest, hungry Jack.

On one occasion, I was very much surprised and delighted, as we were sitting in a circle with the natives around a large wood fire, to see some young boys bring in several large Crabs, having their chelæ, or foot-claws, covered in a very remarkable manner, with a quantity of coarse silky hair, so very dense and thick that they more resembled rabbits' feet than the claws of a Crustaceous animal. These curious Crabs, which were the *Eriocheir Japonicus* of De Haan, were immediately, even before I could rescue a specimen, thrown upon the embers alive, and when burnt crisp and brown, broken by the teeth of the assembled islanders, and consumed, with a few exceptions, shell and all. They appeared very much to relish this primitive, and somewhat savage kind of feast.

Among the new and interesting *Crustacea* met with by us on the coasts, were numerous species of *Leucosiæ*. These handsomely-marked creatures generally affect a sandy bottom, and live at considerable depths among Corallines and Madrepores. They are seldom found in muddy or turbid water, but love the deep sandy banks, where they move in a sluggish manner, and seem destitute of acute perceptions. Sufficiently protected by their porcelain shields, they want the quick progression and threatening attitudes assumed by many Crustaceans. One of the most beautiful of the species is the *Leucosia hæmatosticta* (Adams and White), which is of a dead white colour, covered with numerous round crimson spots.

Among the *Orthoptera* noticed by us among the islands was an apparently new genus, between *Tropidinotus* and *Teratodes*, beautifully marbled with crimson, brown, and yellow; a *Phylloptera*, of a dirty, dull, green colour, having four dark spots on each elytron; a *Mantis*, of a light brown colour; and a large species of *Phasma*; thus again illustrating the curious intermixture of temperate and tropical forms, even among the world of insects. One of the most common *Hemiptera* was a genus of *Coricidæ*, of a delicate emerald green, with two bright golden spots on the body. A genus of *Orthoptera*, allied to *Truxalis*, but with the antennæ, nearly cylindrical, and the head not so much produced, was a common inhabitant of the grassy summits of the hills.

There is a large and handsome Glow-worm (*Lampyris*) which hides, during the daytime, under dead leaves and stones; but which is beautifully luminous during the night. The penultimate segment, slightly gibbous, constitutes a bilobate lamp of great brilliancy, emitting a much yellower light than the generality of this tribe. It has a voluntary power of suppressing or evolving the shining property of its lantern, and when handled, feigns death, at the same time hiding its light, until the danger is passed. There are yellow non-luminous spots on all the other segments, and the upper part of the body is dark brown, approaching to black. The legs are brown, with the exception of the distal ends of the femur and the tarsus, which are of a lighter colour. The head is furnished with a retractile proboscis, having a yellow sheath.

The Centipede of this group lays her eggs under flat stones, to the number of about twelve or fourteen. They are of a semi-transparent straw colour, and the female coils herself around them like a snake. In the egg, the young one is pale, transparent, light-yellow, perfectly globular, with a slit or mark like the hilum of a seed; this slit afterwards forms a deep furrow, and then a wide fissure, one side of which is somewhat more produced and becomes the head, and the other, folded inwards, is the tail and remainder of the body. A large dark spot then appears on each side of the head, which are the eyes, and three short legs protrude from the skin towards the anterior part of the body. Immediately after their extrusion from the egg, the helpless young are nearly pellucid and yellowish, with great black eyes, rounded bodies, big heads, and rudimental legs; the segments are but faintly marked, and the little animal is bent upon itself like a larva of a Cockchafer; the antennæ show themselves by degrees, the other members make their appearance, and, as well as the body, become distinctly articulated; the integument becomes hard and opaque, and the, as yet, harmless little insect crawls about, languidly at first, but afterwards more briskly. The mother appears as attentive to her offspring as an Earwig; and as jealous of their safety, as a hen over that of her chickens.

There is a small *Scolopendra*, with equal-sized segments, of a dull violet colour, found under stones in these islands, and another small species perfectly black.

The small Scorpion found in rotten wood, under bark, and under stones, is of a delicate form, and is, I believe, a species of *Androctonus*. There is another darker and larger kind, found also, but more rarely, under stones, that appears almost identical with the *Scorpio Europæus*. Although held in great abhorrence by the natives, neither of these Scorpions possesses much venom, as I had the misfortune to be stung by one species, and one of the boat's crew by the other.

The Spiders of the Meïa-co-shimah Islands exhibit some very remarkable forms. There is a curious *Epeira*, with the dorsal surface of the abdomen furnished with a radiated crown of hard pointed processes, and the epidermis richly painted with brown and gold. It spins a large and regular web in every brake and bush.

Another large and singular Spider, with long, slender legs, and an elongated body, black, and marked with yellow lunules and patches, crawls among the foliage of the trees in the low woods that occur in some parts of Pa-tchung-san. Another species of the same genus is altogether black. I noticed this kind also in the Bashee Islands.

The *Theliphonus caudatus,* a curious osculating link between the Scorpions and *Tarantulas,* is not uncommon in the islands. It remains concealed generally under logs of wood and stones, and seems to love dark, damp forests as the seat of its depredations, living in the society of the larvæ of Glow-worms, the Scorpions, the *Scolopendræ,* and a dingy coloured species of *Blatta.* It is slow in its movements, and when alarmed raises its stingless tail in a threatening manner, but never attempts to use its cheliceræ, as organs of aggression or of defence.

I am aware that persons have been accused of allowing their imagination to trifle too freely with the reins, in describing submarine scenery; but I shall simply state the matter as I found it, and in language that came freely on the spot, and educed from first impressions. Dendritic Zoophytes, with their slender branches loaded with innumerable richly coloured *polypi,* like trees covered with delicate blossoms, uprose from the clear clean bottom of the bay, distinct and characteristic in their specific forms, and contrasting strangely and powerfully with those most apathetic and stone-like combinations of the plant, the animal and the rock, the Madrepores, the Millepores, and the Nullipores. Flat, and immovably extended on the sand, in the bare spots between the Corallines, were impassive large blue five-fingered *Asterias*; and crawling with an awkward shuffling movement, like an *Octopus,* were numbers of the slender *Ophiuri,* with their snaky arms, groping their way among the weeds, and striving to insinuate their writhing forms beneath the coral masses. Fixed flower-like *Actiniæ* were expanding their fleshy petals on the rocks; the slender *Nereis*; the long-armed *Comatula*, and the languid, slow-moving *Holothuria*, together with numerous fish and Crustaceans, contributed to prove that nature is ever weaving the subtle woof of existence beneath the surface of the waves.

CHAPTER IV.

THE PHILIPPINE ARCHIPELAGO.

Anecdote of a Python—Exploration of Sesarma—Curious Cavern—A ramble about Samboanga—Villages—Scenery—Vegetation—Aborigines of Mindanao—The Flying-Fox—Remarkable Crabs—Habits of Spiders—Insects—Mindoro—Hostility of the Natives—Use of the bow and arrow—Ylin—Poisonous Plant—Insects—Habits of Molluscous Animals.

On the 4th of February, 1844, we left Koo-kien-san, one of the Meïa-co-shimah Group, and arrived at Manila on the 16th of March, where we remained until the 1st of April. While lying in the truly delightful bay at this place, a trifling incident occurred, showing the extreme vivacity, and rapidity of movement, in the larger Serpents, even in those of the Boa tribe, especially when first captured. They are, indeed, then very different from those apathetic listless monsters one sees coiled up in blankets, at Zoological Gardens, and in Menageries. Sir Edward Belcher had a very beautiful specimen of the *Python Schneideri* presented to him, about twelve feet long, and having one day given it a chicken, the reptile, as usual, compressed it nearly to death, within the muscular folds of its body, when one of the bystanders, more tender-hearted than the rest, begged the life of the fowl. I had no sooner, however, introduced my arm with that benevolent intention, than throwing back its head, and unwinding its body from its prey, "the spirited, sly snake," as Milton would have termed it, darted at my hand with the greatest velocity, and held me fast with its teeth, by the ball of the thumb, nor was it without some trouble, that I was able to extricate myself, owing to the fact that the long, sharp, curved teeth of a serpent, all point backwards. Some time after this event, the death-warrant of the poor reptile was sealed, and I appointed myself his executioner. The question was how to persuade a snake so large and active, to enter a stone jar, filled with spirits of wine, without making a vigorous resistance. However, quickly seizing it by the neck, I drew the reptile from its cage, and had his body held down by a party of volunteers. The muscular contractions, however, proved somewhat too powerful for their weight and strength, and the caudal end escaping wound itself about my leg, which, perhaps, would have got a squeeze, but for an accession to our force, in the person of my friend Mr. Charles Richards. "*Vi et armis*," the doomed serpent was now consigned, without mercy, to a death somewhat similar to that selected by a certain duke of Clarence.

If the enormous Boa-Constrictors described by Pliny as warring against the Elephants of India, with perpetual discord, "tantæ magnitudinis, ut circumplexu facile ambiant nexuque nodi praestringant," were as lively in their movements as our *Python* of Leuconia, they must indeed have been "dragons" in every sense of the expression!

Schlegel, in his 'Physiognomy of Serpents,' observes, in a note p. 98, "Professor Reinwardt has witnessed, at Java, a spectacle which proves that it is not always right to trust to these animals (Boas). A Javanese had carried to the house of M. Van der Capelle, a large *Python*, and wishing to make it come out of the basket in which it was, the serpent, by a single stroke, gave him a very considerable wound, laying open his fore-arm through all its length."

On the 1st of April we left Manila, and on the 5th examined the reefs about Panagatan, and while here examined the small island of Sesarma.

We passed a very agreeable day, wandering about collecting plants, catching insects, and hunting lizards, until we were fairly tired out, and then reclining at our ease, took a siesta in a cool cave, which we accidentally discovered in the rocks along the sea-shore. This cavern had a very narrow entrance, but when once you had found your way into the interior, there was a high, arched roof, with numerous stalactites hanging pendent from it, and, arising from the bottom, stalagmites of various shapes and sizes; myriads of dark flitting bats fluttered in the uncertain light, vibrating their leathery wings with a low, murmuring sound, while others clung in huge, dark clusters to the chasms in the roof; the calcareous floor of the cavern was whitened with the accumulated excrement of these twilight-loving animals. As nothing is to be done in these expeditions without lighting a fire, I assembled the jolly-boat boys, left under my command, and, with incredible labour, brought together a vast heap of drift wood, dried leaves and grass, which soon became a blaze, and illuminated gloriously the interior of our cavern; but, alas! short-sighted mortals that we were, forgetting the necessity of a chimney, and the aperture being small, we were completely smoked out, to our no small discomfort.

On the 6th of April we touched at the Cagayanes, and on the 8th we anchored off Zamboangan, or Samboanga, a penal settlement of the Spaniards on the Island of Mindanao, or Majindanao, as it is sometimes written, and notwithstanding the somewhat equivocal character of many of its inhabitants, one of the most pleasing places we visited among the Philippines, a few observations on which may not be displeasing to my readers. Owing to the kindness of Sir Edward, and the liberality of the Governor, I was enabled to enjoy a very pleasant little excursion, of several days, in the neighbouring country. Mounted on an excellent horse (which, however, on starting, managed to rear so high as to fall backwards upon me, without doing me much injury, as I had time to slip away before his hoofs could reach me,) and accompanied by a very intelligent guide, one Mariano Alvirez, I proceeded, at an easy pace, through the villages of Varris el San Juadedios, Tesseros, Canelar, Cantador, Prenza, Santa Maria, Tumogan, Paraguiaba, Voal, Lama-Lama, Tirando-àlerte, and, lastly, Tugbugan, admiring in my progress the wild luxuriance of vegetable life in these latitudes, here spread out in all its prodigality, in the form of splendid trees and

> "flowers as wild and fair
> As ever dressed a bank or scented summer air."

Here and there the naked, muddy skins of large-bodied

Buffaloes were seen wallowing in weedy ponds, or browsing placidly among the bamboo mazes, or, with enduring patience, engaged in drawing burdens; here and there, at various turnings, quaintly carved and antique wooden crosses would remind you of being in a Catholic, though savage country, while the open hospitality of the villagers, and the vows of brotherhood and eternal friendship proffered you in every direction, brought to mind the prodigal liberality of their noble-minded Spanish subjugators.

It would be endless to enumerate all of the botanical beauties of Samboanga, but the handsome scarlet flowers of the *Poinciana*, the feathery foliage of the Tamarind, the grateful Guava, and the Palms, those "magnificent offspring of Tellus and Phæbus;" the agreeable subacid fruit of the *Tambeio*, the large dense foliage of the Breadfruit, and the aromatic Lime and Orange, were all worthy of the passing notice of the student of nature.

To these may be added the Bugo, or *Piper Betel*, climbing gracefully in the gardens; with its less illustrious compeer the Sanquilo (*P. obliquum*), the *Dyospyros embriopteris*, or Luya, the Mango (*Mangifera Indica*), the Lumboi (*Calyptranthes*), the Bixa, or Achote; another species of *Dyospyros*, called by the natives "Mabolo;" the Balibago, a kind of *Hibiscus*, the Balod, or *Nauclea*, the Tubadalag, or *Callicarpa*, and the luxuriant groves of the Caurayan, or *Bambusa*; the graceful hanging foliage, and brilliant berries of the *Abrus precatoria*, the lofty trunk, and stupendous pods of the *Cassia grandis*, the long and pendent fruit of the singular *Stravadium album*, the bell-shaped flowers of the succulent viviparous-leaved *Bryophyllum calycinum*, the elegant climbing *Clitoria ter-*

nata, with its large blue butterfly-flowers; the white and purple blossoms of the *Cleome viscosa*, the golden *Coreopsis*, adhering like a parasite to the trees, and twining epiphytic *Loranthi*; the compound leaves and yellow spikes of the medicinal *Cassia alata*, and along the sea-beach the trefoil leaves and the blue flowers of the *Vitex trifolia*, the clustering trunks of the Banyan tree, and the golden downy fronds of a gigantic fern. I did not fail to recognize the Gogo (*Entada pursætha*), an infusion of the spongy fibres of the trunk of which, is used by the natives for various affections of the skin, and which I have also seen employed with some advantage. The pods of the *Theobroma cacao* were ripening on the trees. A most delicious chocolate is manufactured at Samboanga from the seeds; many parts of the plant are also used medicinally. The glutinous sap of the *Bombax pentandrum* is here applied to parts affected by Rheumatism, and the cottony seeds are used as soporific pillows, like those famous poppy ones of Somnus. The down, moreover, forms an excellent moxa.

The fresh fruit of the Butong (*Barringtonia speciosa*) is bruised and thrown into the water to benumb fish at Samboanga, and fishing-nets are made of the dried fibres. The flowers are large, and very beautiful, the long stamina forming an elegant scarlet tassel. The other species (*B. racemosa*) flowers in May. The seeds of the Camonsilis (*Fuga lanceolata*) are used in alleviating the painful punctures of the venomous spines of the Ray and other fish.

Among other trees, a variety of the Banga, or *Areca Catechu* (*humilis*), was pointed out, distinguished by its flattened fruit, and diminutive size. The *Rosmarinus*, "Romero," or Rosemary, is carefully cultivated in pots, and much esteemed by the natives as a stomatic.

Near the village of Tugbugan I had an opportunity of seeing two of the aborigines of Mindanao "los Indios," as the Spaniards call them, to distinguish them from "los Negros" or Papuans, and "los Moros," or Malays. They are also named *Manabos* by some, although so numerous are the tribes, that it is difficult to determine them with any precision, for they appear to be almost as numerous as those of Borneo. Those I saw were stated by the villagers to live in the mountains, to acknowledge no authority, to go nearly naked, and to live chiefly on the Sago and Indian Corn. Their arms, which I likewise inspected, consisted of large painted shields, the sumpitan, spear, and parang or chopping-knife, which all bore a striking resemblance to those used by the Dyaks. The men were of fine proportions, and somewhat noble bearing, of a light black colour; the nose straight and well developed, the facial angle and lips like those of the negro, and the hair crisp, and disposed in distinct masses over the head. Their eyes were large and black, and their faces smooth and shining, without any vestige of a beard. The people of Samboanga and the neighbouring villages affect to hold these natives in the utmost terror and disdain. Like the Arafuras of New Guinea and the Aru Islands, the Dyaks of Borneo, the Monaboes inhabiting the interior of Malaya, and the Rajangs and Battas occupying the mountaing of Sumatra, these aborigines of Mindanao, according to the information of my guide, and certain village gossips, who seemed well acquainted with them, live in separate communities, each governed by an independent chief. Their dress resembles that of most savage tribes, being simply a strip of cloth encircling the waist, with one end brought down in front, passed between the legs, and fastened behind. Their hair being crisp, wavy, and growing in separate tufts, or bunches, in the same manner as that of the Papuan or Pelagian negroes, would seem to indicate that in Mindanao, as in Borneo, negro-like races inhabit the interior. I do not think the people I saw belonged to any of those savage tribes alluded to by Prichard, "who are supposed to belong to the race of Harafaras, and are said to have some analogy in dialect and physiognomy with the Idaan or Dyaks of Borneo."*

Although it may have been satisfactorily proved by the researches of Prichard and others, that the races of Oceanica are distinct, and cannot be derived either from the Peruvians on the eastern boundary, or from the tribes of South Africa, which bound them on the west; yet it is curious to trace analogies between people apparently so very distinct as the Malayo-Polynesians, and the various tribes disseminated over the continents of the two Americas. I never visited a horde of Dyaks without involuntarily thinking of North American Indians, probably, from some similarity of feeling that exists between them, as to the necessity of either scalping their enemies or of chopping off their heads. In many points their religious belief is also the same. "That enigmatical subdivision of the natives into an almost countless mul-

---

* Phys. Hist. of Mankind, vol. v. p. 59.

titude of greater and smaller groups, and that almost entire exclusion and excommunication with regard to each other, in which mankind presents its different families to us in America, like fragments of a vast ruin," alluded to by Dr. Von Martins, likewise reminds one of the scattered wandering tribes of beings, that rove from place to place in the interior of Borneo. It has been said that the astronomy of Mexico is of Asiatic origin, and philologists inform us that the Malay and Peruvian dialects have many words that may be referred to common roots; and it is singular that in many of their habits and customs may be traced a sort of similarity. For instance, the use of the sumpitan and poisoned arrows is in vogue among the wild people of Guiana, as it is among our friends the Dyaks; the habit of filing the teeth sharp, and of using a constant masticatory, as lime with a narcotic leaf, is peculiar both to Peruvians and to Malayo-Polynesians. As with languages, so it is with the aborigines of any climate, the more primitive their condition, the more nearly they approximate a simple common type; and we may thus account for the casual resemblance observed between the savages of America and those of the Indian Archipelago. Amongst the Malays and Bugis, civilization has imprinted certain moral and physical peculiarities, which enables them, although of the same family of mankind, to stand out in bold relief from their more ignorant, primitive, and less-fortunate brothers.

The "Filipinos," or the peaceable people of Bisayan origin, that constitute the principal portion of the population of the Philippine Islands, believe that the aboriginal races of the interior came originally from Borneo, and it is a curious fact that the legends and traditions of Java assert, that the inhabitants of that island came from Borneo; and indeed some writers believe, that all the different races belonging to the Asiatic Islands were derived from this common focus, although it is far more likely, in my opinion, that, as Dr. Prichard conceives, all the various races of these islands may originally have been derived from the peninsula of Malacca, which constitutes the south-eastern extremity of Asia; for that is the only continent which contains men at all resembling in physical characters the Oceanic tribes.

The *Pteropi*, or Flying Foxes, take their departure at the fall of day, from their places of concealment, among the low islands, in thousands, all steadily wending their way towards the huge forests of the interior, where their favourite fruits are found, and at the early blush of dawn they are seen returning, in like manner, to their diurnal haunts, where they hide in hollow trees, or caverns among the rocks, or hang suspended by the thumbs from the under-surface of the trees among the dense foliage. When the *Pteropus* flies, he generally chooses an exalted station in the air, and his motions are deliberate, noiseless, and crow-like.

At the watering-place not far from the small village of Calderas, among other interesting specimens, I captured the rare *Utica gracilipes*, (White) which has the very remarkable habit of strongly contracting all its members when caught, with what may be termed a cataleptic rigidity; and this trick, together with its singular tabular brown carapace, enables it to escape detection among the dead leaves and rotten pieces of wood, which almost invariably fill the ponds and rivulets in the tropics. This mode of feigning death to escape its enemies, is the more curious in this Crab, as it appears to be allied to the *Grapsidæ*, which are very energetic in their endeavours to escape. The under-surface is dark brown, of a lighter tinge on the legs and post-abdomen; which latter has a light yellowish line down the middle.

Near the same spot, and not far from Calderas, a species of *Sesarma*, of a brown colour, with the tips of the chelæ orange, and the cornea of the eye perfectly concave, is very common. It lives in the fresh-water rivulets, among weeds, like the *Utica*; while another species is found under damp logs, and stones, at a considerable distance from any water.

Never have I been better amused than when observing, in the forests of Mindanao, the habits of the extraordinary spiders that abound there, to figure and describe the varied forms of which, would require the pencil of Abbot, and many years of unwearied application.

The bodies of the *Epeiræ*, seen in the tropics, are often most splendidly ornamented, I might almost say illuminated, for many of them remind you of the gaudy ancient missals, painted by monks in the dark ages. You may have white figures on a red ground; red, yellow, and black, in alternate streaks; orange marbled with brown; light green, with white ocelli; yellow, with light brown festoons; or ash-coloured, and chesnut bodies, with crescents, horse-shoes, Chinese characters, and grotesque hieroglyphics of every description. Then, again, the shape of their bodies is endless in variety; they are round or oval, flattened or globular, angular, tuberculated, lobed, spined, or furnished with hairy tufts. These examples,

> "Whose shapes would make them, had they bulk and size,
> More hideous foes than fancy can devise,"

taken at random during one or two excursions in the woods, will tend to show what a wide field is open to the naturalist in these regions of the sun, provided he has nothing of more importance to engage his attention than the investigation of Apterous insects.

In the forests about Calderas, I collected some splendid species of gold and silver-marked *Tetragnatha*. One, which might be named *T. nitens*, has a dark, shining-brown thorax, and a glittering silvery body, with five black spots; the legs banded with dark brown, and the under side light black. It constructs a large, ingenious, symmetrical web, and drops, when touched, to the ground; taking care, however, at the same time, to suspend itself by a web, by means of which it ascends again, when the enemy has departed. In the centre of its web, it spins concentric circles, and thick, irregular mazes, of a fine yellow colour, and often of very complicated devices. When it falls to the ground, it folds up its legs, and feigns death, all its members being perfectly rigid. The *Tetragnatha* have a remarkable habit of dividing their eight legs, as they cling, head downwards, to the centre of their toils, throwing out four directly forwards, and four directly backwards. Some species, however, have the third pair of legs extended straight out, in a lateral direction. Another common species had a body mottled with dark brown, and covered with white markings; legs brown, banded; the thorax burnished bright green, with darker markings. I have named it, provisionally, *T. refulgens*. Numbers of the genus *Theridion*, of a black colour, were running actively about among the dry, dead leaves that strewed the ground; and some handsomely-coloured species were discovered crouching among the foliage of the trees. One was marked like the *T. Sisyphus* of Haan (Tab. 58. fig. 132.); and another large-sized species was of a bright emerald green. The *Attus formicoides* (Walckenaer), or an allied species, was basking on the dead leaves in the sunny spots; and numerous pretty species of *Salticus*, allied to *S. crux* (Haan, Tab. 17. fig. 52.), but of much larger dimensions, were common spiders. A species of *Attus*, allied to *formicoides*, which may be called *splendens*, was taken here. It was of a brilliant metallic green-gold, with the under-surface fine metallic purple; the legs banded with light brown, and burnished green. It was springing about the foliage of the low trees. Another *Attus* was of a shining black, with several bright ultramarine spots on the abdomen, and light brown legs, banded with darker brown. Numbers of black-coloured *Theridia* were running about over the dead leaves, simulating, at a little distance, so many odd-shaped Ants; numerous other species of this genus, which were seen living among the flowers and foliage of the trees, had their abdomens variegated with beautiful colours. One species, with a hairy body and legs, and shining chesnut-coloured chelicera, runs quickly when pursued, and uses these organs in self-defence. Its body is of a dark olive brown, and it appears to love dark nooks and holes of the bark of trees, and frequently hangs suspended from the under-surface of the leaves. I observed another species, which knew it was being watched, place itself upon a diseased leaf, where it remained quite stationary until after I had taken my departure; and had I not seen the sidelong movement of the cunning little creature, in the first instance, I should not have been able to distinguish its body from the eroded surface of the leaf. Those that live among the foliage and flowers, are vividly coloured, and many flies and other insects are, no doubt, attracted towards these Spiders, by reason of their gaudily-tinted bodies. I have seen the abdomen of one marked with lilac, yellow, and crimson, three powerfully contrasted colours. Others are green, and actually reticulated, like the veined surface of a leaf, with the midrib running down the centre, and the secondary nervures proceeding outwards from each side; the bodies of others resemble the splendid variegated blossoms of the sorts of *Calceolarias*, grown in our gardens.

Several timid, soft, retiring, long-legged *Pholci*, with fawn-coloured bodies, and semi-transparent red-brown legs, covered with long hairs, formed large, loose webs among the rotten wood and leaves that strewed the ground. The legs of these arachnidans appear too weak to support their bodies in running; therefore they resemble their aquatic marine analogues, the *Pycnogonidæ*, which remain stationary among the tangled and thread-like Keratophytes, which constitute the webs of those spider-like Crustaceans, and thus watch cautiously their prey; and when it is caught in the toils, consume it at their leisure, thus making up by cunning and persevering watching for the want of that strength and force possessed by some of their consimilars. Most of the *Crustacea* would appear, on a careful comparison, to have very distinct analogies with the families of Arachnidans.

The nimble-limbed *Dolomedes*, that run after their prey, and catch them by swiftness of foot, rather than by stratagem, have slender legs, and, living on the ground, are generally of dingy colours; with the exception, however, of those very large and powerful species, which, if not rendered somewhat conspicuous to the sight of other insects, might do too much damage to the tribes they are destined to keep in check; most of these, therefore, have the thorax and abdomen margined with a light colour, that contrasts strongly with that of their bodies. The *Saltici* generally resemble, more or less, the colour of the places they inhabit. I noticed a species among the dense thickets, formed by *Abrus precatoria* and other trees, with a black abdomen, marked on each side with dull scarlet, curious as being the colours of the seeds of *Abrus*, which are called by children "black-a-moor beauties;" those species that live on the bark of trees are mottled grey and brown, and those which you find upon the ground, are altogether black or dingy coloured.

It is an interesting fact, that those gay insects, which love to sun themselves in the open parts of the forests, exposed to view upon the leaves, like the brilliant *Buprestidæ*, and other splendid beetles of the tropics, are glorious in their hues, while dingy-coloured *Coleoptera*, like the *Helluo*, in his funereal dress, hide in obscure holes and corners, where the sight may never reach them. The Necrophagous *Silphidæ*, again, are most commonly of obscure colouring, and conceal their dingy bodies in putrid carcases, while their consimilars, the *Nitidulidæ*, that spend their lives among the gaily-coloured petals of flowering plants, are splendid with metallic tints. In like manner there is a wide difference between those Lamellicorn beetles, which fly by night, like *Lucanus*, or burrow in the ground, like *Geotrupes*, or conceal themselves under dung, like *Aphodius*; and those glittering insects, which, like the *Stephanorina*, *Coryphocera*, and *Cetonia*, revel amid the blossoms of the most lovely flowers.

On the 6th of December, the 'Samarang' was once more anchored in Manila Bay; on the 30th of January, 1846, we again examined the Panagatan shoals, and on the 4th of February, commenced surveying the small islands of Ambolon and Ylin, situated at the south end of Mindoro, one of the Philippines.

The people of this part of Mindoro, privately pursuing piracy, imagined we were possessed of the same propensities. On one occasion, a party armed with bows and arrows, attacked the crew of our jolly-boat; and not far from the principal village of Ylin, some natives shot an arrow at the captain's gig, which fell in the water alongside. On our approaching the village the people were prepared to give us a hostile reception; but on our landing with loaded muskets, they retreated, soon laid aside their useless bows and arrows, and became very good friends. Their fort, situated at the top of a steep hill, was filled with their women, who had run up there for shelter. A market was soon opened, in a large house under the surveillance of the chief of the village, and it was a very amusing sight to see a number of old women bringing in their pigs for sale, tied by a string; others offering tempting bunches of bananas; many praising their fighting-cocks, and others the freshness of their eggs. The scenery from the fort was very beautiful; soft green hills, in many parts crowned with a dense mass of noble trees, extended for miles, in every direction, behind the village.

This is the only time I have seen the bow and arrow in use among the Malayo-Polynesian tribes; and although the Javanese are said by Crawford to be extremely fond of the exercise of the bow and arrow, as an amusement; yet we do not find either the bow, the club, or the sling, among the primitive Dyaks, or any other aborigines of the Indian Islands, except the Bisayan race. At the Bashee Group, the inhabitants of which belong to the same stock as those which people the coasts of Mindoro, although at present an unarmed population, yet retain a recollection of the bow and arrow. We were shown several very long and powerful bows, in the house of the native chief of the mission of San Domingo. Those primitive weapons, the bow and arrow, have given place, among most of the islands, to the more refined invention of shooting envenomed arrows through a long cylindrical tube; and for hand to hand weapons of aggression, they have fashioned the useful iron into kris blades, and the heads of spears. In Crawford's account of an attack made on Manila by the British, in 1762, it is stated that five thousand Indians " presented themselves, armed with javelins, and with bows and arrows, for the relief of the garrison." *

In our survey of Ylin, we occasionally regaled ourselves

* Hist. Ind. Archipel. vol. ii. p. 475.

with the boiled leaves of the *Colocasia esculenta*, which we found very palatable. One of the seamen, thinking they were equally good in an uncooked state, incautiously chewed some of the leaves, thereby producing great pain and swelling of the tongue, with an inflammation of the fauces, that lasted several days. At Hong-Kong, where the tubers of the same plant are eaten, under the name of Cocoas, several marines came to me with the same symptoms. It is a curious fact, that most edible roots are yielded by plants possessed of poisonous qualities. The Potatoe is allied to the Deadly Nightshade; one species of Sweet-Potatoe, the *Batatas paniculata*, is a violent cathartic; the nutritious *Cassava* and *Tapioca*, are prepared from a root, the expressed juice of which is dangerously poisonous; and it would be easy to multiply examples, proving the same fact. In Hampshire, the poor people gather the leaves of the "Lords-and-Ladies" (*Arum maculatum*), which belongs to the same natural order as the *Colocasia*, and esteem them, when boiled, excellent eating.

A ramble at a little distance from the village, furnished me with a very handsome *Lamia*, allied to *Ceratites*, of a dark-brown colour, with numerous yellow eye-like spots on the elytra, most probably an entirely new species. The dark purple *Pachyrhynchus moniliferus*, with numerous small ultramarine markings on its gibbose elytra, and another species, of a light chesnut-brown, were found clinging to the leaves of the low bushes; and lurking under loose bark, was a species of *Uloma*, one of the *Tenebrionidæ*, with reddish antennæ, and black polished elytra. In the river that runs through the village,

I noticed several species of *Melania* and *Neritina*, and one species of *Ampullaria*.

During many agreeable boat-expeditions among these islands, I had numerous opportunities of observing the habits of molluscous animals. I shall only add here, however, a few remarks on the *Mitra* and *Calpurnus*, reserving other details for the 'Zoology of the Samarang,' where figures of the animals of many species of shells will be published.

In its habits, the *Calpurnus (Ovulum verrucosum)* is a very slow-moving, and sluggish mollusk, with all the peculiarities of the Cowries, and exhibits a singularly beautiful and striking appearance under the calm, shallow water, as it glides tranquilly along the bright sandy bottom. The spots on the mantle are much smaller, and more irregular in form, than those on the foot. The head is pure opaque white, with the exception of one large black spot, placed in the centre of the forepart, which, with its large black eyes, and black-tipped tentacles, gives it a very peculiar appearance. It was taken alive by us at the extreme southernmost end of the Island of Mindoro, not far from Ylin, in shallow water, and on a sandy bottom. The *Calpurnus* appears to be rather numerous among these small islets, though, in other parts of the Philippines, I only met with specimens dead, and thrown up along the beach.

For a mollusk furnished with such a heavy shell, the *Ranella* is by no means an inactive animal. It moves with considerable animation, thrusting out its head, protruding its tentacles and proboscis, and ascending even perpendicular surfaces with considerable facility. One species, dredged from twenty fathoms water, was furnished with a very extensive proboscis, which it was able to exsert to the distance of two inches from the head, using it as a perceptive organ, in the same manner as the Elephant does his trunk.

I have observed the animal of *Eulima major*, in the living state, at Looc Bay, in the Philippines, at Cagayan-Sooloo, and at the Panagatan shoals, near Apo Island. This mollusk, which I have described in the 'Annals and Magazine of Natural History,' is slow-moving, and excessively timid, retreating quickly within its shell on the slightest alarm. The animal is entirely of an opaque pearly white; the eyes black, and generally concealed under the front of the shell, as are those small, reflected lobes of the mantle, which produce the polished surface of the *Eulima*; the tentacles are yellow at the tip, orange in the middle, and white at the base. It would remain for hours after capture without moving, and emerge from its polished castle with the utmost caution and distrust.

The old stakes of the numerous fishing wears laid down by the natives among the shallows of these islands, are incrusted with Oysters of a very delicious flavour; and it was a source of much amusement, after the labours of the day were done, to collect a number of these oyster-loaded stakes, and cook them in the fires which we had lighted to cheer our bivouac. Seated in a circle, we watched, with hungry interest, the opening of these delectable mollusks, when scooping out the savoury morsels with our knives, we enjoyed the feast kind nature had provided us.

In the animal of *Lima*, the long, slender finger-like

foot, developed from the centre of that portion of the body which includes the viscera, is furnished with the power of producing a tenacious kind of secretion, which hardens in something like the same manner as the cobweb, after leaving the spinneret of the spider, and thus constitutes a temporary kind of byssus; which is somewhat remarkable, as the *Lima* is a most locomotive mollusk, and endowed with as much animation and vivacity as a Pecten; and from another reason that most lamellibranchiate mollusks, which spin a byssus, have the foot in general but very little developed. The *Limæ* usually live quietly at the bottom with the valves widely extended and thrown flat back, like the wings of certain butterflies, when basking in the sun; but when disturbed, they start up, flap their light valves, and move rapidly through the water, by a continued succession of sudden jerks. The cause of alarm over, they bring themselves to an anchor by means of their provisional byssus, which they seem to fix with much care and attention, previously exploring every part of the surface with their singular leech-like foot. When many hundreds of these curious bivalves are seen at the bottom of clear pools, surrounded by living branches of party-coloured coral, their crimson spotted mantles and delicate spiral appendages that fringe the edges, cause them to exhibit a very rich and beautiful appearance.

Although M. Quoy has rightly termed the *Mitra* an "animal apathetique," yet among the Philippines, and in the China Sea, about the low coral islands, I have seen the small longitudinally-ribbed species crawl about pretty briskly over the smooth sand. The *Mitra episcopalis*, probably on account of the small size of its locomotive disc, and the ponderous nature of its long shell, is decidedly a very sluggish mollusk. I have observed some of the auricula-shaped Mitres, that live among the Philippines, in the shallow pools left by the receding tide, crawling about the stones, out of the water, in company with the *Planaxis* and *Quoyia*. The Mitres, however, in general, like many of the larger Volutes, crawl in societies of many dozens, over the sandy mud-flats in shallow water, and are more particularly active just before the flood-tide makes. When the tide recedes, they bury themselves superficially in the yielding soil, and are with difficulty discovered. Some of the small, ribbed species cover themselves entirely with the sandy mud, and in that disguised condition, travel about in comparative security. On one occasion, in the small island of Ambolon, at the south end of Mindoro, I was walking up to my ankles in water, over a firm, sandy mud-flat, taking little notice of the Cones, *Strombi*, *Meleagrinæ*, and Volutes which people the water in great numbers, but looking about anxiously for the rarer Mitres, when I first perceived these small species, under their ingenious disguise, marching in towards the shore, as the tide flowed rapidly over the level surface. Persons, by the way, should never venture in places of this description barefooted, as there is a species of *Pinna* which buries its sharp end in the mud, but leaves the thin, trenchant edges of the gaping extremities exposed, which, when trodden on, inflict very deep and painful incised wounds. Both myself and several of the boat's crew suffered in this way.

The Philippines would seem to harbour the greatest number of these elegant and beautiful shells, although a great many species were obtained by Mr. Cuming in Tropical America. They appear to be chiefly confined to the equatorial regions, scarcely any being natives of cold climates. I have met with several among the Meïa-co-shimah Islands, at Loo-Choo, Japan, and at the Keeling, or Cocos Islands. They are most generally to be found in somewhat shallow water, among the ledges of rocks, between small islands, where the water barely covers the land, and within the shelter of coral reefs, sometimes preferring a clear, sandy bottom, and at other times affecting a hard, muddy, sandy soil. The transversely-ribbed species, such as *Mitra circulata*, are frequently found in very deep water, and many were dredged by us in twenty and thirty fathoms, at Sooloo, and in the China Sea.

The animal of *Mitra circulata*, one of these deep-water species, is very prettily marked. The body is grey, varied with round, well-developed, white spots, and a series of dark-brown blotches, of a pyramidal form, arranged round the lower edge in a Vandyke pattern, and below that, a white rim, with a row of small, linear, horizontal, black spots; the head is white, marbled with grey-brown; the eyes black, and the tentacles white, with a large oval, black spot in their middle; the siphon is brown, edged with black, and with a broad white band at its free extremity. The operculum is very minute, horny, and transparent. In general, however, the Mitres, notwithstanding the elaborate markings of their shells, are not remarkable for bright colours on their bodies.

Another species, with the same habits, the *Mitra circulata*, is semi-opaque-white, faintly mottled with light brown; with the eyes at the outer base of the tentacles, and black.

The animal of *Conohelix*, of Swainson, does not differ from that of *Mitra*. One species, probably new, I have found buried rather deep in the soft, black mud, under the roots of the trees in Mangrove swamps, above high-water mark, in the Island of Basilan. The *C. marmorata* is found in company with many species of Mitres, crawling slowly over the sandy mud, in shallow places, among the Islands of the Philippine Archipelago.

St. Pierre, in his 'Studies of Nature,'* has very truly remarked, that the animals of shells which crawl and travel, and which can, consequently, choose their own asylums, are in general those of the richest colours; such are the gaudily-tinted Nerites, and the polished marbled Cowries; the Olives richly ornamented with three or four colours; and the Harps, which have tints as rich as the most beautiful Tulips; while among the bivalves the vivacious Pectens coloured scarlet and orange, and a host of other travelling shells are impressed with the most lively colours. But those which do not swim, as the Oysters, which are adherent always to the same rocks; or those which are perpetually at anchor in the straits, attached to the stones by their byssi, as the *Pinnas* and Muscles; or those which repose on the bosom of Madrepores, such as the *Arcs*; or those which are entirely buried in the calcareous rocks, as the *Lithodomi*; or those which immovably, by reason of their weight, pave the

* Vol. iii. p. 67.

surface of the reefs, as the *Tridacna*, and those great univalves, such as the *Turbos*; or, in short, those which always remain motionless, like the Limpets, which are attached, by forming a vacuum on the smooth surface of rocks: all these species of shells are of the colour of the bottoms, or floors, which they respectively inhabit, in order, no doubt, that they shall be less perceived by their enemies.

CHAPTER V.

THE SOOLOO AND MOLUCCA ARCHIPELAGOES.

Sooloo—Appearance of the People—Gigantic drum—The Tsjampaka—The Sooloos poison the water—Their fondness for Pearls—Fanciful origin of those concretions—The Sultan's fable respecting them—Sea-Snakes—Origin of "Great Sea-Serpent"—Water Spouts—Shells, and their inhabitants—Apo Island—Malay fishing village—Questionable character of its occupants—Shooting excursion in Basilan—Hostilities in the Island—Habits of Spiders—Curious Shell-fish—Unsang—Wild Animals—Apes — Gigantic Crane—Lace-Lizard—Crocodile—Insects—*Celebes*—Cape Rivers—Marine Animals—Manado—Forest Scenery—Adaptations—Anecdote of a Bee—Curious Insects—Land-Crabs—Habits of Crustaceans—Island of Meyo—Whale—Turtles—Fish — Lizard — Shells — Ternate—The Malukus—Habits of Spiders.

On the 16th of April, 1844, we arrived for the first time at the city of Sooloo, which we again visited in December of the same year, and in February, 1845. The unconquered Sooloos, considered the bravest warriors in these seas, and whose chief city has been termed the "Algiers of the East," invariably go armed, being usually provided with a formidable spear, as well as wearing in their sarongs their ever-constant companion, the murderous kris. The countenance of the Sooloos is not agreeable; there is something more morose, fierce and vindictive-looking about them, than is to be noticed among other varieties of the Malay race. Their figures, moreover, are taller, better proportioned, and of a bolder aspect than those of the generality of Malays. Some of the young girls are very nearly white, and many of them tolerably good-looking; though, as is most generally the case in these countries, they lose their fair proportions, as they advance in years. They manufacture a fine stuff from the fibres of the Plantain, in a very simple and primitive sort of manner, their loom being composed of a few sticks, and the woof being secured around their waists. With this exception, they appear to do nothing but pound *padi* for the use of their lords and masters.

Near the city are numerous grassy plains, where Water-Buffaloes, and a small, well-formed breed of horses graze, in considerable numbers. In the huge, rudely-constructed temple, where the followers of Mahomet meet together, is a gigantic drum, like that one in the city of Brunai, formed of the trunk of an enormous tree, and covered with a buffalo's hide. This summons the Mussulmans to daily prayers, in lieu of the call of the Muezzin. During an audience with the Sultan, I could not help admiring the gorgeous dresses and fine forms of some of these Sooloo warriors, many among them evincing much taste in the selection of their colours, &c. The road to the "Hall of Audience" was rendered very attractive by groves of Cocoa-nut trees, mingled with the fragrant Tsjampaka (*Michelia Champaca*), that splendid member of the Magnolia tribe, the flowers of which, together with the *Nyctanthus*, or Malati, and the Tanjung (*Mausops elengi*), are worn in the glossy hair of the

Indian maidens; or thrown on the tables, mingled with citron-flowers, and Jasmines, at the banquets of the great, for the delicious perfume exhaled by the petals; and whose foliage affords such a grateful shade in the villages of the Malays in these burning regions.

The men of Sooloo, like the Malays and Bugis of Celebes and Borneo, are passionately fond of cock-fighting, frequently staking the whole of their personal property on the result of a battle. The spurs they use are scythe-shaped, long, sharp, and made of steel, and are sometimes fastened to one leg, and frequently to both. Groups of these arch-pirates, the warlike Sooloos, may be always seen in the mud-streets of their chief city with game-cocks under their arms to be pitted "against all comers," thus fostering their love of fighting and gambling, even in their pastimes. Frequently the owner of the victorious bird carries away, as the prize, the vanquished hero of his brother gamester.

While lying off their city, the Sooloos poisoned the springs, from which the boats of both French and English ships were watering, by throwing into them large quantities of the fruit of the Aran, or Gomuti Palm (*Borassus Gomutus*). After some tons had been brought on board the 'Samarang,' many of the men complained of a painful heat, and stinging sensation of the skin of the hands, legs, and other parts exposed during the duties of this day's service, and the officer commanding the boats, having brought on board some of the fruit, I pointed out the poisonous nature of the pulp, and the water was accordingly started. Fortunately, no serious harm was done, although some of the men who had partaken pretty freely of the poisoned water, complained of excessive thirst, and burning of the throat. The Sooloos employ the same fruit, and another plant, which grows wild, and which they call "Tubli," for the purpose of poisoning fish, in the same manner as the "Butong," or *Barringtonia speciosa*, is used at Samboanga, and the *Tephrosia toxicaria* in Borneo.

The Gomuti Palm, on account of the numerous uses to which it is converted, deserves here a more extended notice. This Palm, besides the names of Aran and Gomuti, is also called sometimes Tuack, Gumatty, or Cabo-Negro. Although the outer covering of the fruit is possessed of such poisonous qualities, yet it is in reality one of the most useful Palms indigenous to the Indian Islands. The interior of the fruit is used as a sweetmeat; the cut extremities of the peduncles of the inflorescence yield "toddy," a cooling, grateful beverage, much patronized by the natives of these thirsty regions; from the toddy, according to Crawfurd, "the only sugar used by the native population" of Java is prepared; the reticulum at the base of the petioles of the leaves constitutes a kind of Coir, a substance most admirably adapted to the manufacture of cables, and extensively used for cordage of every description. This substance, which is described by Dalrymple in his 'Natural Curiosities of Sooloo,' although an important product of Sooloo, is met with in the finest state at Manado, in Celebes. It is generally confounded with Coir, which is produced from the husk of the Cocoa-nut, and is a substance known to few who have not passed the strait of Malacca, and to fewer still the manner in which it is obtained. Mr. Dalrymple, moreover, informs us that the Cabo-Negro (Black Head) resembles the Cocoa-nut tree in the figure of its leaves and trunk; but the former are of a dead dark green, in comparison with the Cocoa-nut leaves. Like all other Palms it shoots out its leaves at the top only, and as the tree grows up, sheds the lowest. From the lower part, or stalks, of these leaves (which, he observes, form the bark of all Palms) "the *gumatty* shoots out on both sides like black hair, being, in fact, nothing more than the extension of the finest fibres, whereof the stalks and ribs of the leaves are composed: these fibres bind the dead leaves around the tree, so that the trunk has a very odd appearance, being confined in a rough black coat." These leaves being taken off the tree, are stripped of the hair, and it is said the *Gumatty* must be beaten to free it from dirt, and then spread in the sun; two or three days after which, the larger threads, being unfit for cordage, are picked out. The *Gumatty* is black as jet; the hairs extremely strong, and resemble the *Coir*, except that they are longer and finer. The finest hairs make the best cordage, which ought not to be too hard laid; the small hard twigs found mixed up with this material are employed as pens, and form the shafts of the sumpits, or little poisoned arrows; and underneath the reticulum is a soft, silky material, used as tinder by the Chinese, and applied as oakum in caulking the seams of ships; while from the interior of the trunk a kind of Sago is prepared. St. Pierre observes, in speaking with admiration of the Cocoa-nut tree, "Tout le monde sait qu' on y bâtit un vaisseau de son bois, qu'on en fait les voiles avec les feuilles, le mât avec son tronc, les cordages avec l'étoupe, appellée caire, qui entoure son fruit, et qu'on le charge ensuite avec ses Cocos;" but, perhaps, all the world does *not* know that the Gomuti Palm is nearly as valuable.

The people of Sooloo appear to be very fond of amassing pearls and bezoar stones, and there is scarcely a man of any pretensions among them, who will not, after having been in your society a short while, produce mysteriously from the folds of his sarong, two or more of these precious concretions. The pearls are of different sizes and very various in colour. Those from the *Pinna*, are black and red; from the *Tridacna gigas*, dull opaque white; from the *Placuna placenta*, of a lead-colour; from the true Pearl-Oyster (*Meleagrina margaritifera*), they are frequently of a light semi-transparent straw-colour.

Dalrymple, in his account of the pearl-fishery of Sooloo, gives an amusing statement regarding the *Pinnotheres* which inhabit the pearl-shells. He terms them small lobsters, and says there are two in each shell; that their beautiful transparent bodies have red spots, the female white; and that the latter has, under the tail and belly, many eggs, which appeared under the microscope to be "Teepye" shells (Pearl-Oysters). "There is from hence room," he adds, "to conjecture that shell-fish, in general, are generated by such lobsters; for the several species common in the Sooloo Seas, as Manangcy, Teepye, Bato, Capees, Beelong, Bineong, Seedap, &c., &c., I have been assured always have two lobsters, though every species of shell-fish has a distinct species of the lobster." To confirm his hypothesis, by an appeal to the philosophical judgment of the natives, he adds "It was obvious to all the Sooloos, who saw the egg of the Teepye lobster, that it was a proper Teepye; and they were from thence convinced, that these fish are generated in this manner." The Sultan, on this occasion, mentioned a fable they have amongst them. "A monkey sitting very pensive on the shore, with his arms crossed, as they often do, being asked what was the matter, replied; 'He was considering how the Mangancy* are produced.'"

I have detected a species of *Pinnotheres*, hitherto undescribed (*P. orientalis*, Adams and White,) that inhabits the large Avicula so common in these seas.

The Sooloo Seas appear to be swarming with Sea-snakes, perhaps on account of the calmness of the water, and heat of the atmosphere here, which tend to produce astonishing fecundity in the world of waters. Sea-snakes always appear to prefer calms, swimming on the still surface, in an undulating manner, never raising the head much from the surface, or vaulting out of the water. They dive with facility on the approach of danger, but do not appear to be particularly timid. Their progression is tolerably rapid. The Malays term them "Ular gerang." The *Pelamis bicolor* is common all over the China and Indian Seas. I have seen them in the Seas of Mindoro and Sooloo, swimming by thousands on the top of the water. They appear especially to delight in calms, and are fond of eddies and tide-ways where the ripple collects numerous fish and Medusæ, which principally constitute their prey. Their lungs resemble the air-bladders of fishes more than the breathing organs of Reptilia, in general being simple, elongated sacs, with blood-vessels ramifying over their parietes, but having no cells. Their

* Mangancy, a kind of Pearl-oyster.

tongue is white and forked, differing in respect of its colour from the tongue of other Snakes which is generally black. The two forks are retractile within the root, and are covered with two horny sheaths which, during the casting of the slough, can be drawn off like the scales of the eyes. In some genera, as *Hydrophis*, there are true poison fangs, but of small size compared with the *Colubri* and others; others are innocuous as the *Chersydrus*, while others (*Pelamis*) have two apertures at the base of the two terminal palatine teeth, which may perhaps serve for the exit of venom. Dr. Cantor says, in speaking of marine serpents, (Annals and Mag. of Nat. Hist. vol. iii. p. 138.) that "all the species are, without exception, highly venomous." Schlegel, also includes the Sea-snakes in his second family of *Venomous Serpents* (page 184 of his Physiognomy of Serpents). Captain Cook in one of his Voyages "saw abundance of Water-snakes, one of which was coming up the side of our ship, and our men beat it off. The Spaniards say there is no cure for such as are bit by them; and one of our blacks happened to fall under that misfortune, and died, notwithstanding the utmost care was taken by our Surgeons to recover him."

In the Sooloo Seas, I have often witnessed the phenomenon which first gave origin to the marvellous stories of the great Sea-serpent, namely lines of rolling porpoises, resembling a long string of buoys, oftentimes extending seventy, eighty, or a hundred yards. These constitute the so-named protuberances of the monster's back, keep in close single file, progressing rapidly along the calm surface of the water, by a succession of leaps, or demi-vaults forwards, part only of their uncouth forms appearing to the eye. At the same moment of time, I have seen beautifully-banded Water-snakes, of the thickness of a man's leg, lying extended supinely along the glassy surface, or diving and swimming gracefully, with slow undulating, lateral movements of their vertically-compressed bodies.

Waterspouts were very common phenomena, in these beautiful seas, many dozens occurring all around us at the same time. They were of small size, and varied considerably in shape, some being like a trumpet, some like a very wide-mouthed funnel, and some resembling the curved form of the *Cornucopia*.

To give some idea of the splendour in the colouring of tropical fishes, I here copy from my journal the colours of a species of *Balistes*, taken by us at Sooloo. Upper half of body pale brown, with two broad stripes of deeper brown extending backwards towards the dorsal fin; four well-defined and narrow streaks descending posteriorly to anal fin; a bright spot of ultramarine blue round the anus; iris golden; a dark greenish-brown, triangular mark, margined with deep blue, reaching from beneath the eye to the base of the pectoral fin; over the eye and summit of the head, a deep blue colour, with a lighter streak running down before the eye to base of pectoral fin; a bright blue stripe above the upper lip, reaching to the angle of the mouth; from this point to a little below the pectoral fin, a deep orange-yellow stripe; all below this, and on the belly, pure dead white; a pale oval mark on the tail; all the fins light semi-transparent brown. A *Scorpæna*, of a fine brilliant scarlet, and with very poisonous spines, is also very common at Sooloo A *Pegasus*, of a light sea-green, mottled with darker green;

an *Ostracion*, of a light yellow green, with minute black spots; a *Platax* of a pink-brown, spotted with black towards the head, and the rest of the body covered with opaque white spots; and a remarkable sharp-nosed species of *Rhinobatis*, of a dark, rufous-brown colour, were also procured during our sojourn at this place.

Among other interesting contributions to the Conchological collection obtained at Sooloo, the dredge furnished us with a large and handsome new species of *Cardium* (*C. Bechei*, Adams and Reeve).* This, which was from about forty fathoms water, and from a muddy bottom, is of a lovely red-rose colour, with a semi-transparent, thin, soft, velvety epidermis, the anterior and middle portions of the shell smooth, but the posterior part, which is destitute of epidermis, covered with ribs of short compressed spines. Several very large and beautiful specimens of *Conus thalassiarchus*, and a large rare species of *Stomatia*, together with many new and interesting Crustaceans, likewise rewarded our research.

The animal of *Conus aulicus* has the proboscis beautifully varied with red and white, and there is a square and very minute operculum on the dorsal surface of the hinder part of the foot. Its bite produces a venomed wound, accompanied by acute pain, and making a small, deep, triangular mark, which is succeeded by a watery vesicle. At the little island of Meyo, one of the Moluccas, near Ternate, Sir Edward Belcher was bitten by one of these Cones, which suddenly exserted its proboscis as he took it out of the water with his hand, and he compares the sensation he experienced to that produced by the

* Ann. and Mag. Nat. Hist. vol. xix. p. 417.

burning of phosphorus under the skin. The instrument which inflicted the wound, in this instance, I conceive must have been the tongue, which in these mollusks, is long, and armed with two ranges of sharp-pointed teeth.

The Cones become more numerous and more varied in their colours, as we approach the equatorial seas, and they form bright and beautiful ornaments to the shores of tropical islands. They seem to prefer obscure holes in the rocks, where they lead a predatory life, boring into the substance of the shells of other mollusks, for the purpose of sucking the juice from their bodies. They crawl but slowly and usually with their tentacles extended in a straight line before them. They are very timid, and shrink within their shells quickly on the approach of danger. Some affect deep water, and one was dredged by us in the Sunda Straits, in thirty fathoms; and another, the *Conus thalassiarchus*, at Sooloo, in about forty fathoms, as I have before mentioned.

To be convinced of the comparatively trifling importance of the calcareous secretions, called shells, in the philosophical study of the Mollusca, we have only to glance at the different genera of the grand Gasteropodous division, where we shall find the same organization scarcely at all modified by the calcareous deposits, which here assume every variety of form, from a simple, internal, horny, dorsal plate, to a complicated, spiral, turbinated shell. It is only by investigating the structure and peculiarities of the soft parts, and studying the animals as they are seen crawling about, unmolested in their native element, that we can arrive at any distinct notion of their Protean forms, and of their relations one with another.

What can be more different than the shells of *Phorus, Terebellum, Strombus*, and *Rostellaria*? and yet my observations of their animals have proved them to be intimately connected, with the same habits and necessities, and living in the same peculiar manner. Since the labours of Cuvier, Blainville, Gray, and others, naturalists have never doubted the importance of studying the animals that construct the beautiful shells preserved in our cabinets, and which serve the purpose of protecting the more delicate viscera of the inmate, or for affording a safe asylum for their eggs; but the peculiar details of the animals have not been sufficiently made use of as generic and specific distinctions.

The employment of the dredge gave me an opportunity of here first observing the animal of *Ficula*, which very much resembles that of *Dolium* in the large, thin, flattened foot, rounded in front, with two sharp, angular, lateral processes, and extended and acuminated behind; in the long, recurved siphon, and slender, tapering tentacula; in having a long extensile and retractile proboscis; in the position of the organs of vision; and in the general shape, structure, and lightness of the shell; while the singular fact of the mantle covering the sides of the shell, would seem to approximate it to *Calpurnus, Ovulum, Marginella* and the Cowries.

Although exceedingly timid and sensitive, the *Ficula* is a very lively animal, when observed in its native waters, crawling along with considerable velocity, and, owing probably to the lightness of its shell, able to ascend with facility the sides of a glass vessel, which held it captive. The proboscis is rarely exserted when the animal is in motion; but the long, tapering tentacles are stretched out to their full extent, and the siphon is directed more frequently forwards than over the back of the animal. The animal of *Ficula ficoides* is light, marbled violet, and the head and tentacles are white; six white, opaque spots are arranged round the upper surface of the edge of the foot; the rest of the body is light delicate pink, with marbled markings of a darker pink.

In another species which I observed, and of which I also made a drawing, (the *Ficula lævigata*, Reeve) the mantle is bright pink, mottled with white and deeper pink, the under surface of the ventral disc being of a dark-chocolate colour, with yellow, scattered spots; the head and neck are pink, and also coloured with yellow spots.

The *Ficula* shells, seen in cabinets, convey but a poor idea of these handsome mollusks, observed in the living state, crawling rapidly along, bearing their light, elegantly-formed shells, easily and gracefully, with their siphon erect, their foot expanded, like a broad flattened disc, and their bodies ornamented with delicate colours, beautifully marbled, and moving their long, flat heads, and peering about with their large, bright black eyes, in a manner which is surprising, when one considers the position these animals occupy in the scale of creation, and that but a very small share of intelligence is, in general, supposed to be the lot of most mollusca.

At Sooloo, I first had the good fortune to discover and describe the animal of *Terebellum*, and thus to solve the enigma of the true position of this shell in the conchological system. Although it should be placed, most probably, between *Conus* and *Strombus*, it has been variously situated, in the different systems. Linnæus referred it to the *Bulla* family, that "refuge for the destitute;" Cuvier placed it between *Ovulum* and *Oliva*; Lamark, between *Cypræa* and *Ancillaria*; Férussac, between *Cypræa* and *Terebra*; Blainville between *Conus* and *Oliva*; Latreille, between *Oliva* and *Ancillaria*; and Rang between *Mitra* and *Ancillaria*. The animal is described by me in the 'Annals and Magazine of Nat. Hist.' vol. xix. p. 411.

In its habits the animal of the *Terebellum* is exceedingly shy and timid, retracting its body into the shell on the slightest alarm. It will remain stationary for a long time, moving its tentacles about cautiously in every direction, when, suddenly, it will roll over with its shell, and continue again perfectly quiet. They appear to have all the muscular energy, vivacity, and, doubtless, predatory boldness possessed by the *Strombi*, which they also resemble in their perfectly organized eyes, and quickness of vision. Mr. Cuming informs me he has seen them leap several inches from the ground, exactly as I have seen the animal of *Strombus gibberula*. On one occasion, a beautiful specimen was lost to the above-mentioned enthusiastic collector, by the animal suddenly leaping into the water, as he was holding and admiring it in the palm of his hand. Those I kept in confinement died in a few days, and appeared to be of a more delicate constitution than the hardy Strombus. There appears to be a very trifling muscular connexion between the animal and its shell.

From my observations of the animal of *Terebellum*, I should imagine the spotted variety to be perfectly distinct as a species. In this, which may be called

T. maculosum, the proboscis is of a whitish-brown colour, reddish towards the tip; the body is of an opaque pearly white; the mantle transparent; the foot semi-pellucid white; the ocular-peduncles are mottled with dark red; the iris is brown red, and the pupil black. The front of the mantle, edging the anterior part of the shell, is coloured with a black line, forming its margin.

In the common species, *T. subulatum*, the eye-peduncles are punctulated with red-brown, as is likewise the upper and under part of the fore-portion of the body. The body is opaque pearly white, with three large, irregular-shaped red-brown blotches on the fore part. The under-surface of the foot is light brown, with a white cross-like marking of a deeper brown. Doubtless, when the animal of the variety covered with zig-zag markings shall have been discovered, it will also be found to be specifically distinct.

We landed one day in April on the little island of Soolaree, in the Sooloo Archipelago, where the Mangrove trees grow in the water along the shores, and strange crabs, and fish of monstrous forms, live beneath their branches. The interior of the island we found to be a salt marsh, in one part forming a lagoon, on whose banks was a pretty little Malay village, peopled by fishermen. Emissaries were sent inviting us to visit their hamlet; and on our proceeding to the spot, we were received by the chief, and some twenty other Malays, all armed with the lance and kris. Having presented him with a trifle, in the form of a handkerchief for the head, he very civilly escorted us to our boats, and affectionately took his leave. These men were probably pirates, and had our force been smaller, their character might have been very different; but there is guile even in a savage! and might with them is ever right. Many a true tale of the crews of merchantmen, slaughtered in cold blood by these merciless freebooters, that constitute the curse of Malayan Asia, might be mentioned in confirmation of this sad truth.

On the 21st of April, 1844, we touched at Basilan, which we also again visited in March, 1845, and March, 1846, on which last occasion I had an opportunity of catching a glimpse of some of the scenery of the island, and thus it happened.

While lying off Passan, a new establishment of the Spaniards on the island, I had occasion to visit the Commandante, who was very ill of fever and dysentery, and after doing him all the good in my power, I was persuaded to remain and spend the day with the Officers in their newly-erected wooden castle. After partaking of a capital dinner, where wine and choice liqueurs were not wanting, on my expressing a wish to obtain some specimens of the Flying-Foxes, which are very numerous in the island, a little expedition was immediately planned, and, in a very short time, a strong party of us started on foot, armed with fowling-pieces, into the interior of the forest behind the fort; and I confess I was amused at the very motley group we formed. One Spanish gentleman, very stout and with enormous moustaches, wore a huge "Sombrero," and carried a thick club-shaped stick; another, a shrivelled little man, with a sharp nose, was dressed in white, even to his hat, which was made of thin pith, and covered with white calico; another carried two guns, and was dressed like a sporting gentleman on the first of September; while another wore a loose blouse, and a wide-brimmed straw hat.

Having advanced a considerable distance into the wood, and traversed some of the most romantic glades I had seen, even in the tropics, without observing anything but a wild pig, and a small species of civet cat, we came to the banks of a small, deep, still, dark-coloured river, with the lofty trees meeting over our heads, and crowded with pigeons. Here, as if to compensate ourselves for our disappointment in not meeting any *Galeopitheci*, we all eagerly commenced firing at the poor doves, and the result was the death of a considerable number, and among them several *Vinagoes*, with splendid metallic-green plumage. While engaged in this recreation, several women and children, with two men, belonging to the hostile parties on the other side of the island, passed timidly by us, and, stepping into a canoe, paddled rapidly out of sight. These poor people had come, at the risk of their lives, with eggs and vegetables for the use of the Spaniards, and I was informed that if their own people were acquainted with the fact, they would all be "krissed." A sharp look out was kept by all our party, for the natives, stealing through the wood, often lie in ambush for those that venture out of the fort, and shoot them; any mode being justifiable in their eyes, in getting rid of their European invaders. One of the Spanish soldiers was shot in this manner two days before. So sudden are the Malays of Basilan, and so secret in their movements, that the Spaniards are constantly on the watch to guard against surprise, and unexpected attacks. Although very large in numbers, and very brave, the natives are easily repulsed on account of their want of fire-arms, and their desultory mode of warfare. The friendly Basilan people I saw reposing in groups about the fort, appeared to be a very fine, and even handsome race, both men and women.

The ground in this part of the forest, was literally over-run with a small black, agile, species of *Lycosa*, many of which had a white, flattened, globose cocoon affixed to the ends of their abdomens. It was most amusing to watch the earnest solicitude with which these jealous mothers protected the cradles of their little ones, allowing themselves to fall into the hands of the enemy, rather than be robbed of the silken nests that contained their helpless progeny. All Spiders are gifted with the same "storgé," or maternal instinct, and resort to various methods for the purpose of securing their cocoons. The *Theridion*, when a seizure of the precious burden is threatened, tumbles, together with it, to the ground, and remains motionless, guarding it with solicitous anxiety; and the *Thomisus* covers the receptacle of its offspring with its body, and when robbed of it, wanders about disconsolate. Did the minute size of these poor Spiders admit of the same psycological dissertations, anecdotes as interesting, no doubt, as those told of the she-bear, when robbed of her cubs, or the violent emotions of the Lioness, when disturbed in her maternal duties, by the hunters in the jungle, might be recorded, proving how strong is the love of offspring, even in animals the most insignificant.

While staying at Basilan, I had an opportunity of observing the animal of *Ovulum volva*, in a living state, and shall shortly mention its habits. The *Radius* is slow and languid in its movements, sliding along deliberately, and is not more sensible to alarm than *Cypræa* or *Calpurnus*.

From the foot being rather narrow, and folded longitudinally upon itself, this animal, no doubt, is in the habit of crawling upon, and adhering to, the slender, round, coral-branches, and fuci, in the manner of certain other *Ovula* and many *Dorididæ*. Dredged in five fathoms from a rocky coral bottom. One barren island rock, not far from Basilan, was covered with vast numbers of *Ostræa crista-galli*, firmly attached by calcareous matter, to the surface of the coral masses, which were pierced, moreover, with *Lithodomi, Petricolæ*, and other boring Mollusks. The sharpened appetites of ourselves and men, were pleasantly appeased by knocking off the upper valves, and devouring the coarse, though not unsavoury contents of these dishes, spread by nature for our entertainment and gratification.

Anchored off the eastern coast of Borneo, in the province of Unsang, for the purpose of surveying, and taking observations, I had an opportunity of examining many new and interesting productions of that little-known Island. On either side of the encampment on shore, was a vast extent of untrodden forest, abounding with wild animals of various descriptions. Tracks of enormous apes appeared in the sands; tiger-cats and lynxes were seen roaming about in the shade of the matted jungle; and boars, of large dimensions, came rooting and grunting in the immediate vicinity of the tents. An adjutant or gigantic Crane (*Ardea Mirabou*), four feet high, was shot, and brought on board; a huge Monitor Lizard (*Hydrosaurus giganteus*), five feet long, and spotted with dull yellow, was also killed and converted into soup. The Crocodile (*Crocodilus biporcatus*), must occasionally attain to a very large size in Borneo, judging from an enormous skull found whitening on the beach. The owner must at least have been twenty-eight feet long.

Among the insects, I noticed, as being most common in this province (Unsang) was a species of *Monochama*, with the elytra elegantly marked with longitudinal, red stripes, alternating with opaque-white stripes marked across with deep black, triangular, spots, and brick-dust-coloured thorax, with three longitudinal black bands. Another truly splendid insect, was a *Catacanthus*, of the subgenus *Chalicoris*, with a scarlet body, and head of burnished green; a thorax of a purple-green with a metallic lustre, having a broad, bright scarlet, semi-lunar, transverse band; the long scutellum, half green and half scarlet, and the elytra white, with green and scarlet marks. Another remarkable form, belonged to *Platyrhinidæ*, a connecting link between the *Curculionidæ* and the *Longicorns*. It was of a dull, dark, olive-brown, with a bronze-coloured head and antennæ, with alternate black and white rings. A species of *Mastax*, allied to *M. vitrea* (West. Arc. Ent. t. 22. f. 2.) but differing in the ends of the elytra being incised, was also procured. This species I have named *M. Whitei*, after that enthusiastic entomologist, Mr. Adam White of the British Museum, to whom I am indebted for the scientific names of many insects previously unknown to me. It is of a dark brown colour, with two transparent white spots near the ends of the elytra, and wings of a light, semi-pellucid brown. A new species of *Scyanus*, entirely of a black colour, with light brown, semi-pellucid wings, and several species of *Reduvius*, a genus which appears in Borneo, and I believe elsewhere, to assume every conceivable modification of montrous form. One species had a yellow body, green thorax, and wings nearly opaque; another had golden-brown wings, and a shining coal-black body. Under the shade of the Casuarina-trees, and burrowing in the ground, was a handsome *Gymnopleurus*, a remarkable looking insect of a black colour, and like all the insects of that family, possessed of enormous strength. To this may be added, a species of *Popilia*, closely allied to the *P. cyanea* of Hope, but most probably a new species; of a bright polished-steel blue, inclining to deep purple, viewed in certain lights; and, in the same locality, under leaves on the ground, was detected a handsome, polished black *Passalus*.

At *Cape Rivers* in the Straits of Macassar, were seen the star-like tentacles of the *Tubipora musica*, of a pale delicate white, striped with light blue, expanded in large masses; the red *Pinnatula*, lying dead upon the beach, with the pellucid plates of the beautiful *Velella* and fragile *Porpita*; the elegant jointed *Isis*, throwing its branches in every direction, among large beds of other corals, and various madrepores strewing the margins of the pools. The large and ugly "biche de mer" (*Holothuria tremula*), lay extended on the sandy patches, and, to every stone, the sea anemonies, with their brilliant tentacles, were exploring the warm, shallow waters for their food. The dark and slug-like bodies of *Parmophori*, and the crawling forms of *Stomatellæ*, were seen moving and sliding among the coral beds, while scarce a stone was turned, without observing *Chitonelli* crawling on the under surface. In every part where solid rock was seen, the bright, blue branchiæ of *Tridacnæ* were visible in their stony houses, while crabs, of every form, were found concealed in corners, greedy, rapacious, and devouring.

There is some very fine forest scenery in Celebes. I have wandered several times in the uninhabited parts of the coasts for whole days, with no other company than my own thoughts, and the sights and sounds of nature. I have already endeavoured to picture the forests of Borneo: those of Celebes are very similar. The trunks and branches of the trees here, as elsewhere in the Tropics, are covered with *Bauhiniæ*, and other huge climbing plants, which suspend themselves, like monstrous serpents, from the trees, twisting their folds sometimes so tight as to strangle and eventually destroy the plants they embrace; on every side you notice that fragrant

> "parasites
> Starr'd with ten thousand blossoms, flow around
> The grey trunks;"

gigantic *Lycopodiaceæ*, or club mosses, are frequently met with, rearing their elegant heads from among the damp beds of decaying leaves; the prostrate trunks are covered with *Opegraphæ*, and other Lichenoid plants, which spread their distempered-looking *thalli* over the loose bark; while on the shaded side, and often concealed by the tree, minute and delicately formed *Fungi* of the most extravagant forms, live their little hour, and are succeeded by a crop equally as ephemeral. Bamboo thickets are common in some parts, and the slender branches, and light quivering leaves, produce those peculiar changing shadows you often see in dense forests where the sun partially shines through the foliage; a fact which did not escape the observant eye of the Bard of Avon;

in 'Titus Andronicus,' he thus alludes to this peculiarity:—

> "The green leaves quiver with the cooling wind
> And make a chequered shadow on the ground."

I have frequently seen the Bamboo, that magnificent member of the grassy-tribe, waving aloft its feathery sprays in groves, more than forty feet high. The appearance of the epiphytic vegetation, in these forests, exactly resembles, in some spots, the vineyards full of trees so eloquently mentioned by Dickens:—" The wild festoons; the elegant wreaths, and crowns, and garlands of all shapes; the fairy nets flung over great trees, and making them prisoners in sport; the tumbled heaps and mounds of exquisite shapes upon the ground; how rich and beautiful they are! And every now and then, a long, long line of trees will be all bound and garlanded together, as if they had taken hold of one another, and were coming dancing down the field!"*

What must ever strike a European observer in tropical forests, is the singular want of any of those autumnal signs of partial decay, or vernal indications of gradual development, seen in climes more temperate. There are no mellow tints, or boughs covered with young green buds; no red withered leaves falling from the trees; but always renovation and dissolution, always the same quantity of dead rotting leaves, and the same dense mass of dark green foliage, wherever the woods are entered, whether in the dry or rainy season. In many parts of these forests I noticed a vast number of *Fungi*, those scavengers of the vegetable kingdom, which insignificant,

* Pictures from Italy, p. 90.

and unpretending, spring up on every fallen tree, and, disguised under a thousand grotesque forms, prey upon, and consume the decayed and putrefying wood. But though these tall trees, shorn of all their pride and beauty, as the poet Shelley says, in his poem of 'Queen Mab,' in a beautiful simile:—

> "Lie level with the earth to moulder there,
> They fertilize the land they long deformed;
> Till from the breathing lawn a forest springs
> Of youth, integrity, and loveliness,
> Like that which gave it life, to spring and die."

Whatever of grand or beautiful may be seen in the forests of the torrid zone, yet the observer of nature, if he be of European origin, will always sigh in vain for certain simple signs of landscape scenery, and woodland peculiarities once familiar to him in other lands. Where will he find in Borneo or Celebes, commons covered with purple blooming Heather, or brown dusky glens ornamented with the drooping bells of the Fox-glove, or snug little coppices where the Wild Rose and the Hawthorn mingle with the graceful Ash and silver-barked Birch? Sombre, dense, and towering masses of foliage, trees beyond trees in never ending avenues; these take the place of more lively rural scenes. And among the feathered race, what birds, however gaudy their plumage, or vivacious their movements, can vie with pretty Cock-robin, the saucy Jay, or the pert chattering Magpie with its long black tail? Can the harsh scream of the Parrot compare with the sweet melody of our summer songsters, their plaintive monotony, or shrill pipings, or even with the clamorous cawings of the Rooks that build their nests on the tall Elm trees?

What can be more delightful, than to enter a forest abounding in examples, for the purpose of satisfying your mind whether there is any truth in the statement that the tongues and jaws of Lepidopterous insects, or Butterflies, are adapted in length to the corollas of the flowers they suck; so that a tubular blossom is rifled by an elongated proboscis, and a salver-shaped corolla by a short obtuse muzzle. In the Silk-worm Moths, which do not require food in the Imago state, the mouth is not developed; but in the Humming-bird Hawk-moth, which hovers about tubular flowers, and greedily extracts the nectar, the tongue is of enormous length.

The beautiful adaptation of insects, at large, to the flowers on which they feed, is well shown by St. Pierre, in the Bee. He observes:—" Nous voyons avec plaisir les relations de la trompe d'une *abeille* avec les nectaires des fleurs; celles de ses cuisses creusées en cuillers et hérissées de poils, avec les poussières des étamines qu'elle y entasse; celle de ses quatre ailes, avec le butin dont elle est chargée; enfin l'usage du long aiguillon qu'elle en a reçu pour la défense de son bien."*

During a stroll one day into the forest of Celebes, I was very much struck with the ingenuity of a large species of Bee, which frequented, in great numbers, a tree loaded with monopetalous corollas, furnished with a very long tube. The slender trunk of the Bee was, doubtless, too short to reach the honied store concealed in the nectary at the bottom, and therefore its "long, narrow pump," as Paley terms the promuscis of Hymenopterous

* Etudes de la Nature.

insects, was of no avail; our Bee, nothing daunted, sawed through the base of the corolla, where it joins the calyx, with its fore legs, and then shoving it to the ground with its head, sucked up the honey "ad libitum." Speaking of the Bee, Paley observes, "The harmless plunderer rifles the sweets, but leaves the flower uninjured;" this wicked insect, however, not only robs the blossom of its nectar, but leaves ruin behind. Many years ago, I remember noticing that the Humble-Bee of England, as he

"Sits on the bloom, extracting liquid sweets,"

employs frequently his feet for the same purpose, in cases where the tube of the corolla is of greater length than usual; as, for example in the Jasmine.

In the forests of Celebes, I procured, also among many other insects, two *Elaters*, one with yellowish-brown elytra, and the other with the wing-cases covered with mouse-coloured hair; a *Languria*, with a green head, an orange thorax, and burnished green elytra, marked with punctulated, longitudinal striæ; a *Lucanus*, of a tawny yellow colour, with a reddish-brown head, and three black marks on the thorax, and the elytra margined with black; an *Anthribidous* of a greenish-ash colour, with dull, opaque, dark, black markings; an *Elater* of the genus *Calais*, Laporte, *Alaus*, Eschsch; most probably a new species, with the head and body covered with a hoary pubescence, and on the thorax, a large, shining, longitudinal, oval, black spot, and four smaller round spots arranged about it, and the elytra marbled and mottled with black; a *Cicindela*, very near *C. Chinensis*, of a dull sap green, and yellow marks on the elytra; a remarkable species of *Apocyrtus*, of an ash colour, covered with minute black spots; a *Micraspis*, one of the *Coccinellidæ*, with bright orange elytra, margined at their inner edges, with black, and having a large, curved, linear, black mark in the centre of each. To these may be added a *Galeruca*, of a pale straw colour, with black spots on the thorax; a *Languria*, with a reddish-brown head, and dark metallic green, brightly polished elytra, which alights on the blades of the *Zea mays*, and leaves of other plants, in open sunny places, and is very active on the wing; a curious genus of *Anthribidæ*, entirely covered, when alive, with a white mealy powder, which, when rubbed off, leaves the elytra of a dark gray, and shows longitudinal rows of alveoli, or pits; an *Agrilus*, with a brilliant green head, and dark bronzed, black elytra, and a body of the most vivid blue, which flies rapidly, and alights to sun itself on leaves; an *Anthraxia* of a burnished emerald green, which is very active in its motions, alighting on the leaves and stalks of plants in the sunny glades of the forest. Besides these, a *Brentus* of a red chesnut brown, and highly polished body struck me as being a most remarkable form among the Coleoptera, which abound in these woods, so fecund in these "resuscitated worms," as Cowper terms insects in their perfect state.

Near Manado, there is a woody tract, not far from the river that runs through the town, which abounds in *Gelasimi* of the most beautiful colours. I have described and figured one species, allied to *G. bellator* (White), of a green colour, with black markings; another, black, with two bright ultramarine spots in the centre of the carapace; and another grey, marbled with white, with an enormous light yellow chela. These cover the ground by thousands, stalking about and holding up their single huge claws in a most ridiculous manner. Notwithstanding, they appear to be overburdened with this unwieldy member, they are by no means easy to capture; but on the slightest attempt upon their liberty they run quickly to the mouth of their burrows for protection, where they will boldly wait and see if the enemy makes any further advances; and, if he does, they retreat quickly backwards, holding out their pincer as a weapon of defence. In the pools of fresh water, and under damp stones, a dark olive-green *Sesarma*, with bright yellow blotches, may be seen concealed; but on the slightest attempt to take the stranger captive, he is off with the greatest velocity, darting under the leaves, and scrambling over sticks, until he finds security either in a hole of the ground, or under the mud of the pools; while on the coast, the observer cannot fail to be delighted and amused with the elegant and agile *Thelphusa grapsoides*, which, by its beauty and brilliancy, gives life and animation to the coral flats, left dry by the receding tide.

Another Crab, which appears to be rather common also, among the Philippines, is the *Chasmagnathus convexus* (De Haan). It lives in the firm black mud of Manila Bay, and in other parts of Luzon, in company with the *Lingula anatina* and *Arca inequivalvis*. Like the *Xenophthalmus pinnotheroides* (White), it doubtless forms oblique, cylindrical holes in the surface of the mud, somewhat in the manner of the *Macrophthalmi*, and *Scopimera globosa*.

On the 23rd we arrived at the little island of Meyo, which appears to be not very long recovered from a state of volcanic sterility, bearing scarcely any traces of vegetation on its blackened, scoriaceous surface. The light porous rock, that composes the principal part of the island, is raised in heaps of jagged points and pinnacles, and has, altogether a most unpromising appearance to the naturalist; and yet, even on such a barren spot as this, nature holds out some objects for our entertainment.

As the boat approached the abrupt and barren shore, a young Whale bared its back, and spouted close alongside of us; and a little nearer the island, two Turtles, of the right sort, came floating by, with lazy, flapping fins, and narrowly escaped being turned into soup by the boat's crew. Close in shore, myriads of banded *Chætodons* and party-coloured *Scari* glided through the calm water among the rocks; and, as we landed, a large black Lizard, a species of *Hydrosaurus*, upwards of four feet long, scaled the rocks immediately above us. On the right, heavy rollers came tumbling in from seaward, between huge perpendicular rocks, rushing impetuously through a wide, time-worn chasm, and receding as violently as they entered, forming a perfect "Maelstrom," and looking like the interior of some enormous caldron, in a state of ebullition. In another part, the sea recedes, and leaves exposed a long, flat, stony beach, with shallow pools, dug in the rock, abounding with small fish and molluscous animals of various descriptions. The large and showy *Cypræa tigris* was here seen crawling about by hundreds, generally in the shade of the steep banks of the ponds, or hiding away in crevices. *Trochi* and *Turbines*, *Cones*, and *Turbinellæ* were equally numerous, and offered, as may be readily supposed, a rich treat to the conchologist, who walking among them as they gemmed the rocks, like so many animated flowers, gathered the prettiest and most brilliant, leaving the others to pursue their nearly vegetable lives unmolested.

Among the fish procured by me in the pools left by the tide on the shores of this little island, was a *Scorpæna* of a dark, mottled brown, with darker grey-brown spots, and a light brown belly; a *Chætodon*, of a blue silvery grey, darker, and with a greenish tinge towards the back, and a bright silvery belly; a *Blennius*, of a dark olive green, rufous towards the head, and greyish towards the back, and both body and fins covered with vivid, linear, ultramarine spots and markings; and a species of *Hippus*, with a blue-grey body, darker towards the dorsal region, and with broad oblique bands of black and white on the tail.

Our very brief sojourn among the Spice Islands did not enable us to gather much information concerning the inhabitants of that group; but from those I had an opportunity of observing at Ternate and Gilolo, I should say that they are of a darker brown than the Malays, with larger heads, longer upper lips, smaller and more sunken eyes, and broader and flatter noses; but these observations may not be generally characteristic among the entire population, but apply to individuals only. They are called Malukus of which the term Moluccas appears to be only a corruption. There were many of this race of men among the Illañons on board the fleet of prahus that attacked the Samarang's barge and gig off the Island of Gilolo, as was proved by the capture of their shields which are narrow, bent in the form of an arc, made of hard black wood, inlaid with bits of shell and mother of pearl, and provided with a single handle, placed in the centre, by which it is held; while the Illañon shield is very large and wide, and of an entirely different construction. The Malukus speak the Tarnata, the language of the Moluccas, the name of which is evidently derived from Ternate. Once free and formidable as pirates, these natives in times past must have offered a curious example of a paradise peopled by devils; of a group of islands probably the most delicious in the world, with a soil the most fecund, abounding in spices and other commodities of enormous commercial value; enjoying a climate at once healthful and undisturbed by hurricanes or violent alternations of temperature; but, alas! inhabited by a set of fierce, vindictive, blood-thirsty savages, whose only delight was in rapine and murder. They are now fortunately almost deprived of the power to injure, are reduced to a state of servile vassalage, and even their Rajahs are but regal slaves, whose pomp and state are maintained by the dollars of the Dutch.

Mr. Brooke in his Journal gives a short account of the war-dance of the Malukus, which he witnessed at Saräwak. He observes that it is of a more gentle nature than that of the Illañons of Mindanao, and that instead of the sword or "kempilan," they prefer the spear, advancing with it stealthily, casting it, and then retreating with the sword and shield. The dancers mad with rage and opium, whom we observed stamping, turning, and yelling on the fighting-deck of the pirate prahus, during our engagement, were most probably Illañon "Datus," or "free men," commanding the expedition. Mr. Brooke states that the sword of the Malukus of Gilolo is similar to that of the Moskokos of Boni Bay, in Celebes.

At the Island of Ternate, I made a capture of a large and splendid undescribed species of *Nephila*, which spins a very wide, strong web among the bamboos. The body is liver-coloured, with a silver horse-shoe mark; the thorax is covered with a downy, hoary pubescence; the shanks of the tibiæ of the two first pairs of legs, have a broad yellowish-white band; the other legs are black. Besides this, I have drawings of numbers of species not yet described, as I always took an interest in these remarkable insects. Spiders are among the most artful of living creatures; their whole life consists of one unvaried course of craft and stratagem; whether they sneak about on the surface of leaves, as green as their own emerald bodies, and surprise the poor flies that venture to approach within the range of their fatal spring; whether they gloomily lurk in dusky holes, or under the shade of dingy tents, and spring upon unwary insects that chance to pass their door; whether they lie supine in the broad daylight, motionless, in their wide-spread treacherous toils, and having seen their victim fairly entangled, wrap him up in a winding-sheet of their own manufacture; or whether, simulating the surface of the ground on which they live, they course their prey with untiring assiduity, and, having run it down, suck its blood with tiger-like ferocity. In the Island of Panagatan, I made a capture of another species of *Nephila*, which I also consider as undescribed. The head is blackish; thorax silvery, with black spots, and covered with a downy pubescence; legs chesnut-red, with the last joints black. The body is of a light emerald green, with numerous bright yellow spots. The under-surface is dull black. It forms a large, strong, geometrical web, spreading from bush to bush, in the centre of which it remains motionless, with legs stretched out, and the head downwards. In a beautiful wood behind Calderas, in Mindanao, I observed a dingy little species of Spider, of the genus *Clubiona*, concealing itself in very snug retreats, formed out of a dead leaf, rolled round in the shape of a cylinder, lined with a soft silken tissue, and closed at one end by means of a strong, woven felt door. When hunted, it was amusing to see the frightened little creatures run for protection into their tiny castles, where they would doubtless be safe from the attacks of birds, owing to the leaves not being distinguishable from others that strew the ground.

CHAPTER VI.

SINGAPORE AND BORNEO.

Singapore—The Sensitive Plant—The Nutmeg Tree—Gutta Percha—Trees yielding Caoutchouc—Jatropha Manihot—Gambier—Useful Plants—Lizards and other Animals—An Opium-smoker—Effects of Opium on the brain—Royal Children—Curious mode of catching Snakes—The Sun-birds—A Tree Slug—Cerithia—Dragon-flies—Nondescript Spider—Remarkable Caterpillar—The Horse-shoe Crab—A Land Lobster—*Borneo*—Excursion up the Linga—Scenery—Insects—The Long-nosed Monkey—Village of Bunting—The Balows—Dried Human Heads — Diseases — Excursion to Tungong—Native Boar-hunt—Singular Fish—Crabs and Shells—Land-Crabs—Habits of Crustaceans.

On the 28th of June, 1844, we were again at Singapore, or, as the Malays term it, Singhapura, where we remained sufficiently long for us to examine some of the numerous objects of interest peculiar to this important little island. Rambles, in any direction, always well repay the naturalist; and a walk, even in the immediate vicinity of the town, is very agreeable. In some parts you will find the ground covered with the Sensitive plant (*Mimosa pudica*), and, as you walk along, you leave a quivering track behind you, caused by the shrinking of a thousand leaflets, making you almost believe, with Darwin and Dutrochet, that plants indeed have feeling; and tempting you to exclaim with the poet Wordsworth,

> "It is my faith that every flower
> Enjoys the air it breathes."

The Nutmeg tree (*Myristica officinalis*, Linn.) appears to thrive equally as well in this island as at Pulo Penang; and everywhere around you, if you wander a little to the back of the town, you will perceive plantations of these valuable trees, which, disposed in clumps, have a very pretty appearance, particularly when the large green fleshy pear-shaped fruits have burst, and the crimson aril, or mace, shows ruddy through the fissure in the rind. The bark abounds in a yellow juice; the long shining oval leaves are powerfully aromatic when bruised; and the inflorescence consists of axillary racemes of small green flowers, the males having thick, cup-shaped calices, and the filaments united together, and the females possessing a solitary pistil, with a very short style. The oval seeds, or nutmegs, are stripped, like ripe walnuts, of their fleshy valves; the aril or mace is carefully removed, and spread on mats to dry; and the nuts, with their hard oval shells, are placed in lofts, under which fires are kept burning; but are not steeped in lime-water for the purpose of protecting them from insects, as is done in some countries. A few Clove trees (*Caryophyllus aromaticus*, Linn.) seem to thrive tolerably well, but they have not been very extensively introduced. In an excursion into the woods of the interior, I had an opportunity of observing the tree which yields the material called Gutta Percha, although properly speaking, the first word should be written "Gatah," which is the Malay name for any gummy exudation, and is likewise applied by them to the Dammar and Gambier. The tree (*Icosandra gutta percha*) belongs to the Natural Order *Sapotaceæ*, and has lately been described by Sir W. J. Hooker. It is a large, high tree, with a dense crown of rather small dark green leaves, and a round smooth trunk. On incising the bark with a chopping-knife, a quantity of rather thin white milky fluid exudes, which gradually hardens on coming in contact with the air, in which state it is the Gutta Percha of commerce. A West Indian tree belonging to the same tribe, *Achras Sapota*, abounds in a thick white tenacious milk, which might possibly be applied to similar purposes; and another Sapotaceous plant, the *Bassia longifolia*, also yields a milky sap, which is used on the continent of India in rheumatic affections. The sap of *Icosandra* is not viscid and tenacious like that of the *Ficus elastica*, which is common in Borneo, and of the other trees which yield a similar substance, as the *Urceola elastica*, which grows at Penang, and affords an excellent kind of caoutchouc, and that other climbing plant, *Willoughbeia edulis*, which is found in the same island, but produces a very indifferent sort. The advantage the Gutta Percha seems to have over the other descriptions of caoutchouc, appears to consist in its great tenacity, and in its retaining its form and solidity, even in the tropics; but on the other hand, it wants elasticity. It is easily moulded into any form, by steeping it in hot water, and forms very good catheters, bougies, soles of shoes, riding-whips, gas pipes, ornaments for picture-frames, &c. Several other plants yield sap with similar useful properties, as the *Hevea Guianensis*, which produces the Demerara and Surinam caoutchouc, and the Bastard Manchineel tree (*Cameraria latifolia*), which is common in Cuba, and other West Indian Islands. In the plantations about Singapore you will see the *Jatropha Manihot*, with its white, brittle, warty stems, and large, deeply-divided, heart-shaped leaves; a plant which yields, at the same time, a dangerously poisonous juice, and a wholesome fecula, which, in South America, forms an important article of diet, under the name of *Cassava*; the useful Gomuti Palm, and graceful Plantain, the elegant, feathery Bamboo, the Betel, and the climbing Yam, mingled with Papayas, Citron, and Lime trees, and various useful Scitamineous plants, as the Turmeric and the Ginger, may be also mentioned; nor must that very important Cinchonaceous plant, the *Uncaria Gambir*, which yields the substance named *Terra Japonica*, a kind of Catechu, be omitted; the extract being most extensively employed by the Malays, mixed with Betel leaf, *Areca* nut, and Lime, as a masticatory. At Singapore, the Malay fishermen make a very strong cordage out of the leaves of the *Pandanus lævis*; and here, as elsewhere, among the Eastern Islands, the leaves of the *Nipa fruticans* are universally used for thatching their primitive and fragile dwellings. The island, moreover, abounds in Pine Apples of several varieties, the common sort, in my opinion, being the best flavoured; the long, red, conical ones being the next in esteem; and those with variegated leaves being the worst of all.

Among the dry, withered leaves that strew the ground, hundreds of large, brown, shining Lizards rush about with the greatest velocity, reminding the timid of the rustling of serpents beneath their feet; and, in the trees, the flying Squirrel (*Pteromys Petaurista*) or, by a rarer chance, the beautiful *Galeopithecus variegatus* may be seen towards the evening, besides the pretty little active *Tupaia Tana*, and Squirrels and Monkeys of one or two descriptions. Many rare animals may occasionally be observed confined in the menagerie of the Governor, and other places; I have seen the black variety of the Leopard, the Orang-Utan, and Wou-Wou, the Argus Pheasant, Black Cockatoo, and several large *Pythons*, exhibited in this manner; the Dugong has been caught off the island, and I have seen the Sword-fish in the boats of the fishermen, who also bring off for sale numbers of 'Neptune's Cups,' a species of *Alcyonum*, and vast quantities of Corals and shells; among the latter, *Aspergilla, Fistulanæ, Cardissæ, Lithodomi,* and *Gastrochænæ* are very numerous.

In a certain large Caravansary, belonging to the Malay village near Singapore, a place where Buffaloes and Goats occupy the centre, and where pallets are arranged around for its human occupants, I had a good opportunity of observing the effects of Opium on the physical aspect of the Malay. I was particularly struck with one old confirmed Opium-smoker, with whom I enjoyed a "hubble-bubble." He was a feeble worn-out old man, with an unearthly brilliancy in his eye. His body was bent forwards, and greatly emaciated; his face was shrunken, wan, and haggard; his long skinny arm, wasted fingers, and sharp-pointed nails, resembled more the claw of some rapacious bird, than the hand of a lord of creation; his head was nodding and tremulous, his skin wrinkled and yellow, and his teeth were a few decayed, pointed, and black-stained fangs. As I approached him he raised his body from the mat on which he was reposing, and filling an antiquated pipe with tobacco, courteously presented it for my acceptance. There was something interesting, and, at the same time, melancholy, in the physique of this old man, who, now in rags, appeared from the silver ornaments he wore, and by his embroidered jacket, to have been formerly a person of some consideration; but the fascinating influence of the deadly drug had fastened on him, and a pallet in a Caravansary was the reward of self-indulgence. In my experience of Opium, which has not, however, been very extensive, I cannot say I found as much pleasure as De Quincy, the "English Opium Eater," in his 'Confessions,' would lead us to believe fell to his lot. After three or four Chinese Opium-pipes, I found my brain very much unsettled, and teeming with thoughts, ill-arranged, and pursuing each other in wanton dreamy play, without order or connexion; the circulating system being, at the same time, much excited, the frame tremulous, the eye-balls fixed, and a peculiar and agreeable thrilling sensation extending along the nerves. The same succession of image crowding upon image, and thoughts revelling in strange disorder, continues for some time, during which a person appears to be in the condition of the madman alluded to by Dryden, in his play of the 'Spanish Friar:'—

> "He raves, his words are loose
> As heaps of sand, and scattering wide from sense:
> So high he's mounted on his airy throne,
> That now the wind has got into his head,
> And turned his brains to frenzy."

Unutterable melancholy feelings succeed to this somewhat pleasurable period of excitement, but a soft languor steals shortly across the senses, and the half-poisoned individual falls asleep. The next day there is great nausea and sickness of stomach, headache, and tormenting thirst, which makes you curse Opium, and exclaim with Shakespeare's King John:—

> "And none of you will bid the winter come
> To thrust his icy fingers in my maw:
> Nor let my kingdom's rivers take their course
> Thro' my burnt bosom; nor intreat the North
> To make his bleak winds kiss my parched lips,
> And comfort me with cold."

At the residence of the Ex-Rajah of Singapore, I was introduced to a young Prince and Princess, children, as as I was informed, of the Rajah, and likewise to their mother. These scions of departed royalty were perfectly naked, and adorned with silver ornaments; the boy wearing an amulet about his neck, and rings on his arms and legs; and the girl having an ornamented silver heart-shaped fig-leaf depending in front, and attached by a silver chain around the hips. They were both very pretty children, and good-tempered; but I observed that young as he was, perhaps not more than five years old, this small brown prince had commenced the habit of chewing the betel-nut and sïrih leaf; for his lips and teeth were already stained with the universal masticatory.

In an excursion with Sir Edward Belcher and Dr. Oxley into the interior of the island, for the purpose of collecting some of the numerous and beautiful epiphytic Orchids that abound in the forest, I noticed a very novel and ingenious method of capturing snakes. A small, but highly-venomous reptile of this description, of a bright green colour, having a row of white spots along the sides, and with the triangular head, and enormous fangs, which characterize the genus *Trigono cephalus*, was detected by Sir Edward peeping from among the tangled leaves of a bunch of *Epidendra*, which he was about to gather. On pointing it out to our Malay attendants, one of them immediately procured a long tapering twig, and formed a running noose out of a fine grass, which being fashioned according to his satisfaction, he passed it over the extended head of the reptile, drew the knot tight, and thus secured the prize, which I immediately seized between the finger and thumb, and divided the spinal cord with the point of a pen-knife; for the natives, if they could have had their way, would have crushed the head, and so ruined the specimen,

At Singapore I first had the pleasure of observing those tiny paragons of the East, the Sun-birds (*Cinnyris*), which, like their brilliant representatives of the West, are etherial, gay, and sprightly in their motions, flitting briskly from flower to flower, and assuming a thousand lively and agreeable attitudes. As the sunbeams glitter on their bodies, they sparkle like so many precious stones, and exhibit, as they turn, a variety of bright and iridescent hues, "like atoms of the rainbow fluttering round," as a poet has described them. As they hover round the honey-laden blossoms, they vibrate rapidly their tiny pinions, producing in the air, a slight whirring sound, but not so loud as the humming noise produced by the wings of the *Trochilidæ*. Occasionally, I have seen them clinging by their feet and tail, busily engaged in rifling, of their insects and nectar, the blossoms of the trees; in the stomachs of many which I examined, were the partially-digested remains of dipterous, coleopterous, and tetrapterous insects. These lovely and active little ornaments of the feathered tribe serve, by the rapidity of their movements, and the brilliancy of their colours, materially to enliven the monotony of a noon-day walk. I well remember a certain dark-leaved tree with scarlet, tubular flowers, that especially courted the attention of the Sun-birds, and around its blossoms they continually darted with eager and vivacious movements. In the course of an hour's watching, I have counted more than a dozen different species of *Cinnyris*, *Nectarinea*, and *Certhia*, coming and going to and from this honied banquet. The Sun-birds seemed particularly delighted, clinging to the slender twigs, and coquetting with the flowers, thrusting in their slender beaks, and probing with their brush-like tongues, for insects and nectar, hanging suspended by their feet, throwing back their little glossy heads, chasing each other on giddy wing, and flirting and twittering, the gayest of the gay. Some were emerald green, some vivid violet, and others yellow with a crimson wing. In the vicinity of this tree, which was in the town, were numbers of Sparrows, in their every-day dress, apparently engaged in disdainfully contemplating these gaudy-coloured birds of pleasure. Darwin's capital description of the Humming-bird applies also to the *Cinnyrides* :—

> "So where the Humming-bird in Chili's bowers,
> On murmuring pinions, robs the pendent flowers;
> Seeks where fine pores their dulcet balm distil,
> And sucks the treasure with proboscis-bill."*

Among molluscous animals, the *Onchidium* of Singapore offers a curious instance of what may be termed an Arboreal Slug. It is a limaciform animal, which is found crawling among the foliage of the trees in the woods, and appearing more particularly after heavy showers. During the heat of the day it collapses its broad, flattened body, and retires under the shade of large leaves, where it remains apparently in a half-torpid condition. It leaves no slimy trail behind, when it crawls, as the Limax and Snail do. It is of a chesnut-brown colour, minutely tuberculated, with numerous small, dark, scattered spots, and with the raised middle line of a pale brown; the eyes are terminal on the long superior pair of tentacles.

Another remarkable molluscous form is the *Cerithium truncatum*, which is found generally in brackish water in Mangrove swamps, and the mouths of rivers. Sometimes it crawls on the stones and leaves in the neighbourhood, and sometimes it is found suspended by glutinous threads to the boughs of trees, and from the roots of the Mangroves. The animal of *Megalamastoma suspensum* has been found in the West Indies, by the Rev. Lansdowne Guilding, hanging from trees in the same manner; and Mr. Gray states that he has found the *Rissoa* similarly suspended. There is another very handsome species, closely allied to the preceding, which I have frequently found crawling in a slow and languid manner on

* Botanic Garden.

the leaves of the *Pontedera,* and of *Calami* and Sedges, found among the fluviatile marshes, and on the low banks of rivers in several parts of Borneo, even many miles in the interior, where the water is perfectly fresh. In this species, the eyes are likewise terminal; the proboscis is elegantly marked with crimson and yellow; there is a vivid scarlet edge extending round the lower part of the body, where it joins the foot; the under surface of which latter part is of a dark brown. They live, in general, quite out of the water, and have a very pretty appearance when seen crawling among the leaves.

In the insect world nothing surprised me more than the large number of *Libelulæ,* and analogous forms of *Neuroptera.* Dragon-flies, however, are not only numerous here, but in China, and among all the islands of the Eastern seas. On every barren bank, on every flowery plain, over oozy bogs and stagnant pools, may be seen all day long, flitting on their untiring wings of gauze, these beautiful creatures, or as Shakespeare would term them:—

> "Those gay creatures of the element,
> That in the colours of the rainbow live,
> And play i' the plighted clouds."

Volatile and erratic, their chief resort is about some dull, sequestered pool, where rank weeds luxuriate, and where, springing from the mud and slime, the air teems with living forms. These are the food of the Dragon-fly, and in their pursuit and capture consist his pastime and delight. I have frequently regarded with astonishment the dexterity of the little Dyak boys, who catch these sprightly *Neuroptera* by means of a noose formed of human hair, and fastened to the end of a long, slender stick. They will lassoo adroitly their tiny game, and bring them to you with the hair neatly secured around the insect's neck, which does not prevent it from fluttering about, to the great delight of its captor; for boys are cruel, even in a state of nature.

In the woods of Singapore I made captive a very large and handsome species of *Nephila*, which I do not find described. The thorax is covered with a rich golden pubescence; the terminal half of the palpi are deep black, the proximate half red above, and yellow beneath; the chelicera are large and shining black; the abdomen has a black band at the anterior part, and posteriorly, and on the sides large bright patches of yellow; the cephalothorax, where not hid by the silky hairs, is dark green, with yellow striæ; the legs are black, with bright yellow rings at the joints, and the thighs, on the under surface, are bright yellow, and the eyes are black and shining. It forms a large, geometrical web, extended vertically between low bushes. Another remarkable insect was seen feeding on the bark of a tree, and appeared to me to resemble, more than anything else, the larva of one of the *Geometridæ*, which, being destined to live on a rough, green bark, and not among twigs and slender stems, instead of the usual brown colour, was of a bright green, with the segments of the body dilated laterally, giving it somewhat the appearance of a number of fronds of the *Lemna*, or Duck-weed, strung together. When this strange-looking caterpillar crawled, it hooped its body in the manner peculiar to the members of the *Geometridæ* family.

Near Point Romania, on the Peninsula of Malacca, among several other curiosities of nature, I observed numbers of the *Limulus Moluccanus*, or Horse-shoe Crab. It progresses in a very awkward manner, beginning its onward movement by raising its enormous cephalo-thorax, or carapace, several degrees from the ground, by extending the joints of its legs, and standing on its toes or ungual joints, which operation is, however, entirely concealed from common observation; thus reminding one of the manœuvering operations of the ancient Testudo, a sort of machine employed by the Romans in besieging cities, under the roof of which the soldiers worked when undermining the walls. When the anterior part of the shell, or carapace, is sufficiently elevated, the whole weight of the animal is thrown forwards, the shell is then again raised, and the operation repeated. It carries its spiniform tail and flattened abdomen trailing on the the ground; but when irritated, it raises the latter at an obtuse angle with the body, while the tail is elevated perpendicularly in the air, and moved from side to side in a threatening manner, When alive, the animal is of a dull, greyish, leaden colour, and dirty brown on the abdominal surface. I have sometimes been amused in putting to flight a whole army of little *Limuli*, just after their emergence from the ova. Their raised and threatening tails, angry menaces, and uncouth efforts to escape, are truly ludicrous. These young fry are frequently met with among the shallow bays of the islands in the China Sea, and I have found those of another species, (*Limulus longispina*,) at Leegeetan, on the coast of Borneo. Among the Japanese, the *Limulus* is employed to indicate the

Zodiacal constellation of Cancer; in China the *L. heterodactylus* is esteemed choice eating; and I have seen the Malays use the carapace as a drinking cup, at the springs, the long straight tail forming a capital handle.

The *Thalassina scorpionoides* is common both at Singapore and Borneo; living in vertical, cylindrical holes in the ground, in marshy places, and on the banks of rivers. During wet weather, and particularly after heavy rains, it issues from its habitaculum and comes to the surface. In its movements it is slow and feeble, and when taken, is, apparently, defenceless, not making use of its chelæ as organs of aggression. In some parts of India it is said to spoil the roads, and do considerable damage to the plantations. It is exceedingly tenacious of life, one in my possession existing upwards of an hour in proof spirits.

On our return to Sarāwak, in July, I had the pleasure of accompanying a boat expedition up the Linga, for the purpose of capturing, if possible, the noted Arab pirate, Sheriff Sahib. On our passage up this river, the scenery was very splendid, and, as in many parts, we grazed the bushes, I had excellent opportunities of gathering epiphytes, and observing the different insects that fluttered around us. The spectral-looking *Phasma*, like some withered stick, moved slowly and deliberately among the branches; while his more lively congeners, the pink-winged *Empusa*, and emerald-green *Mantis*, as closely simulated the foliage of the trees on which they hung, ever greedy for prey and rapine. It is very amusing to watch a large-sized *Mantis* saw off the head of some dipterous insect that has just become its prey: he does it in such a surgical and business-like manner!

Numerous *Grylli* and nimble-limbed *Locustæ*, of large dimensions and of splendid colours, spread their gauze-like wings, and flew, with whirring noise, from spray to spray. Hosts of merry, never-wearied *Cicadæ*, flitting about on their silvery membranous elytra, and sitting on the twigs among the leaves, raised their shrilly voices above, below, and around :—

> " Hinc querulas referunt voces, quîs nantia limo
> Corpora lympha fovet; sonitus alit aëris echo,
> Argutis et cuncta fremunt arbusta *cicadis*." *

Large *Lepidoptera*, with flapping wings, rose and sunk amid the vistas of the wood, with that lazy way these gorgeous creatures always have in tropical forests, sailing slowly across the open spaces, and gradually disappearing like lovely visions, amid the leafy labyrinths.

We came at length to the last bivouac of the fugitive Sheriff, at a point of the river where the banks were under water, and where there was an open space, bounded by enormous forest trees, whose quaint and knotted roots appeared above the swamp, in the form of brown and wrinkled twisted serpents, arches full of extraordinary contortions, and other strange forms usually assumed by the roots of the *Rhizophora Gymnorhiza* and similar trees. The pursued and persecuted remnant of the enemy had chosen this miserable spot for its last resting-place, having with native ingenuity thrown trees from root to root, several feet from the surface of the water, with cross pieces of bamboo, secured with rattans and strips of pliant bark, and on these rude and slender platforms had erected huts of branches. Here they had

* Virgil, Culex. l. 150.

lighted their fires, and squatted for the night among the creatures of the swamp.

During our ascent of this river, I had numerous opportunities of observing the habits of the Kahau, or Proboscis Monkey, in his native woods; for in the forests of this part of Borneo, he forms a very conspicuous feature, and occurs in great numbers; and although the *Semnopithecus nasicus*, or *Nasalis larvatus*, is tolerably well known, yet I am inclined to make a few observations on its history, from having had so many opportunities of examining it in a state of nature. The best account of the animal I have seen, is in an excellent work called the 'Menageries.'

In their native woods these *Semnopitheci* are not so agile as many of their quadrumanous consimilars, but climb and walk in a more deliberate manner. Their physiognomy is of a melancholy aspect, to which the prominent nasal organ lends a somewhat ludicrous expression. When excited and angry, the female resembles some tanned and peevish hag, snarling and shrewish. They progress on all fours, and sometimes while on the ground, raise themselves upright and look about them. When they sleep, they squat like the Dyaks on their hams, and bow their heads upon the breast. When disturbed, they utter a short impatient cry, between a sneeze and a scream, like that of a spoilt and passionate child; and in the selection of their food, they appear very dainty, frequently destroying a fruit, and hardly tasting it. When they emit their peculiar wheezing or hissing sound, they avert and wrinkle the nose, and open the mouth wide.

In the male, the nose is a curved tubular trunk, large, pendulous, and fleshy; but in the female, it is smaller, recurved, and not caruncular. In the latter, moreover, the organ is grooved in the middle line, and ends in a sharp point, from which it slopes abruptly to the upper lip, forming a truncate surface, in which are placed the nostrils. The eyes are small, and not much sunken; the pupil is large and circular, and the iris of a bright yellowish brown. The following description of the colours of an adult female seems to differ in some particulars from that generally given. The hair on the frontal region was of a deep chesnut colour, inclining to red; the shoulders and outer part of the upper arm red; inner part dirty white; throat breast and belly white; hair long, soft and silky; fore-arms, legs, and inner surface of thighs dirty grey, in some parts inclining to silvery; hairs on the back thick and soft, and resembling in colour the fur of an old hare; on the sides, loins, and outsides of the thighs, it inclines to rufous; over the lumbar region is a triangular grey patch, and the tail also is grey, inclining to whitish towards the tip; the naked skin of the face, when the animal is alive, is a bright red brick-dust colour, but after death, is a pale dirty pink. The palms are black. Wormb says its cry resembles "Kahau," which name it very frequently goes by. They do not, however, hold their nose when they leap, nor do they seem to be particularly gregarious.

On our return from this pirate hunt, we visited the village of Bunting, and walked about admiring the native ingenuity of the Dyak forges, the bellows of which are formed of two hollow cylinders, with feather-suckers to the pistons; observing with admiration several large and handsome War prahus, building under sheds, of great length, and having elevated and highly-ornamented prows; and more especially did we find amusement in examining the interiors of those large Caravansaries raised on poles, where the Balows live. The cabins allotted to the married couples, are garnished with furniture of a very simple and primitive description; a rude bed-place in one corner, and a few jars for holding water in another, seemed to constitute the chief essentials for the toilet and repose of the Dyak. These Balow dwellings, which may be compared to enormous bee-hives, have places under the kedjangs of the corridor, or gallery, common to the whole swarm, where might be seen fowls roosting by the dozen; various implements of war; cooking utensils; canoes unlashed, and taken to pieces; rush-woven mats; looms for weaving sarongs; huge baskets of rice and corn; and last, not least, among this singular "omnium gatherum," at all events in the estimation of the owners, numerous smoked and dusty human heads, hanging suspended from the rafters, and some of which I noticed of very recent capture. An examination of their teeth and cranial peculiarities, apprised me that one among them was the trophy of a European; several were Malayan, and by far the greater number Dyak, with their black, stained, shark-like teeth. Dalton, alluding to the propensity these people have for hoarding up the heads of their enemies, says that his friend Selgie, a Dyak chief of Coti, had as many as one hundred and fifty; and one of his sons, only twenty years of age, was possessed of nine.

As we were reposing after dinner, in our boats, a party of Balows came off in a canoe for medical advice. I was fortunate in being able to give relief in a bad case of Entropion, by removing a transverse flap of skin and muscle from the eyelid, a proceeding which seemed to give much satisfaction to the spectators; and, as usual in these cases, presents of fruits and fowls were forced upon my acceptance. Among these unfortunates was a man with that tubercular form of Lepra, called Elephantiasis:

> "corpore adeso,
> Posterius, tremulas super ulcera tetra tenentes
> Palmas, horriferis adcibat vocibus Orcum." *

Leaving the Batang Lupar on the 4th of September, we returned to Sarãwak, and shortly after, ascended the river Lundu, and visited the town or campong of Tungong, on that river, inhabited by the friendly Sibnowan Dyaks, one of the mildest and most amiable of the tribes to be found in the Sarãwak territory. Here I had the pleasure of accompanying His Excellency, Rajah Brooke, the Hon. Capt. Kepple of the Dido, and some others, in an excursion, when a party of Sibnowan Dyaks was assembled to hunt the Wild Boar in native fashion. Headed by Kalong, eldest son of Sejugah, Orang Kaya, or chief of the village, we proceeded in canoes to the hunting-ground, near the mouth of the river, accompanied by some numbers of a small, fox-like breed of dogs, very active, bold and sagacious; and after paddling for some distance, landed beneath the shade of the dark-leaved Casuarinas, and other forest trees, where the sand was marked with the foot-prints of hogs, and covered with the tracks of deer.

* Lucretius, De Nat. Rerum. Lib. v. l. 993.

Each Dyak hunter carries a stout Nibong spear, with a well-sharpened iron head, and when the eager dogs have sniffed the game, and pressed into the tangled jungle, fierce in the ardour of pursuit, the Dyak follows up the chase, and bursts impetuously through the brushwood. Meantime, the dogs have surrounded the frightened boar, and while they are worrying and keeping him at bay, the keen-edged spear of the hunter penetrates his side, and an end is put to the moonlight foragings of the boar for ever. In this manner six or seven pigs were dispatched in the course of the day.

The Boar of Borneo (*Sus barbatus*) has, when full-grown, rather a formidable appearance. It is furnished with enormous whiskers, a huge tuft upon the nose, and a shaggy main; and it has a fierce, red eye, and a singularly elongated head and muzzle. It runs with great rapidity, is very wild and wary, and is chiefly nocturnal in its habits. It appears to be very partial to crustaceous animals, which it finds on the muddy banks of the rivers after the fall of the tide; and is frequently seen at dusk, wandering in large numbers along the flat sandy coasts, evidently bent upon the exciting errand of searching for these delicacies. Some are perfectly grey in the colour of their skins, and a large specimen, captured by one of the crew of our jolly-boat, as he was swimming across the mouth of the Morataba river, was entirely of a dirty white colour. This animal, which remained with us some days, stood very high on his legs, and had a remarkably long head. He was secured between two guns on the main deck, but always continued very savage and refractory. As we were leaving the anchorage, he broke his tether, leaped out of the port, and was most probably drowned, although we saw him strike out lustily for the shore. One of this species was killed by Lieut. (now Commander) Inglefield, at Unsang, on the east coast of Borneo, of enormous dimensions. It was a full grown boar, and weighed more than five score.

Many very interesting specimens may be procured at low water, in the flat, sandy bay near the mouth of the Lundu. It was here that we had the good fortune to discover a new species of *Amphioxus*, or Lancelet. This interesting link, between the annelides and the fishes, has been described by Mr. Gray,* who has named it *Amphioxus Belcheri*. Here also we procured a very elegant and beautiful species of Crustacea, also new to science, *Amphitrite argentata* (Adams and White);† while any person walking along the shores in the immediate neighbourhood, might have collected numbers of very perfect specimens of *Tellina Spengleri*, beautiful violet-coloured Mactras, (*Mactra violacea*,) *Solenocurtus radiatus*, and frequently a tolerably perfect specimen of *Rostellaria rectirostris*. Olives and Nassas cover the moist sand, and a brilliant dark-coloured *Rotella*, a species not yet described, may be detected lurking by thousands immediately below the surface in company with another species. Several specimens of that strange genus, *Calappa*, were taken by us in this locality.

Near the Dyak village of Samarhtan, not far from the mouth of the Lundu, there are certain mud-banks left dry at low water, and which are perfectly cribriform with

---

* Ann. and Mag. Nat. Hist. vol. xix. p. 463.
† List of Specimens of Crust. in Brit. Mus. p. 126.

the cylindric holes of *Gelasimi, Ocypode,* and *Gonoplax.* When their communities are no longer flooded by the water, these bustling little Crustaceans make their appearance in dense crowds, but retreat on the slightest alarm to their subterranean burrows. They are of every variety of colour, some of them being milk-white, some purple, others reddish, and many perfectly black. So numerous are these Crabs, that seen at a little distance, they give the soil a variegated aspect, nearly obscuring the original blue colour of the mud. A Crab, with a triangular carapace, of a light brown, is also common among the tufts of grass in the vicinity.

A few remarks on the habits of certain genera of Crustaceans, which I have noticed in the course of our wanderings, may be deemed of interest by some of my readers, although the subject will be more fully treated of in another work. The *Grapsi* are more varied in their habits than is generally supposed. The common species (*G. varius*) and others, are found running over the rocks near the sea, feeding on the *Periopthalmi, Blennies,* and other fish, that quit the water for short intervals, and attacking occasionally the sessile Cirrhipeds, as *Balanus* and *Conia,* fixed on the surface, or that pedunculated one which fills up the fissures, the *Policipes.* Darwin tells us, he has seen them come to the nests of Sea-birds, and without ceremony help themselves to the fish which the parent birds had brought to feed their nestlings. They run with the greatest rapidity, and are very cunning and difficult to capture. There is one species, however, (*G. latifrons,* White) that I have found inhabiting fresh-water rivulets and ponds, which has all the quick, vivacious movements of its wary consimilars, and when hotly pursued hides under weeds and stones, remaining perfectly quiet till the enemy is supposed to be gone. The most common species on the coast of Borneo appears to be the *Grapsus plicatus*, which differs, however, in colour in a very remarkable degree, even in localities not very distant from each other.

Some of the large, powerful species of *Grapsidæ* are very bold, active, and predacious. I have seen them steal with an almost imperceptible motion, and in a cautious sidelong manner, towards a *Periophthalmus* basking on the rock, and before the fish had time to plunge into the sea, the pincer of the crab had secured it in a vice-like gripe, and the unfortunate victim was consumed at leisure. While watching the evolutions of this lively and sagacious Crustacean, I could not help comparing it to an enormous *Attus* or Jumping Spider, which, in a somewhat similar manner, creeps towards the flies on which it preys, and suddenly surprises them, by leaping on their backs, and sucking their blood.

The *Lambrus*, owing to its similarity to the gravelly floor on which it is generally found, must readily escape detection by its enemies. Its body and members, in fact, appear to be made up of a conglomerated mass of small stones. It is a curious fact that so many animals, living upon the submerged beds of broken shells and muddy gravel in the China Sea, should present a similar appearance. Such is the case with *Phoridæ*, *Amphitrite*, and many species of *Alcyonia*. Two new species of the genus *Lambrus* were obtained from the Java Sea, and the coast of Borneo, and have been named by Mr. White and myself *L. rapax* and *L. segnis*.

Where one of the mouths of the Sarāwak disembogues into the sea, at low water, there is a very extensive mudflat, the entire surface of which is perforated in every part by a hitherto undescribed species of *Gebia*, which hides in a perpendicular position, in a superficial burrow, with the extremities of the chelæ at the orifice for the purpose of securing whatever prey may offer. Thousands of *Macrophthalmi* and other crabs live in the same spot, with a small species of *Lingula*; while upon the slimy surface, crawl thousands of little brown *Cylichnæ*, several *Mangeliæ*, and *Columbellæ*.

The *Spheromas* are generally obtained in company with *Cymodoceæ*, *Cassidinæ*, *Amphoroideæ* and others, among dense masses of floating Sea-weed, where they appear to live an active predatory life among the populous mazes of their small, floating forest. They are constantly spinning and darting about, rolling up their bodies into a ball, then straightening them, and crawling among the Algæ and Keratophytes, with a great deal of vivacity. Among the collection brought home in the Samarang, are several species not before known to Crustaceologists.

The very handsome genus *Sicyonia* of Edwards, swims in a slow and deliberate manner forwards, and occasionally with a sudden jerk propels itself vigorously, in a backward direction. It keeps at a considerable distance from the shore, and appears to love deep, still water, never appearing when the sea is at all ruffled. The species obtained by us is new, and is deposited, with the other Crustaceans, in the British Museum.

Like the genera *Thenus* and *Ibacus*, the *Scyllarus* lives at some distance from the shore, and in tolerably deep water. It swims in the manner of a *Crangon*, by rapid inflections of the abdomen. It will occasionally spring through the water with the greatest velocity, in a backward direction, and when caught wounds the hands with the tail, which it throws about with violent jerks.

Among numbers of new and interesting genera of Crustaceous animals found by us in the province of Unsang, Borneo, was a new species of *Alope* (White), a remarkable shrimp-like animal, with one foot-claw rudimental, and the other enormously developed. It is an active and restless little creature, darting and whirling forwards and backwards, and frequently producing a loud clicking noise by snapping the pincer at the end of the large foot-claw, in the manner of the *Callianassa* and *Squilla*. Specimens may be found under nearly every stone which is turned on the beach at low-water mark, and the loud noise it makes, when discovered, would astonish persons ignorant of the cause of its production.

The *Gonodactyli* appear to differ from *Squillæ* in their habits, inasmuch as they are generally found in deeper water, whereas the *Squillæ* affect the shallow, weedy, and sandy bottoms, within coral reefs, and on flat beaches, where they hide in holes of the banks of pools, across which they dart occasionally in straight lines, leaving a turbid track behind them. They both, however, have the same power of producing a loud clicking noise with their chelæ, and of inflicting very severe wounds with those organs, using them in a scythe-like manner, like the *Mantis*.

The *Cryptopodia dorsalis* (Adams and White) is found on a stony bottom, in deep water. It has the habits of

Calappa, feigning death, and concealing the legs under the edge of the carapace, and folding the chelæ upon themselves to protect the eyes and mouth.

The *Trapeziæ* are tolerably lively in their habits, with the same manner of hiding, and shuffling under stones, as the *Porcellanæ*; but unlike them, they inhabit the coral branches of deep sunken reefs.

Many species of *Idotea* and *Iara* would appear to inhabit the Sea-weed along the shores, as well as that found floating in the high seas. At Quelpart, I found a large and singular species, not yet described, in the former situation; and in the sea of Celebes, I met with another new form among Algæ far from land.

The species of the genus *Lupocyclus* (Adams and White) are very active in the water, and keep rather close in shore. They swim by quick, rapid jerks along the bottom, and when caught, pinch rather severely, and wound the fingers with the spines of their chelæ. Their habits, indeed, are very similar to those of *Lupa, Neptunus*, and other swimming crabs.

The *Chorinus acanthonotus* (Adams and White) inhabits, like the *Mithrax*, deep water, and prefers those localities where the bottom is covered with weeds; it is inactive in its movements, and becomes rigid in all its limbs when first captured.

CHAPTER VII.

BORNEO.

Ambong—The Badjows—The Illanons—Appearance of the Country—Wild Men in the Mountains—*Tampassook*—Scenery—The haunts of Pirates—New species of Lantern-Fly—Lantern-Flies not luminous—A beautiful Flata—Gigantic Tent-Caterpillar—Habits of certain Ants—The dwellings of the White Ants—Habits of Scarabi and other Mollusks—*Brunai*—The Upas-Tree—The Pantai—Scenery of the River—A deserted Village—The Rajah's grave—Bats and other Animals—*Bulungan*—The Orang Sagai—Wild and cultivated Plants—Terrestrial Leeches—The Nibong Palm—Vegetable Tallow—Aromatic Barks—Plants used for benumbing Fish—Singular mode of fishing—Insects—*Leegeetan*—Scenery—Poisonous Plants—Insects—Birds—Habits of Crustaceans.

On the 25th of September, the Samarang was again at Singapore, leaving which we arrived at Borneo on the 13th of October, touched at the Island of Labuan on the 22nd, and on the 3rd of November, the ship was towed into the snug little bay of Ambong, our business being to rescue, if possible, an English lady, said to be detained prisoner at this place. The village is miserably poor and dirty, with about fifty houses, and a few squallid, leprous Badjows, or Sea Gypsies, for inhabitants. So badly off for comforts were these poor people that they willingly gave us a bullock for a piece of calico, and a fowl for an empty wine-bottle. They told a pitiful, and no doubt perfectly true, story about a famous Illañon pirate-chief, having come from the neighbouring Tampassook, and taken away the young men of the village, leaving those that remained nearly destitute. The adjoining country is beautiful, exhibiting in its sea-ward aspect more especially, gently undulating hills, covered with a long, rank, green-looking grass, in many parts higher than a man's head; little rivulets trickle down the sides, and form refreshing springs under the shade of the trees that overhang the beaches of little coves and bays. The mountains in the vicinity are inhabited by a wild and savage race of Dyaks, possessed, by all accounts, of a much larger stock of energy than the poverty-stricken gypsies of the village. The bay abounded with fish of the most beautiful colours and striking forms, keeping my pencil pretty well employed.

On the 10th of November we touched at Tampassook, a lovely, fertile plain, with a river running through it, from its source in the huge mountain of Kini Balu, which towers above the plain, and forms a most imposing back-ground. The towns about here, and on the river's banks, are stated to swarm with Illañon pirates, a brave and bold set of buccaneers, who keep the entire coasts of Borneo and other islands in a constant state of alarm. Those we saw were fierce, proud, and well-made men, handsomely clothed, and fully armed.

Among several other splendid insects captured by me in the course of this short cruise, I may mention a large and handsome new species of Lantern-Fly, which I have named *Fulgora (Hotinus) Sultana*.* The form of the beak, or rostrum, is intermediate between that of *H. clavatus* and *H. pyrorhynchus*, and like the upper surface of the thorax, is of a rich blood-red colour; the elytra are blackish, brown at the base, with the tip ochraceous, and traversed by numerous veins of the same colour; the wings are of a deep carmine, fading to pink towards the anal angle, the tips being brown, with four or five roundish white spots. The body above is straw-coloured, and, when the insect was alive, was covered with a white mealy substance, which I have noticed on many other insects in the tropics. This showy-looking addition to our known Lantern-Flies remains in a torpid state during the day, and becomes more active in the evening; in this respect being analogous to its consimilar genera *Aphenia, Flata, Pœciloptera,* and *Euriptera,* which generally select the early part of the night for their flittings. None of these insects, according to my observation, are luminous in the slightest degree; I have kept the *Hotinus Sultana*, and the common Chinese species, for many days, but have never seen the vestige of any luminous property, either about their so-called lanterns, or elsewhere. Madame Merian has stated, however, that the Surinam species is luminous.

I have figured a very lovely unpublished species of *Flata*, which I procured in the jungle immediately behind the village of Ambong, the elytra of which are of a light semi-transparent sepia, with a darker brown circle and a broad diagonal white linear mark, and yellowish tips; the wings are of a light, silvery, semi-opaque

* Ann. and Mag. Nat. Hist. vol. xx. p. 204.

white, the head is fawn-coloured; the eyes and the antennæ are black; the thighs pale-yellow, and the legs and tarsi black. This truly elegant species flies by night in a weak and fluttering manner, and with a peculiar oscillatory movement of the wings; by day it is sluggish, and reposes on the surface of leaves. Near Ambong an *Oiketicus* is found feeding on the trees with a case an inch and a half long, composed of dead and withered leaves, forming externally a compact and hollow cylinder, closed at the posterior end, and lined with a well-woven, downy felt, of a dirty brown-colour, fabricated from a finely-comminuted, vegetable substance. The larva is tolerably active and very voracious, and the imago is a large, dull-brown moth. Among the high grass, I noticed the active black-and-yellow *Gryllus elegans* (Guér) and, alighting on the leaves in sunny spots of the forests, may be seen the *Phytomia chrysorrhœa* (Guér) of a beautiful metallic-blue, with a golden tail, and the large carnivorous *Milesia gigas*.

During a ramble into the jungle, I was very much amused by observing the great variety of Ants that abound in these forests of Borneo. An Ant, usually more solitary than its neighbours, which I have named the "Bombardier," has a mode of defence similar to that of *Brachinus crepitans*. When irritated, it turns up the caudal segments of the body in the manner of an angry *Staphylinus*, and forthwith emits a continuous stream of dense, white, acrid vapour. This Ant is nearly half an inch long, with a large head and enormous mandibles. It is of a shiny black colour, and has no sting.

There is another ingenious species which constructs its

domicile out of a large leaf, bending the two halves by the weight of united millions, till the opposite margins meet at the under surface of the midrib, where they are secured by a gummy matter. The stores and larvæ are conveyed into this arboreal home by regular beaten tracks, along the trunk and branches of the tree.

On the banks of the Linga, the trees are covered with black-coloured nests built by an insect of a red colour and of large size. These aërial habitacula are formed of prepared vegetable matter, mixed with a tenacious secretion, and peopled with inhabitants furnished with a most tormenting sting.

In many parts of Borneo, there is a shining black Ant about the sixth of an inch long, whose habits are altogether nocturnal. During the day, it remains concealed within its subterranean galleries; but as the night advances, it covers the ground in moist and sheltered places with its myriad hordes. Its sting is very severe, though the pain and irritation soon pass away.

The habitations of those ingenious little architects, the *Termites*, or white Ants, have been often mentioned by travellers. One species occurring among these islands builds its city of finely-comminuted leaves and mud, forming a huge hemispherical nest on the trunks of trees. The interior consists of myriads of *cancelli*, separated by walls and passages, which are all thronged by the tiny soft-bodied inhabitants. On being disturbed, the big-headed soldiers make absurd and impotent attempts to defend their Queen and helpless workers, who immediately retire within the recesses of the city. Seen from a little distance, this arboreal insect-metropolis looks like an enormous vegetable excrescence, or wen growing from the bole of the tree. There are, moreover, covered galleries from the ground, made of mud, leading to the city gates.

Cuvier says the *Scarabi* feed on aquatic plants, but I have never observed them among the Algæ that lie along the shore; but in the dark, damp woods, more particularly along the sea-coasts, they are very numerous. They love a humid soil, and crawl languidly like the snail. They are fond of congregating together under stones and tree-roots, or in holes of the ground. They feed on partially decayed leaves, and lay their eggs under damp rotten logs, and the young shells may be found concealed, in large numbers, in the crevices of dead trunks. The *Scarabi* assume various shades of colour, from a mottled reddish brown to pale yellow, and I have even seen them white.

The species of *Conovulus*, which lives entirely in the salt water, has a shell of a much firmer character than that which is found amphibious, among the mangrove swamps. In fact, it generally follows, that shells, which inhabit both the land and the water, are intermediate in density of structure between marine and terrestrial species, and are covered in general with an epidermis. Thus we find *Telescopium, Potomis,* and *Terebralia,* covered with a kind of epidermis, and their calcareous dwellings less solid than their marine analogues, the *Cerithia*. In like manner, I have found a shell in the rivers of Celebes, named *Melatoma,* by Swainson, which bears the same relation to *Pleurotoma*. The *Potamomya* is a thinner shell than *Corbula*, which it represents, and *Neritina* than *Nerita*. I have found a species of *Pholas* in the fresh-water rivers of Borneo, living in dead trunks of trees, which is partially covered with a thick brown epidermis.

It is a curious fact that the nearer mollusks live to the sea-water, the more dense their shells generally become. This may be noticed in those species of *Auricula* and *Melampus*, found among the loose stones on beaches; and among the Korean Islands, I have found a *Cyclostoma*, in heaps of stones, near the sea, of a very compact appearance, compared with the terrestrial species. The *Cyclotrema* and *Scalaria*, their marine analogues, are yet more calcareous and dense in their structure. Among the Philippines, I have observed some auriculari-form *Mitræ* crawling about the stones, which the receding tide had left exposed, in the manner of the *Quoyiæ* and certain species of *Planaxis*. These *Mitræ* have an epidermis, and are hardly of so dense a nature as other members of the family. The exception to the foregoing rule is to be found in those pelagic animals, in which the extreme lightness of the shell constitutes their best security; for the ocean may toss them in its fury, but, unless a foreign body interpose, their tenuity saves them from being injured.

While residing at Brunai, I had an opportunity of examining the celebrated Upas-tree which grows on the banks of the river opposite the city, and a short account of it is given in the body of the work; a few notes which I shall here add, may not, however, be deemed altogether void of interest.

Mr. Crawfurd observes* that the word *upas* "is not a specific term, but the common name for poison of any description whatever." He says that *Antiaris toxicaria*, although the common source of the vegetable poison in use, does not yield so intense a poison as the *Chetik*, a large creeping plant found only in Java. This is the same plant *Strychnos Tieute*, "Tshettik" or "Tjettik," I have alluded to in my notice of the Upas-tree, as the *Upas-Radja* of the Japanese. The symptoms produced by the Strychnos poison are nervous, while those produced by the juice of the Antiaris act chiefly on the vascular system. The violent effects of the latter are certainly very much exaggerated, and from what I have noticed myself and gathered from hearsay, I am inclined to agree with Mr. Crawfurd, who observes very truly that "it proves hurtful to no plant around it, and creepers and parasitical plants are found winding in abundance about it;" and in another place "beneath the shade of it the husbandman may repose himself with as much security as under that of cocoa-palm or bamboo." The supposed remedy which Rumphius mentions under the names of Bakung and Radix-toxicaria is the *Crinum asiaticum* of Roxborough,† the bulbs of which act beneficially by inducing violent vomiting.

Mr. Brooke, in his journal, makes the following observation on this famous poison-tree, and the plants sometimes confounded with it:—"On the authority of Sulerman, an intelligent Meri man, I am told that the tree below the town is the real upas, called by the Meri men *tajim*.

*Hist. Ind. Arch. vol. i. p. 467
† Flor. Ind. Vol. 2. p. 128.

The Borneons call it *upas*. Bina (the name we formerly got from a Borneon for upas) is by Sulerman's statement a thin creeper, the root or stem of which, being steeped in water, is added to the upas to increase the poisonous quality: it is not, however, poisonous itself. There is another creeper, likewise called *bina*, the leaves of which are steeped and mixed with the upas, instead of a stem of the first sort." With this interesting statement, we dismiss the Upas, by admitting in the words of Crawfurd that, "Every thing we know of the true history of the *Upas* tree proclaims the egregious mendacity of the man who promulgated the fable respecting it, which has obtained currency in Europe, and the extraordinary credulity of those who listened to his extravagant fiction."*

On the 27th of November, we left Manila, for the purpose of rescuing from the hands of the Sultans of Bulungan and Gunung Taboor, the crew of the 'Premier,' a merchant ship which had been wrecked on a shoal near Pulo Panjang, on the coast of Borneo, first touching at Sooloo for the purpose of procuring a pilot. On our passage to the Pantai river we perceived the remains of the ill-fated vessel. As we ascended the river, the scenery was observed to be very wild and romantic, conveying a striking view of the vast extent of vegetation which exists in every part of this island. Meeting with no traces of habitations, however, in this long branch of the river, we returned to the ship, and on the following day proceeded to explore the other branch, which, as we ascended it, expanded in one part of its course into a large, wide,

*Hist. Ind. Arch. vol. i. page 471.

navigable river, with numerous islets dotting its surface, and having the banks clothed with the most superb timber-trees, and the most beautiful and luxuriant vegetation imaginable.

In the course of our progress up the river, we came to a deserted village, and while the captain was observing, I joined an exploring expedition, and examined the country around. Our attention being directed to a building on a hill surmounting the ruined hamlet, we scaled the height, and found it to consist of the tomb of a Rajah or other great man. It was neatly palisadoed round, and covered with a kedjang roof, while, in the interior, over the grave, was a faded canopy of silk. In the course of our scrutiny a large and handsome Snake was espied among the rafters, and an animated hunt ensued, which ended, however, in the escape of the serpent. In our eagerness to obtain the specimen, the shed was unroofed, and, as I was anxious to ascertain the mode of sepulture among the Malays, I got permission from the captain to dis-inter the Rajah, and examine the grave. Some men being placed at my disposal, we proceeded in our unholy work, and, at about four feet from the surface, came to a board placed in a diagonal manner across the shaft, on carefully removing which we perceived a square lateral chamber, or cavity, where the mortal remains of the deceased "Orang Kaya" were reposing. The skeleton was that of a very old man, and is now in the Museum of the College of Surgeons. Not a vestige of clothing, not even the wrapper of white cloth which is said to be generally employed, nor any arms, amulets, or ornaments of any kind were found in the grave. The body was laid upon the right side, with the knees in a bent position; and the flesh was mummified and adhering firmly to the bone; the ligament connecting the hyoid bone to the styloid process, and also the thyroid and cricoid cartilages were completely ossified; the hair was thin, and the alveolar processes of the jaws absorbed, thus proving the extreme old age of the exhumed.

I was very much astonished at the great numbers of bats which were here concealed in the heads of the Banana trees, and which flew forth, when disturbed, on feeble, fluttering wings, many among them having a couple of little ones clinging tenaciously to the pectoral mammæ of their mothers. The swampy ground in the neighbourhood abounded in *Assimineæ*, small univalve Mollusks, and was covered in many places by the foot-prints of deer and wild hogs. On raising a tablet suspended to an old tombstone, to endeavour to decipher the inscription, I made captive an enormous black scorpion, which had there taken up his quarters.

Upon passing the first portion of Bulungan, we were desired to proceed no further, or the Sultan would fire upon us. Disregarding these admonitory warnings, however, the boats continued their rapid progress up the river, and finally came to an anchor immediately opposite the palace of the Sultan. Before this edifice was an open space, planted with numerous pieces of cannon, some of large calibre, but old, and badly mounted; these were manned by crowds of brown-skinned warriors, while hundreds of excited armed men thronged the banks in readiness to throw the spear and blow the deadly sumpit. After an attempt to intimidate us by a pretence to fire, they thought it advisable to establish a friendly understanding with their visitors. Accordingly, an old Arab, the Sultan's vizier, or prime minister, came off and civilly enquired our pleasure. On being informed of the nature of our errand, he returned to apprize his Highness, and to prepare a rough salute in honour of the British flag, which latter was performed in a respectable manner, and returned by us in somewhat better style; in short, in such a way as to constrain the natives to behave very civilly while we remained before the city. The officers accompanied the Captain upon a visit to the Sultan, in state, who consented to deliver up the Lascars then in his possession, without demanding ransom. As many of these unfortunates were distributed throughout the country, some at a considerable distance from Bulungan, we were necessitated to wait in the river more than a week before the entire number could be collected, which afforded us an opportunity of seeing something of the neighbourhood. In the town I noticed the *Phœnix farinifera* and in the jungle around *Caryota urens, Borassus caudata, Bambos verticillata, Pandanus lævis*, a species of *Calamus*, and various plants altogether new to me; offering a rich harvest for an enterprising collector, and a rare intellectual treat to the Botanist.

During our stay at Bulungan, we had numerous opportunities of observing the "Orang Saghai," or wild men of Borneo, who came from the mountains in great numbers, probably to offer their services to the Malays, in case of any warlike operations ensuing with the English. On our proceeding up the river, long before the town came into view, isolated canoes betrayed its vicinity. As we drew nearer, however, the boats became very numerous, some containing hunting and fishing parties, and others fully equipped for war. Among the most striking of these latter, were several long and narrow canoes, manned entirely by Dyaks, arrayed in all their savage finery of plumes and skins and beads and other uncouth ornaments, armed invariably with the blowpipe or sumpitan, and carrying quivers of sumpits, or small upas-poisoned arrows, a long light spear, a shield of wood, and their constant companion, the sharp-edged parang; being thus prepared, as they thought, either for attack or defence. Displaying in their manner neither the guile nor caution of the treacherous and wily Malay, these untutored denizens of the interior showed an evident and lively curiosity about our visit, striving to approach the boats and engage in conversation with the white man. As they propel their narrow canoes rapidly along the river, they always stand upright, using the paddle with a peculiar jerking motion of the body. Many among them, particularly those holding the rank of chieftains, were very gaily and fantastically ornamented. In the feather caps, worn by some, the long tail-feathers of the Argus pheasant appeared to be a favourite ornament. In the rude and showy head-dresses of several were toupees of the tail-feathers of cocks and other birds, giving these Orang Saghai very much the appearance of a party of North American Indians, dressed for the war-path. Many of their caps were made of monkey, lynx, and tiger skins, and adorned with the beak of the large Hornbill (*Buceros Rhinoceros.*) Some of the men were regularly tattooed being ornamented, more particularly on the fore-arm and instep, with various figures, frequently very graceful in their design, and very neatly executed.* The ears of the great majority were wonderfully metamorphosed, and greatly disfigured, by the insertion of tigers' teeth in a hole of the summit of the pinna, and of rings, sometimes single and sometimes as many as four or five, composed of tin and very massive, appended to the lobe, forming cumbrous ear-rings. These enormous metallic pendants, being very heavy, greatly distended the aperture in the lobe, which frequently descended as low as the shoulder. They dress variously in the skins of animals, or in jackets made of the bark of trees; some, however, were entirely naked, with the exception of a waist-band and perineal appendage. When the jacket or body-garment consists of a lynx or tiger's skin, the hind-paws and tail, or fore-paws and head, hang down behind, which gives the wearer a very wild and picturesque appearance.

A chief, named Meta, was very anxious that we should visit him in his home among the hills. He seemed to take a very particular liking to the English, and was our constant visitor. On one occasion a follower of his was detected in the act of abstracting a piece of white calico, when he was immediately seized, and severely chastised by the indignant chief. The captain forwarded a letter by this savage to Mr. Brooke, at Saräwak, Meta assuring him that it would arrive at Brunai perfectly safe, as he would transmit it across the country from tribe to tribe,

* Mr. Earl says, that he has seen tattooed Dayaks, and that the Polynesian custom of tattooing the skin prevails among the Dayak tribes in the interior of Borneo.—PRICHARD's *Phys. Hist. of Mankind*, vol. v, p. 91.

carefully avoiding those who were his enemies. The same chief blew for our satisfaction some sumpits across the river; the effort appeared to be very great, but the direction of the dart was straight, and its force considerable. Before using the sumpits, they tip them with fresh poison, and steep them in a small vessel of lime-juice, which increases its virulence and activity. Their helmets, or head-pieces, which are made of strong skin and bamboo, are said to be sumpit-proof; so are also the corselets which cover their breast and back, so that only the arms and legs are left exposed. Many have a large polished pearl-shell appended in front, probably to protect the belly and navel. Their shields are of hard wood, variously painted and ornamented with shells and tufts of human hair. Some of these shields are upwards of four and five feet long, and two broad.

These men are much better featured than the Malays, having straighter and more prominent noses and higher foreheads. They wear their hair long and straight, but cut short across the forehead. It is coarse and black, and often confined by a white cincture, especially among the women and boys. Cutaneous diseases appeared common among them, particularly a rough, scurfy kind of lepra, which, however, they are said to produce artificially, and consider ornamental.* The women in this part of the island do not appear to wear the ring-stays of stained

* Mr. Earle observes, that the word 'Dayak' is often used by the Malays to designate a cutaneous disease to which the aborigines of Borneo are very liable, more so than any of the other Polynesian tribes whom I have encountered. I am of opinion that this is the origin of the term Dayak, as applied to the aborigines of Borneo.—PRICHARD's *Phys. Hist. of Mankind*, vol. v. p. 89.

bamboo peculiar to some tribes, as the hill Dyaks of Serambo and others, but have simply a sarong, which extends from below the breasts to about half way down the thigh. Like the men, they disfigure themselves by wearing enormous weighty ornaments of wood, ivory, or tin in the lobes of their ears. In their persons they are usually engaging and well made, stately and voluptuous in their gait and manner, though somewhat too *en bon point* to please the fastidious eye of an Englishman. They are reported by the Malays to be very modest, chaste, and constant to their husbands. Their chief employment here, as elsewhere in Borneo, is pounding and preparing the *padi* for the sustenance of their lords and families. In all the Dyak tribes, the members are usually divided into those who make war, privileged men, the flower of the tribe; those who manufacture arms; and those who cultivate the ground and make ornaments for the women. By means of the Saghai a profitable trade is carried on with certain Bugis Makassars, who come in large well-armed prahus from Celebes. Their traffic consists chiefly of bees-wax and camphor, honey, vegetable-tallow, and areca-nuts; trepang, damma or damer, (the concrete juice of *Shorea robusta*,) sharks'-fins, tortoise-shell, edible birds'-nests, and pearls: the specimens of the latter which I saw, although in some instances of large size, were very indifferent in form and colour.

Though differing in some respects from the rude and savage Scythians who had their flocks and herds, the Dyaks yet exhibit a pastoral wandering life, mingled with warlike habits and sanguinary customs, resembling those of that ancient people. Like the North American

Indians, they also congregate in tribes, and only obey chiefs elected from the wisest and bravest of their horde. Although in a measure addicted to the chase, they yet cultivate the soil, and live upon the produce of the earth. Like the Indians of the West, they are fond of decorating themselves with feathers and trophies, and if they do not scalp their enemies, they deprive them of their heads. Amongst themselves they are quiet and gentle, but in war their passions are frightful, fierce, and vengeful.

The females are better treated than is generally the case in savage tribes; they grind the *padi* and fabricate the clothing; nor does the whole burden of tilling the ground devolve entirely on the weaker sex, as is the case in some countries not yet civilised. In the terrible excitement of war, the fierce yells of the Dyaks, like the whoops of the Red-Man, are demoniac. Instead of the quiver and bow, the tomahawk and scalping-knife, the Dyak arms himself with sumpitan and sumpits, spear, and parang. They attack their enemy in the dead of night, without even the fair warning of the red-tomahawk of the American Indian, and with equally as much guile and remorseless compunction. It is a somewhat remarkable fact, that many among the Dyaks fancy heaven is situated at the top of Kini-Balu, and that the pass is defended by a savage dog. The North American Indians likewise imagine their land of souls to be guarded by a furious dog. It is singular that the Greeks of old should have entertained a similar notion, the warder, old Cerberus, at the gates of Hades, being represented as a three-headed dog. The Dyaks believe in one God, whom they, like the Red-Man, regard as the creating and preserving

Spirit of the universe; and they both have in common, moreover, a belief in omens, and hold certain birds in veneration. With regard to the barbarous custom of cutting off heads, we are told that the aboriginal inhabitants of New Guinea, the Horraforas, have precisely the same practice. Dr. Coulter, an American gentleman, in an account of his adventures among those people, observes, that they have "a horrible custom I believe peculiar to themselves: a young man, before he can possess his bride, must present her with a human head, which must not be mutilated, but on careful examination of it by her family, bear the true marks and ornaments of one of an enemy."

Dr. Dalton, in his "Essay on the Dyaks," speaks of some wild men that inhabit the north of Borneo, who neither cultivate the ground nor live in huts, but roam about in a perfect state of nature; who do not associate, save when the sexes meet in the forest. When their children are old enough to shift for themselves, they quit their parents and pursue a similar savage and independent life. They sleep under the overhanging branches of the trees, make a fire to keep off the wild beasts and snakes, cover themselves with a piece of bark, and are hunted by the other Dyaks, who regard them with the utmost contempt. These *nobler* Savages "shoot the children in the trees with the sumpit, the same as monkeys from which they are not easily to be distinguished." Dr. Leyden also observes that "the lofty mountains ranged on the centre of Borneo are represented as occupied by a people named Punams in the very rudest state of savage life."

As you approach a Dyak Village, the splendour of tropical vegetation cannot fail to impress the visitor. The magnificent Maize (*Zea mays*) springs up often in large and vivid patches; the Bird's-eye Pepper and Turmeric are found growing like common weeds. The *Piper Betle*,* the leaf of which is chewed with ripe or green pieces of the nut of *Areca oleracea*, is a graceful, pretty looking plant, particularly when loaded with long spikes of fruit. Some individuals appear however, never to have fruit, and are probably barren or males. The *Piper Betle* either runs like a creeper along the ground, or clings to the trunks of trees in its vicinity. Sometimes you will see it climbing up poles or the stems of the Papyia and Areca palms in little patches which are carefully guarded by rude palisades, and great pains taken by attention to irrigation, &c. to insure a good flavour in the leaves. Crawfurd says that "in the northern parts of Hindostan it is grown almost with as much difficulty as the plants of warm regions in *our* hot-houses." It is a curious circumstance that the use of the *Sirih* leaf diminishes perspiration, while that of the Ava (*Piper methysticum*) is used among the Society Islands to produce excessive diaphoresis for the cure of disease. The Durion (*Durio Zibethinus*) and Mangustan (*Garcinia Mangostana*) will be seen in some campongs amid whole groves of broad-leaved Plantains (*Musa paradisiaca*), graceful Cocoa-nuts (*Cocos nucifera*), elegant Palmyras (*Borassus*

---

* So written by Linnæus (Sp, Plant 40.) Mr. Crawfurd has Piper Betel, although he observes (Ind. Arch. p. 403) that "the word adopted in the European languages is from the Telinga, in which it is indifferently pronounced Betlé or Betré."

flabelliformis), and the slender tapering Betel-nut palm (*Areca oleracea*); while the showy-looking Papaw (*Carica Papaya*), and here and there a Rhambutan tree (*Nephelium Cappaceum*), or a dark-leaved Guava (*Psidium pyriferum*) will contrast with the golden fruit of the "Limau gadàng," or Shaddock. The Bamboo (*Arundo Bambos*) forms extensive groves at the back of many of the houses, and the Pine-apple (*Bromelia ananas*) luxuriates in the dark damp shady nooks. If you leave the neighbourhood of man, and take a stroll towards the river's bank, you may see the showy *Pontederia* brightening the fluviatile swamps with its azure blossoms. Close to the water's edge the "Paku Grudu" (*Cycas circinalis*) frequently grows luxuriantly, and a gigantic kind of Burr-weed (*Sparganium*), whose yellow, compound flowers, form quite a gay relief to the universal green that encloses them on every side, and whose singular fruits are sure to arrest the attention of the traveller. At Bulungan, the forest on the banks of the river, was full of leeches and *Planariæ*, some of them very handsomely marked. The Leeches crawl upon the leaves and fasten to the skin as you brush by the branches, but the *Planariæ* live upon the ground and are found sticking to the dead damp leaves.

The Nibong Palm (*Areca Tigillaria*, Jack) so often alluded to in the course of the work as one of the principal trees which furnish posts, rafters, and floorings of the houses in Borneo, perhaps demands here a brief notice. The tree is surrounded at each girdle of growth by a cincture of sharp thorns, which are more numerous and needle-shaped as we approach the leaves; the head contains, like all other Palms, a soft spike about the hardness of the core of the cabbage, which has hence induced seamen and others to christen it the Cabbage-Palm, and the Spaniards *"Palma brava."* It is certainly a most delicious vegetable, and when boiled resembles Asparagus or Kale; uncooked in its raw state, it furnishes fictitious cucumber and an excellent salad. The tree contains an immense quantity of useless pithy matter or newly-formed wood of the interior, and it is therefore split into four or more parts, and the soft parts cut away leaving only the outer rind of older wood, which is of so flinty a nature as to turn the edge of well-tempered tools. These narrow slightly-curved slabs form the principal flooring of all Malay houses. In England this hard, brittle, and beautiful wood is frequently used for the sticks of umbrellas; and it is capable of being manufactured into very elegant frames for pictures, or for any matters not requiring a greater breadth than twenty-two inches by half an inch, or three-quarters of an inch in thickness. The bows as well as arrows of the Natives of New Guinea are generally formed from this wood.

At Gunung Taboor, I first saw that singular commodity collected by the Dyaks called vegetable-tallow, which is an object of some commercial importance among the Natives of the Indian Archipelago. It is a concrete oil obtained from the expressed boiled fruit of a species of *Bassia*, a Sapotaceous plant, either the *B. longifolia* of Linnæus or the *B. butyracea* of Roxburgh, and belonging to the same genus as the Butter-tree described by Mungo Park. It was brought to us in large round flattened cakes of the consistence and colour of cheese, and also in cylindrical masses, which had assumed the form of the bamboo joints into which it had been poured when in a liquid state. A plant which grows in Java, the *Tetranthera Roxburghii* Nees, also has a fruit which yields a kind of naturally-formed vegetable-tallow, out of which the Chinese manufacture the candles with which ships are sometimes supplied at Singapore and Hong-Kong. To render these miserable apologies for candles more stable, they cover them over with a thin coating of wax. The principal advantage of the vegetable-tallow of Borneo over that produced from animal fat is, that it remains concrete under a tropical heat, whereas the other becomes too soft to serve any useful purpose.

The Natives likewise collect aromatic barks of which we obtained samples. One specimen appeared to have been obtained from the *Cinnamomum Sintoc*, as it differs from the bark of *C. Culilawan*, in having a flavour likewise of cloves. The specific name of the latter plant which yields the clove-bark of commerce, is derived from Kulitlawan, the native name of the bark; the specific name of the former is probably taken from the Javanese name for the same bark "Sendok." The bark generally called cinnamon in Borneo, is from a species of Cassia; the true Cinnamon-tree (*C. zeylanicum*), although grown in Java, is a native of Ceylon.

One of the most remarkable botanical productions of Borneo is the *Tephrosia toxicaria*, common at Kuching and Serambo, the roots of which are used by the Malays for the purpose of stupifying the fish of the rivers, and which, by acting on the nervous system, causes them to be more readily speared by the natives. This root might serve as an excellent substitute for Digitalis.

The *Phyllanthus virosus* is used in some parts of India for the purpose of intoxicating fish, and in Jamaica they employ the root of the *Pisidia Erythrina* for the same purpose. At Sooloo, and in other parts, they select the fruits of the *Borassus Gomutus*; in the West Indies, the berries of *Sapindus saponaria*, pounded and thrown into water, are used with a similar intention; and in Mindanao the *Barringtonia speciosa* answers the same end. Marsden, in his history of Sumatra, observes, that the natives "steep the root of a certain climbing plant called Tuba, of strong narcotic properties, in the water where the fish are seen, which produces such an effect that they become intoxicated, and to appearance dead, float on the surface of the water, and are taken with the hand." The Dyaks are very dextrous in spearing the poor stupified fish which are under the influence of the weed. There is another very singular mode of capturing the finny tribes in Borneo. Floating ducks, made of light wood, have a hook, properly baited, fastened to a line which hangs from the under surface. A man in a small canoe looks after the ducks at a distance, and when he sees one begin to dive and plunge, he paddles up and secures the fish. I have seen dozens of these dumb ducks floating down the rivers with the stream. Sir George Staunton says, that a somewhat similar mode of fishing is practised in China; and La Pérouse, speaking of the Esquimaux, observes, that "their mode of angling is very ingenious. Each line is fastened to a seal's bladder, and set adrift. One canoe has twelve or fifteen of them. When a fish is caught, the canoe rows after it." Dixon, in his Voyage, makes a similar remark regarding these people. He says, "they bait their hook with a kind of fish called by the sailors 'squids,' and having sunk it to the bottom, they fix a bladder to the end of the line, as a buoy."

Crawling on the leaves in the jungle was a very beautiful insect, the larva of a species of *Tesseratoma*, entirely of a delicate, semi-transparent, blood-red colour, with a flattened body, and head furnished with a stinging proboscis, which inflicts a somewhat painful wound. At Gunung Taboor, I procured one of the loveliest species of *Cassida* I have seen in any collection. The dark-green, convex body was studded with round, brilliant, golden spots, while the margin was transparent horn color, and reticulated like a leaf. Among other rare and beautiful insects, the *Lucanus Tarandus* of Thunberg flew at dusk into the boat in which I was sleeping. It is a large stag-beetle, with elongated jaws and bronze elytra, shaded with gold and red, and covered all over with a velvety down. A singular coal-black *Coreus* was also met with, covered with golden hairs.

Returning with our liberated captives from Bulungan, after having examined the reef on which the "Premier" was wrecked, and where we obtained some interesting crustaceous and molluscous animals, we touched at Leegeetan, on the coast of Borneo, for the purpose of watering the ship, at which place I procured many rare insects, and had a good opportunity of seeing some of the wildest woodland scenery in Borneo. In the course of a little trip at this port, I fell in with a scene so singular, that I will endeavour to describe it.

On our right was a vast, sandy flat left by the retiring tide, where several stout-limbed oyster-catchers were screaming and running rapidly along, like small ostriches, while beyond was the ocean, hushed into a perfect calm. On our left extended the huge forest trees, for miles fringing "the beached margent of the sea." Entering a thicket, we threaded the woody maze a little distance, and came suddenly upon a large mangrove swamp, where all the trees had, from some cause unknown to us, perished, and remained, some erect like huge, blackened skeletons arising from an oozy bed; and others prostrate, and lying in vast heaps, forming fit hiding places for the huge Monitors and broad-bellied Lace-lizards that we soon perceived abounded here. The entire surface of the hardened mud, in other parts, was covered with *Cerithium palustre* and the large black *C. telescopium*, while here and there fragments of those bivalve Mollusks, that love the brackish water, strewed the soil.

On the margin of this dried-up Lagoon, were heaps of old decayed and moss-grown trunks, speckled with lichens and sprouting with fungi, rotting piecemeal in the black and slimy mud. Thousands of *Gelasimi* and other land-loving crustaceans, bustled about the surface of the ground, rushing into holes with the greatest trepidation, but nevertheless snapping, as they retreated, their huge single foot-claw, and thrusting it menacingly forth, when they reached the aperture of their burrow. In many parts of the yielding surface, well-beaten tracks were formed by our dingy lacertine friends, the giant *Hydrosauri;* and in other places, the soil was stamped with the foot-marks of deer, and grooved by the snouts of wild boars. The forest beyond was perfectly silent, and, sitting on one of the tall and blasted trees, was a solitary white heron, himself as motionless and silent as the rest of nature.

While cutting wood in the forest not far from the watering place, our seamen and carpenters suffered very considerably from the virulent acrid sap of the *Excæcaria Agallocha*, or a plant closely allied to it, which produced violent itching and inflammation of the face, hands, and wherever it came in contact. I remember, that near the Morotabas entrance of the Sarāwak river, the party sent on shore to cut wood, were also much annoyed by the acrid juice of a plant with a large, brownish, spherical berry, and smooth shining leaves. Not being then in flower, it was difficult to say to what genus it belonged, but most probably it was the *Stagmaria verniciflua* of Dr. Jack. Besides the chance of scorpion and snake-bites, and the certainty of being punished by innumerable musquitoes, a large species of Tabanus is very annoying to the naturalist in these forests, alighting on the exposed parts of the body, and producing a sharp bite; but the pain however is momentary, and not so poisonous as that of the mosquito.

Clinging to the flower-balls of a delicate-leaved Mimosa, were numbers of splendid bronze-green beetles, of the genus *Aromia*, which emitted such a powerful scent of attar-of-roses around, as to impregnate the air for some little distance. That showy looking insect *Purpuricenus* (*Eurycephalus*) *maxillosus* Oliv., or a closely allied species, with black and red velvety elytra, was found clinging to the bark of trees; and, alighting on the leaves in sunny spots, on the slightest alarm taking flight and soaring high above the trees, was a splendid *Therates*, a beetle of the family of *Cicindelidæ*, remarkable for their powers of volitation. The species I obtained had large strong jaws, enormous eyes, a wide head, beautiful dark burnished-bronze elytra, and orange legs and mandibles. One specimen I captured, had just regaled himself with a fly, which I allowed him to eat up, before I attempted to make him a prisoner. He held the unfortunate dipterous insect, which was of the size of an *Œstrus*, firmly with the dilated tarsi of the fore feet, had cut off the head with his powerful mandibles, and was busily intent in consuming the flesh of the inside of the thorax, shaking his prey occasionally like a tiger, which these Cicindelidæ most assuredly represent in the insect-world. Also, on the leaves, but totally unlike its volatile neighbour the *Therates*, was a species of *Cassida*, a pretty tortoise-shaped beetle, with the elytra margined with bright golden yellow, four dark blue spots at the angles, and the central part of the back of a brown bronze, with deep red markings. A most extraordinary-looking hymenopterous insect, belonging to the genus *Stephanus*, with a red head, a black body very much elongated, light brown, semiopaque wings, enormous hind legs, and three long slender stylets at the end of the tail, hovered steadily around the trunks where the sunbeams penetrated, and seemed to delight to crawl up and down the bark. During flight it has a very remarkable appearance, reminding one somewhat of a heron on the wing, with its long legs awkwardly stretched out behind. In the fresh-water pools I obtained specimens of a large water-scorpion, near *Nepa rubra*, more than two inches in length, with a brown body, and blackish elytra. Its sting, the powers of which I unfortunately experienced, is much more severe than that of the *Nepa cinerea* we find in the ponds of Europe. A new species of *Gerris*, with a dull red thorax margined with black, and a dark line down the centre, with opaque black wings, was running, in its peculiar jerking manner, on the surface of the stagnant water. I was pleased to find these aquatic insects, as both water beetles and water lizards appear to be very scarce in Borneo, if we except the *Hydrosauri*, which are not entirely aquatic. I never came across, during the whole course of my wanderings, with a single species of *Salamandra* or *Triton*, or among insects with a *Hydrous* or *Dyticus*.

The woods of Leegeetan afford the large Hornbill (*Buceros Rhinoceros*); a Kingfisher of considerable size and splendid colouring (a species of *Dacelo,*) frequents the river brinks. A beautiful *Cypselus*, with a rich green metallic lustre along the back, soars high above the forest trees; while on the coast the *Hirundo esculenta* hovers incessantly to and fro, uttering its sharp and peculiar cry. A grey Heron perches on the lower boughs of the trees, and delights to fish in the ponds, feeding on crabs and frogs. A small sized Wood-pecker, and a large red-headed species with black wings and back, and a white belly, climbs up and down the forest stems in sequestered places. A black coloured bird, with two long feathers in the tail, skips rarely in the trees from spray to spray. A *Cuculus*, with a greenish-black back; and a small bird, with the feathers of the back and rump pilose and much prolonged, probably a species of *Chaunonotus*, are also found in the woods. In other parts of Borneo, I have met with a Tody with a red and yellow head, and another species with a black and yellow back, and salmon-coloured breast; a Thrush with a yellow back and black head, that utters a very sweet note among the Bamboo groves and thickets; a handsome Pigeon, with a green back and belly, and wings of reddish brown; a black Thrush, with a white abdomen; and a splendid ultramarine blue bird, with the neck, and belly black; a land Rail, prettily marked; a white-headed Falcon with reddish brown wings; a large horned Owl, and the minute Passerine species; the Griffin with a Falcon's beak, is also sometimes met with; and I have seen the Crowned Eagle, the Cayenne Barbett, and species of *Lanius, Bubutus, Garulax,* and *Calorhamphus.* The list might easily be lengthened, were it at all necessary in a short popular notice like this; but long dry lists of ornithological nomenclature would not be likely to interest the general reader. I may however offer a few words on the famous swallow that supplies the Chinese markets with nests, and pay a passing tribute to the extreme beauty of the Pigeons of this part of the world. Many of these belonging to the genus *Vinago*, are covered with feathers of rich metallic hues; in fact, the oriental Pigeons are the most beautiful creatures imaginable. Their air is full of softness, and their eyes of gentleness; their motions are all elegance, and their forms of the most graceful proportions. The turn of the neck and the carriage of the head are fraught with harmony; and the plaintive cooings of their voices, issuing from the dead solitudes of sombre woods, though somewhat mournful is soothing and agreeable to the ear. Playful in their motions, sportive in their caresses, they seem formed for love and dalliance in the dense forests they animate and adorn. The cooing of these birds in the tropics is somewhat different in sound from that of the Wood-pigeon.

About the rocky parts of the coast of Borneo, the *Hirundo esculenta* skims backwards and forwards all day long, uttering its little cheerful chirp as it eagerly pursues its insect prey. I have taken the nests in nearly every state from the sides of shallow caves, where they adhere in numbers to the walls, like so many watch-pockets. The eggs are white, with a slight pinkish tinge, and are generally two in number. The nests are either white, red, or black, and the natives maintain that these are built by three distinct species, with a white, red, and black breast, but this is erroneous. The Malays assert frequently, moreover, that the nests are formed from the bodies of certain sea-snakes, but there is no doubt that "agal-agal," a marine cellular plant, is the material employed. The Chinese lanterns are made of netted thread, smeared over with gum, produced by boiling down this same plant, which, when dry, forms a firm, pellucid, and elastic substitute for horn or glass. Other species of Swallows, besides the *Hirundo esculenta*, employ the same glutinous material in the construction of their nest; but it is always mixed up with grass and matted feathers, so as to render the nests perfectly useless in a commercial point of view.

Collecting the nests is often a very perilous operation, as may be seen on reading the following extract from Crawfurd's History of the Indian Archipelago. He is describing one of the most productive caves in Java, those of *Karang-bolang*, on the south coast of the island:—
"Here the caves are only to be approached by a perpen-

dicular descent of many hundred feet, by ladders of bamboo and rattan, over a sea rolling violently against the rocks. When the mouth of the cavern is attained, the perilous office of taking the nests must often be performed with torch-light, by penetrating into recesses of the rock, when the slightest trip would be instantly fatal to the adventurers, who see nothing below them but the turbulent surf making its way into the chasms of the rock."*

Before taking leave of this part of Borneo, I must make a few observations on the habits of certain crustaceans. On tropical mudflats, I was always very much amused at the multitudes of Crabs that take their pastime there,—those active, predatory, rapacious busy-bodies, presenting forms so anomalous, manners so strange, and motions so grotesque. As soon as the water recedes from the shore on the ebbing of the tide, and the large firm mudflats are left exposed, myriads of crustaceans of every form and colour issue from their various holes and hiding-places, to enjoy the heat, to forage for their food, and to propagate their kind. The males of many species, after looking cautiously about them, stalk a few paces with their huge single pincers raised in the air, which they snap frequently together, producing a slight clicking sound, then rushing eagerly towards their females, they seem to embrace with their arms their smaller and more dingy paramours. The salute is very brief, and is followed by the swift retreat of the lady-crabs into their different habitations. These belong chiefly to the burrowing *Macrophthalmi*. Many of the genera *Sesarma*, *Gonoplax*, and *Grapsus*, are how-

* Vol. iii., p. 433.

ever perceived equally well occupied. Creeping stealthily upon these [are larger and more formidable Crabs, which come with sidelong steps towards their unwary neighbours, chase, capture, tear, and finally consume them. Others are content to forego their amorous dalliance, and help themselves to worms and little shell-fish, feeding alternately first with one hand and then with the other. Many again lie languidly along the mud, seeming very much to enjoy the genial rays of the sun in listless indolence; while others are watchful at the mouths of holes, ready to pounce upon the Jumping-fish and Squillæ that swarm about the mud, and which speedily disappear within their rapacious jaws.

A very splendid species of *Cardisoma*, which I have named *C. Aspasia*, inhabits the steep muddy banks at the mouths of the rivers near this part of the coast, where it forms deep cylindrical burrows. It is excessively wary, retreating on the slightest noise into its subterranean domicile, from whence it is not easily dislodged. It appears to be less shy, however, as the evening advances, and is probably nocturnal in its habits, like some of the species of *Ocypode*. This lovely crustacean, nearly as large as the adult edible crab, has a purple shell margined behind with buff, and feet and claws of a delicate lilac.

The muddy banks of the Batang-Lupar, Sarăwak, and many other rivers of Borneo, are covered at low water by numerous handsome species of *Gelasimus*, among the number of which is an undescribed species which I have named *G. cærulens*, from the beautiful blue colour of its carapace. I have seen the black mud in many parts assume quite a brilliant blue tinge during the heat of the day, at low water, when these crustaceans come forth to feed.

CHAPTER VIII.

LOO-CHOO—KOREA—JAPAN.

Loo-Choo—Mandarins—Visit a Missionary—Gardens of the Temples—
—Burial-ground — Tombs — Loo-Chooan females — Sheudi, the
capital — Palace of the Viceroy — State of religion — Acquainted
with Arms —Language —Money —Medicine —*Korea* —Physical
appearance of the Natives—Costume—Moral Character—Arms—
Boats — Punishments — An Anecdote —Beacon-fires —Island of
Quelpart — Plants — Stone Images — Vegetation — Scenery—
Birds—Fishes—Insects—Habits of Spiders—Molluscous Animals
—Radiata —Sponges —*Sama-Sana* —Scenery —Vegetation—Insects —An Earthquake —*Koumi* — Scenery — Birds —Beetles—
Grasshoppers — *Japan* — Physical appearance of the Japanese—
Costume—Weapons—Shells—Volcanic Archipelago—Inhabitants.

On the 22nd of August, 1845, in company with Mr. Corbett, of the Royalist, I landed at some distance from our anchorage in Napa-Kiang harbour, on the other side of the village of Po-tsang, (or Pot-soong, as Beechey and others write it,) a small straggling hamlet full of temples, tombs, banyan trees, and salt-pans, with a neat, well-built little bridge, and a very long causeway. We were received on the beach by a large concourse of the natives, and as soon as we had disembarked, a venerable and good-natured mandarin of the second class, took us by the hand, and kindly led us towards the village. He spoke to us in broken English, asking us how we did;

what were our ages, &c. We made him understand that we wished to proceed to the residence of a French Missionary, who was living some little distance off, in one of the Joss-houses, occupied by the people of the Alceste at a former period. He comprehended in a moment, and accordingly most politely made us a bow, and led the way. Our road lay through very pleasant woods, where the Bamboo and Acacia, the Areca, Banyan and Cycas trees, formed an agreeable shade. In the temple, occupied by the Missionary, were the usual emblems of the Roman-Catholic Church, and walking about the ground, were numerous Bonzes, or priests of Buddha, apparently very poor and low in the grade of society. One old gentleman seemed very much disgusted with our Catholic friend, pointing with scorn at the parade of paintings and crucifixes made by the good Father. The coadjutor in the labour of this French gentleman, was a young Chinese, educated at the Jesuit College at Penang, who, as the Padre assured us, could converse well in Latin, Portuguese, French, Chinese, and Cochin-Chinese. The gardens of these temples are neatly and tastefully laid out, and among the flowers in the parterres I noticed the beautiful crimson blossoms of the *Hibiscus Rosa-Sinensis*, with the petals of which the Chinese black their shoes; the Prince's feathers (*Amaranthus caudatus,*) the *Gomphrena globosa*, and some very fine Cockscombs (*Celosia coccinea,*) their thousands of brilliant shining bracts glittering in the sun. These gardens and temples, occupied by the officers and crew of the Alceste, are rendered doubly interesting by the graphic and pleasing accounts of Hall and M'Leod. They are quiet, lonely, and secluded, and ornamented with beautiful walks and numerous trees. We rambled on among the tombs of the Loo-Chooans, which form one vast cemetery or city of the dead, and which from our anchorage, appeared as large and conspicuous as the living city of Napa. The tombs are all well-preserved, nicely chunammed, and of a dazzling whiteness. The tombs of strangers, however, are of an oblong shape, not formed like a horse-shoe as are those of the natives, and are embowered in trees; among them I observed the grave of the man who died belonging to the Alceste. Their respect for the dead certainly appears to be very great, and I could not help noticing the solemn demeanour of the old Chief as he pointed out to us the grave of our countryman. Having passed through an archway, we came suddenly upon a square in which were congregated many hundred women, each with a small basket, bargaining for rice and other necessaries, and laughing, chattering, and cheapening in the most discordant and emphatic manner. It was market-day among the good people of Po-tsang. All these lively and energetic females belonged to the lower orders, and rejoiced in countenances by no means attractive; the old hags, on the contrary, were about the most hideous objects I have seen in the course of my travels. An occasional exception to this ungracious and not-at-all-gallant picture, might be found in the person of a young girl or marriageable maiden, and the little brown babies were decidedly very funny. Proceeding on our walk, we arrived at the summit of a hill, from which elevated position we obtained an excellent view of Sheudi or Shui, the extensive and populous capital of the Great-Loo-Choo.

It is very delightfully situated in the bosom of a wooded and verdant valley, and appears to be well and regularly built. At some little distance from the city, we noticed the Prince's palace, a large square building surrounded by a high wall. We were informed that the Prince, or probably Viceroy appointed by the Japanese, is quite a prisoner in this royal abode, never being allowed to travel beyond the precincts of his enchanted castle. Near Abbey Point, in the rude cavernous recess of a rock, we saw the image of the Goddess "Kwan-yan," called by Beechey, the Goddess of Mercy, and of which he has given a representation in his work. The natives did not seem, however, to evince much awe or reverence as they passed this favourite deity; indeed Gutzlaff observes that "they disavow practical idolatry because their reason disapproves the theory; yet they do in fact persevere in their unreasonable worship." There are various other idols in other parts of the island, some formed of wood, and many carved out of stone. La Pérouse, who visited these people, observes, speaking of the inhabitants of Kumi, that "each had a dagger, the hilt of which was gold." Beechey has a variety of arguments to prove they were formerly acquainted with the use of arms, and, in connexion with the same question, Gutzlaff observes: "Upon inquiring, we found that they had among them the same severe punishment as at Korea; that they possessed arms likewise, but are averse to use them." Both Hall and M'Leod, on the other hand, aver that these people are totally unacquainted with the use of arms. Thinking to throw a little light on the subject, I enquired casually of A-sung, our Chinese interpreter, who was much among them, what they would do if they were attacked by an enemy, when he informed me that they had large stores of arms which he had seen, shields, spears, and bows and arrows, but that they wish to keep the knowledge of their existence in the island, a secret, even from their own people. Beechey remarks, that "the inhabitants of Loo-Choo have no written character in use, which can properly be called their own, but that they express themselves in that which is strictly Chinese." They have not preserved, even if they ever possessed in their early state, any original written language, but they have adopted that of Japan. Both the French Missionary and A-sung, our interpreter, assured me that it was strictly Japanese. The Loo-Chooans, certainly must originally have been a colony from Japan, although in the present day they disclaim all connexion or acquaintance with that empire. In a conversation with Gutzlaff, they even affirmed that three Junks from Satsuma in Japan had been driven hither by stress of weather. During our visit, there were numerous Japanese vessels lying in the harbour, no doubt tribute Junks. The Catholic Priest informed me that he had not succeeded in making a single convert, and though his tenets were smiled at as being too absurd for credence, yet he was treated with the greatest respect, mingled, however, with a little jealousy. The higher classes are probably very well contented with the precepts of Confucius, and the lower with the doctrines of Buddha, both systems having numerous proselytes among the Loo-Chooans. Many, however, even among the most wealthy and intelligent, are free-thinkers, and seem to trouble themselves very little about superstition in any form.

They are said to be unacquainted with the use of money, though they received dollars in payment for a horse, pigs, and several descriptions of provisions, from the Captain and some of the officers of our ship; and Gutzlaff says, that "the Chinese tael and cash are current among them, but very scarce." While staying here, the most celebrated native doctor of Napa treated A-sung for rheumatic pains, with hot cataplasms, made of the recent aromatic leaves of the Sansjo (*Xanthoxylon piperitum*) and, as he informed me, with considerable benefit. The Ginseng (*Panax quinquefolium*) is held in as much repute here as it is in China.

During this year, the Samarang was engaged in surveying the large island of Quelpart, and the numerous group of smaller islands constituting the Korean Archipelago; and as our opportunities of examining some of the more interesting ethnographical peculiarities of the singular people inhabiting this little-known region of the globe were rather numerous, I shall here offer a slight sketch of those manners and customs, which, at the time, were regarded by me as worthy of note, and as such committed to paper for the amusement of friends at home.

The Kooraï or Koreans are said to have come originally from a country to the northward of Pe-tche-li, and although now forming a separate nation, governed by a king, they are, in a measure, tributary to China, as before the conquest of Korea by the Chinese, they were the subjects of the Japanese empire. In personal appearance, they resemble the natives of Siberia and Tartary. Like most Mongolians they have a tawny skin, prominent cheek-bones, some obliquity of the eyes; a rather prominent nose, thick at its base, and wide at the nostrils; strong, well-developed jaws, and long, lank, straight, black hair; but like some tribes of northern Asia, their beard is tolerably thick, and their eye-brows bushy. Their physiognomy is less effeminate than that of southern races, their average stature being greater, their bearing bolder, their Tartar-like features more prominent and striking, and their beards and moustaches being frequently long and flowing. One of the most striking peculiarities which all who have seen them have noticed, is the method of confining the hair of the head in a delicate network, beautifully formed of a fine material resembling Coir, and of a glossy black colour. The hair being all drawn upwards towards the crown of the head, is tied at the summit in a neat and rather graceful topknot, without the help however of pins, as at Loo-Choo and the Meïa-co-shimahs. The young unmarried men and boys, however, have the hair parted in the middle, gathered behind, and descending in two long plaited tails, that hang down the back somewhat in the fashion of those of the sons of Han. Frequently a white band of bark or leaf is worn across the forehead, to restrain the loose and straggling hairs.

Their costume, though formed of a uniform peculiar to China, Japan, and all this part of the world, varies considerably from all other nations in unessential details. The Mandarins, or chiefs of the better class, wear long gowns or mantles, with loose hanging sleeves, having red or green cuffs. These robes are often of silk stuff, and have a very pleasing and picturesque appearance. Their pantaloons hang in a rather loose bag below the knee, their gaiters or socks are of white linen cloth, and their neat leathern shoes are very much pointed and turned up at the toes. Their hats are of enormous size, with very broad brims, and are of a slight and slender texture, being ingeniously made of a net-work of bamboo, stained black. The crown is very peculiar, high, and conical, and two or three peacock's feathers appended to a curved ivory ball on the pointed apex, hang gracefully over the capacious brim. The hats of the Mandarins are usually furnished with strings of large amber beads, to fasten them under the chin. An under tunic of white, and a broad silken sash, usually complete the dress of these grandees. They generally carry, moreover, a small piece of black bamboo, with a coloured riband twisted spirally round it, which is their wand of office, and on which their rank is written. The soldiers wear a plaited string from the crown of their hats, with a quantity of red horse-hair depending from it at the hind part of the brim. In winter time, some of the lower orders wear huge fur caps, made of wolf or lynx skin; and the heads of others are covered with enormous brown or black sombreros, fashioned from a kind of felt, while many again affect huge cone-shaped hats, covered with painted oiled paper. Serfs and husbandmen are very loosely clad, and go about with the legs and fore-arms bare, and wear grass sandles on their feet. Both men and boys have a habit of carrying long staves, which gives them an appearance, when seen at a distance, of being armed with spears. The females we saw were very ugly, very dirty, and much more degraded in appearance than the men.

The natives of Korea, or more properly of Chaou-Seen,

are but little advanced in civilization, owing doubtless to the repugnance they have to hold any intercourse with other nations, not even their neighbours, the Chinese, being permitted to settle in their territory, and their trade with that country and with Japan and Tartary is exceedingly limited. They invariably repulsed us in the same spirit on our attempting to invade the sanctity of their towns and villages, not even allowing us to enter within the walls of their cities. With the same exclusive feeling and jealous alarm of foreigners, they also evinced a great objection to receive anything from us as presents. During our surveying duties, where it was indispensably necessary to land and erect marks, they frequently showed symptoms of hostility, and when not opposed in a determined manner, were inclined to assume a hectoring demeanour, threatening and commanding us to retreat; but we always found that their courage consisted chiefly in a system of intimidation. They are, however, very good-humoured, and seem to enjoy anything like a joke exceedingly. All appear to be passionately fond of spirituous liquors, nor can I say much for their morality of conduct. They are great smokers, carrying continually in their hands a long-stemmed pipe, with a diminutive brass bowl, which they fill and empty at brief intervals.*

* The pipes of the Indo-Chinese races, including the Tartars, Chinese, Koreans, and Japanese, are provided with a small metallic bowl, and usually a long bamboo stem, for with persons who are in the habit of smoking at short intervals all day long, a large bowl would be inadmissible. By inhaling but a pinch of tobacco on one occasion, they extend the narcotising influence of a larger pipe over a greater space of time. Nations that smoke larger pipes adopt some other material for the bowls, as metal would become too hot: thus the Chibook of

Their arms consist of bows and arrows, spears, and a few rude matchlocks, constructed in the Chinese fashion; and in some of their walled cities they have forts strongly built of stone, and mounting guns. When they wish to intimidate their enemies, and make a great show of martial power, they collect all the heroes, with their swords and spears, and assemble by hundreds, mingling their shouts with the discordant sounds of gongs, trumpets, and a harsh shrill instrument resembling in noise the bagpipes. I have heard some among them, however, play very plaintive melodies on the flute, with much taste and proficiency.

They do not appear to be a maritime people, their boats being neither large nor numerous. As in China and Japan, the use of oars is unknown among the Koreans, the boats being always propelled by means of sculls, the boatmen standing over the loom, and bending his body backwards and forwards. I have seen as many as ten

---

Turkey is made of " Samian ware," a kind of red-brown clay; the Meerschaum of Germany is formed of a yellowish-white steatite; the pipe of Holland is of porcelain, and that of our own island of unglazed clay. Among the Bashee group, and more particularly on the island of Ibayat, the natives form very elegant and commodious pipes from different species of shells, the columella and septa of the convolutions being broken down, and a short ebony stem inserted into a hole at the apex of the spire. A pipe of this manufacture, in my possession, is formed from the *Mitra papalis*, and I have seen others made out of *Mitra episcopalis* and of *Cerithium* and *Terebra*. At the Cape of Good Hope I procured some pipe-bowls, made by the Kaffirs, from a black and from a green stone, but without sculpture. Old Indian pipes have been found in America also fashioned out of green stone. The sailors belonging to the Samarang having lost their pipes in the Sarawak river, set to and in a very little while manufactured excellent pipes from different sized internodes of the bamboos that grew around them.

men working at one enormous long scull. For landing in the surf and among the rocks they employ a sort of catamaran or raft, with an elevated platform large enough to contain eight or ten persons, which is sculled in the manner of a boat. In some instances they employed these rafts to destroy our surveying marks, when our boats, giving chase, would pursue and capture them, often giving rise to very laughable scenes When a man becomes troublesome or offends in any way, he is brought before the chief Mandarins, who first abuse him, and then order him to be seized and thrown down, when he receives a certain number of severe blows with a flat baton (formed like an oar and about six feet long), on the bare hams. Many carry about them severe traces of this bastinado practice in the forms of scars and ulcers.

On our approach to a village, the poor frightened inhabitants first drive away all their bullocks beyond the mountains, generally, however, leaving one of the leanest behind as a tempting lure. This being effected, they then assemble in crowds upon all the highest hill tops, until they are assured of our pacific intentions, when they cautiously descend and approach, and begin curiously to examine our persons, admiring the fine texture of our linen, wondering at our gold bands and buttons, and still more at the pinkish tinge of our skins, and the brown colour of our hair. On one occasion we landed in a beautiful little bay where there was a village, and along the shore a wood of large-sized fir-trees. By an offer of cloth and sweet wine the Captain obtained permission to cut down some of them; but no sooner did the carpenters lay the axe to the base of one of the finest, than an old man interposed, with gesticulations and tears in his eyes making us signs that the trees were his. On our men proceeding in their work, the poor fellow grew quite frantic, clasping now the trunks of his beloved trees, and then the knees of those who were felling them, using every possible sign and gesture to save his firs from destruction. He was however eventually pacified by bottles of sweet wine.

The same custom occurs along the coast of Korea, as among the Malays, namely, lighting beacon fires on the summits of the hills and projecting points of land, to indicate the movements of a supposed enemy. La Pérouse alludes to the same procedure where he says: "It is probable we occasioned some alarm on the coast of Korea, for in the afternoon we perceived fires lighted on all the points."

The large island of Quelpart or Quelpoert, which we circumnavigated and surveyed in the boats, is the most southern island of the Korean Archipelago. The proper name is the same as that of Korea, namely, "Chaou-Seen," and it is somewhat remarkable that the name of the principal city, King-Ka-Tou, is the same as that of the peninsula. Quelpart may be said to be an oval iron-bound island, covered with innumerable conical mountains, topped in many instances by extinct volcanic craters, and all bowing down before one vast and towering giant, whose foot is planted in the centre of the island, and whose head is lost in clouds. The whole surface, including the plains and vallies between the hills and even that of the mountain-flanks, is carefully, richly, and most beautifully cultivated and covered with a pleasing verdant vegetation, laid out in fields divided by neat walls made of piled-up stones. It is surrounded on all sides by " black waves, bare crags, and banks of stone," covered with limpets and Chitons, and tenanted by troops of dusky cormorants. As we coasted along the land, crowds of wondering natives appeared on every hill-top, staring at the adventurous strangers who had come to visit their far distant country, and perchance disturb the peaceful tenor of their lives. In many parts along the coast the rocks are very lofty, and quite perpendicular, and are adorned in many instances with splendid waterfalls,—

> " Where a wild stream with headlong shock
> Comes brawling down its bed of rock
> To mingle with the main."

In one part only was the coast level, and huge heaps of weeds lay along the shore. Numbers of meagre Cormorants sat in long black rows upon the stones; flocks of dappled wild Ducks were feeding at the margin of the water; a species of Tern, with a long black crest, was hovering above the surf, and at some distance from the shore were hundreds of large white Gulls, sweeping the surface of the sea.

A large and beautiful open blue Campanula was very conspicuous in many parts, as were also the handsome yellow Liliaceous plants allied to *Hemerocallis disticha* and *H. flava*, which grew chiefly on acclivities, and the large and showy Tiger-lily (*Lilium monadelphum*). There was also a small and pretty Hyacinth with delicate blue blossoms; two or three species of Juniper, many of Oak, three of Fir, several of Thuja, two kinds of Hazel, and one of Myrtle. The Fumitory, the Lychnis, the wild Onion and Silver-weed were common everywhere. La

Pérouse speaking of Quelpart, observes: "Unfortunately the island belongs to a people to whom all intercourse with strangers is prohibited, and who retain in slavery all who have the misfortune to be wrecked on their shores. Some of the Dutch sailors of the 'Sparrow-hawk,' after a captivity of eighteen years, during which they had received severe bastinadoes, found means to steal away a bark and get to Japan, whence they reached Batavia, and at length Amsterdam." He observes, moreover, "this island which is known to Europeans only by the loss of the Dutch ship 'Sparrow-hawk' in 1635, was at that time under the dominion of the king of Korea." Mr. Gutzlaff, who visited some of the islands of the Korean Archipelago, with much truth makes the following regretful remark:—"Walking," he says, "over these fertile islands, beholding the most beautiful flowers everywhere growing wild, and the vine creeping among weeds and bushes, we accuse the 'lord of nature,' man, of shameful neglect; for he could have changed this wilderness into an Eden."

In many parts of the Archipelago, the hamlets and houses of the more wealthy members of the population are delightfully situated, being frequently embosomed in groves of umbrageous trees with running rivulets beside them, and all around and towering up behind, gently swelling hills covered with verdure, and with herds of oxen grazing; and when placed near the sea-side, there is generally a fishing-wear close at hand. Their houses consist of a sitting-room, a sleeping-apartment, and a shed used for culinary purposes, where are observed large earthern vessels for holding rice and water. In their towns are frequently seen rudely carved stone-images, and it may be observed that a very striking similarity exists between these graven boundary stones of the cities of Quelpart, and the Hermæ of the ancient Greeks, and the Termini, or Lapides Terminales, of the Romans. The earliest form in which the divinities of classic mythology were represented, was an unhewn stone, which afterwards assumed the modification of a square block, and subsequently grew, when the art of Sculpture became more elaborate and refined, into a polished pedestal, surmounted by the head of the favourite deity. These were placed in the front of temples, and other public buildings, and at the corners of streets and roads, and frequently received the tribute of divine honours. Whether these Korean Hermæ were regarded with religious veneration by the inhabitants of Quelpart, I am unable to state, but I may point out the remarkable fact of the existence of similar sculptured posts in the Dyak villages of the island of Borneo, where they occupy the same relative positions and probably serve the same purpose. Lieut. Kolf, in his Voyages of the 'Dourg,' a Dutch Brig of war, states that among the Arafuras inhabiting the Arru islands, one of his officers found "an image rudely formed of wood, together with a post on which different figures such as snakes, lizards, crocodiles, and human forms were carved, and which the owner stated to be intended for preserving the house from evil spirits."

Crawfurd, in his history of the Indian Archipelago, alludes to the existence of images of a similar nature in Java: "In the least civilised parts of the island, as the mountains of the Sundas, and particularly the eastern province of Banyuwangi, there are found a variety of images extremely rude and ill-fashioned, and which, frequently, by the extensive decomposition which their surfaces have undergone, appear of greater antiquity than those already described. These are, in all probability, representations of the local objects of worship among the Javanese, before they adopted Hinduism, and which probably, as is still the case in Bali, continued to receive some share of their adoration, after that event." The appearance of the basaltic columns that adorn the perpendicular sides of many of the islands was very grand and imposing, simulating in several instances ruined monasteries, old time-worn buildings, and picturesque cathedrals, with high fretted pinnacles,

> "rocks sublime
> To human art a sportive semblance bore,
> And yellow lichens coloured all the clime,
> Like moonlit battlements and towers decayed by time."

On the rugged acclivities of several steep, rocky islets, hundreds of Stone-flowers, as the sailors call them, (*Lycopodium lepidophyllum,*) were expanding their rose-like heads in every direction, and the grey summits were often garlanded with graceful hanging festoons formed of the wild vine and various other climbers.

Pines of several species, oaks, maples, rhododendrons, brambles, azaleas, roses, violets, camellias, myrtles, mulberries, junipers, eugenias, mallows, sages, hypericums, asters, gnathaliums, and hundreds of other plants are observed in these islands; the parasitic *Cassythis filiformis* is found clinging to the low bushes, and weaving them together in an almost impervious mass; the larch and the willow, the *Ficus tinctoria* and the *Diospyros*, the Bamboo and the Cycas are spread abundantly over every part; a few labiate and scrophulariaceous plants were visible, and several species of *Chenopodium* and *Asclepias* were common everywhere. Grasses and compound flowers were not very numerous, but I observed a pretty good sprinkling of Cryptogamia, especially among the ferns and lichens. On the sides of some tombs on a little island near Quelpart, a species of hymenopterous insect of the family *Eumenidæ* builds a neat hemispherical nest of the size of a filbert, composed of clay and comminuted grass made into a kind of mortar; the interior is lined with a smooth polished plaster, and contains a single larva with the body slightly bent upon itself.

On one small island where we watered ship, there were fields of Tiger-lilies, and in another part barley was growing, and clumps of dark-green pine-trees overhung the precipitous side where masses of lichen-stained rocks lay crowded and jumbled together. The whole surface of the island was covered with huge boulders and loose stones overgrown with vegetation. In one part was a large square enclosure with low solid walls of piled-up stones, containing the graves of two individuals, known as such by the most grotesque tombstones I ever saw in my life. As the sun was shining brightly and the day very warm, insects were numerous, more especially the Diptera, which were far more brilliant and in larger numbers than I had anywhere seen, even in the tropics;

"these little bright-eyed things,
That float about the air on azure wings,"

were pitching on the leaves, whirling round the flowers,

and hovering gaily about the bare, sunny sides of the big stones, with the greatest vivacity, imparting much liveliness to the entire scene. In another part of this pretty islet, however, the appearance of affairs became slightly changed, and this occurred in a dull swampy morass where huge reeds grew, and where, as you stooped down and looked curiously, as I did, among their tall, slender culms, dozens of lurid-looking vipers might be seen trailing their slow length along the surface of the ground, and winding their sinuous way quietly into the dull distance of the pigmy forest. It was in truth a noisome place, "redolent," as Dickens would say, " of all sorts of slabby, clammy, creeping and uncomfortable life." Frogs, however, towards the evening were numerous and cheerful, and the glow-worms lighted up their tiny lamps, but still the gloom of that dark spot where the vipers so abounded continued for some time to haunt my mind. It seemed to be a scene such as Spencer must have presented to himself, when he described in his "Faerie Queene" the subsidence of the waters of the Nile after the fertile slime, according to his ideas of the spontaneous generation of animals, had covered the plains:

> "wherein there breed
> Ten thousand kinds of creatures, partly male,
> And partly female, of his fruitful seed;
> Such ugly monstrous shapes elsewhere may no man reed."

In some parts of Korea the land exhibits the appearance of parks and meadows, with clumps of firs and other trees, among which may be noticed the oak. The *Vitis Indica* is seen trailing among heaps of stones; the *Compositæ* begin to appear, among which may be noticed a Coreopsis and an Aster; a few Cacti mingled with Sedums, aromatic *Labiatæ* and *Scrophularineæ*, and here and there a Cruciferous plant, caused the vegetation to assume somewhat the appearance of what we are accustomed to see in Europe, but strangely mingled with such tropical forms as *Euphorbiaceæ, Leguminosæ, Rhizophora Mangle,* and *Hibiscus tiliacus.*

The scenery of these islands reminds one very much of our own woodland haunts; for, when the sky is bright, and the sun is powerful on the ground, the retired dells, and plains, and shady nooks are instinct with life. Gaudily-tinted butterflies sport around, feathered warblers twitter in the trees, and crowds of insects spin about the flowers. Among the birds, " Great Nature's happy commoners," were seen the modest Pigeon, cowering in some deep recess; the Flycatcher and the Butcher-bird, busily intent on prey; the showy Woodpecker, fluttering in its pride, and clinging to the boughs in every kind of fantastic attitude. Troops of white, long-necked Herons ranged themselves along the padi-fields, greedy after frogs; nor were " lingering notes of sylvan music" wanting, as the evening drew on apace; a bird with a note like the nightingale, and a species of Thrush, warbled very prettily; and at early dawn, the Lark, that glorious minstrel-bird, sang loud and joyous. Many other birds, well known in England, were busy in affairs of love. The Raven sat quietly perched upon the stunted trees, or croaking as he sailed familiarly around us; the Wren, the Sparrow, and the Blackbird were common in the thickets; the Kingfisher glided by the narrow brooks; the Swift and the Swallow clung to the rocky cliffs, or wheeled in circles through the air; the Cormorant sat grave and judge-like on the coral reefs; the Sea-gull screamed about the ripple of the tide; and Ducks and Divers were disporting themselves on the waters of the bays. Most of these, however, were of different species from those that inhabit the countries of Europe. When I first saw the Wren in this far-off region, it instantly recalled scenes familiar to me in childhood by the mere force of association, for certain animals are always connected in our minds with peculiar haunts and localities. We never think of the Chamois, but we fancy him clinging to the cliff; of the Antelope, but we imagine her bounding across the plain; of the Tiger, but we ruminate on drear and lonely jungles; of the Wolf, but we dream of forest gloom; or the Hyæna, but we picture to ourselves grave-yards and desolate burial places. The Spoonbill, the Quail, the Curlew, the Titmouse, the Wagtail, and the Teal, are also met with in the Korean Archipelago.

I have but few words to say with reference to the fishes of this group, the habits and economy of these scaly denizens of the deep continuing to remain almost a sealed volume even to the Naturalist. Solitary and retiring, they elude the scrutiny of curious man in the vast regions of old "ocean's grey and melancholy waste," or when "but dimly seen" up rivers and in shallow bays, or playing among the coral reefs, such is in general the rapidity of their movements, that the most eager scientific eye cannot trace the nature of their proceedings.

The fishes of the Eastern Seas glitter with gold and silver, their sides are marked, banded and spotted with the most vivid colours, and as they cleave the transparent water round the coral reefs, sporting playfully or resting motionless on their vibrating pectorals, they fascinate the eye fully as much as the large gaudily-coloured Lepidoptera do upon the land.

Among the Islands of the Korean Archipelago the children use the dried spiral eggs of a species of Skate, or some other cartilaginous fish, as rattles, having first introduced a few small pebbles to assist in making a noise. Beautiful azure Serrani and party-coloured Scari people the calm waters within the coral reefs. Thousands of other rock-fish are also met with in every possible variety of colour. One species swims in shoals, and is of the deepest and most brilliant ultramarine blue; others are vivid yellow, while many again are striped, banded, or furnished with crimson tails or bright green fins, reminding one of the fish Milton alludes to, which

" show to the sun
Their waved coats dropp'd with gold."

Various species of *Carassus, Coboeta, Lenciscus,* and other genera, were observed by us among the islands.

The Entomology of these islands doubtless is very rich in new species. The large black and white butterfly *Histia Leuconome* is common both among the Korean Archipelago and in the Meïa-co-shimah group. It wanders lazily along on heavy flapping wings, a little above the low trees, in shady places. On thistle-heads an elongated polished green *Cerambyx* is seen, which diffuses a very powerful odour of attar of roses, like the agreeable perfume emitted by the *Cerambyx rosalia* of the Pyrenees. Another very common beetle is the *Pristonocerus cæruleipennis*, a beautiful blue insect with a yellow head; while on the ground, in shady places, a splendid new species of Carabidæ (*Carabus monilifer*, Tatum,*) is met with in considerable bundance. Dull green *Cetoniidæ* are also numerous among the grassy parts of the islands; and a species of *Passalus* is found among the dried Algæ along the strand. In the evening *Lampyridæ* and several species of Stag-beetles (*Lucani*) fly about in company with *Geotrupes* and *Aphodii*. Hundreds of the long-horned, beautiful, little *Adelæ*, day-flying Moths, with wings that in glossiness and brilliancy resemble burnished steel, were flying in companies of thirty and forty in rapidly revolving circles above the low bushes, thus disporting themselves in the heat of the noon-day sun, contrary to the usual custom of nocturnal Lepidoptera. Some other insects, as *Œcocophoræ*, *Sesiidæ*, or diurnal humming-bird-Hawkmoths, and various *Uraniidæ* have the same habits. Flying heavily about the lower bushes, or clinging to the stalks of the tall grass, were several species of *Trochilium*, some very handsomely marked, and others apparently similar to those of Europe. A species of Earwig, very closely allied to our *Forficula auricularia*, but somewhat larger, was observed to be common among the dead leaves that cover the ground in the pine-woods; and here the huge *Dynastidæ* and *Onthophagi* of the tropics seemed to have given place to the numerous sub-genera of the *Geotrupidæ* of more temperate regions, and I began to recognise many forms belonging to this extensive family once familiar to my eye in England. A Spider, belonging to the genus *Attus*, was observed by me among the thousands of dead *Truncatellæ*, that occupy the holes and

* Ann. and Mag. Nat. Hist. vol. xx, p. 15.

corners of the rocks in every part of these islands, which forms a convenient abode in these small shells, lining them carefully with a fine silken tapetum. Near the sea-coast, a minute species of *Pagurus* was found occupying these little truncated univalve shells, crawling about by thousands. Our spider, however, is unable to move about with its borrowed house in the manner of those pirate crabs, but either sits sedentary in its den, or ventures forth at intervals on its predatory hunting excursions.

Among the rocks of a small islet near Quelpart, the largest of the Korean islands, there is a species of Spider which forms a very ingenious dwelling, which may be compared to that of the Swallow, whose nest affords such an important article in the gastronomy of wealthy Mandarins, (the *Hirundo esculenta*,) but adhering to the rough surface of the rock in a reversed position, resembling a watch-pocket upside down. It is composed of a substantially-woven silky material, and firmly secured by means of a glutinous secretion. The ingenious little builder and proprietor of this strange castle in the air, lets himself down by a rope-ladder, or, to speak less fancifully, by a fine spun web, which he manufactures for the purpose out of the substance of his body as required, he himself serving the purpose of a weight; "deducit stamina, ipso se pondere usus," as Pliny observes, when treating on these animals in his chapter "De Araneis." In the eaves of the thatched houses of the Koreans, I observed that a large black-coloured species of hymenopterous insect forms long cylindrical holes, lined with comminuted straw made into a kind of mortar by being mixed with a glutinous secretion; at the bottom of this tube the mother deposits her eggs, which are shut out from any external communication by means of a thin partition made of a substance resembling "papier maché." Another Wasp constructs a mud hut for its future progeny against the sides of the walls, having a small round perforation on the lower part, which serves as a door.

A milk thistle with long spiny leaves, is rather common on some of the islands of the Korean Archipelago, on the large purple flowers of which I frequently found one or two specimens of a species of *Aromia*, which diffuses a powerful odour of attar of roses. In markings it approaches to the *Polyzonus bifasciatus*, but differs from it in having the thorax spined and in other characters. Among other insects met with by me in these islands, were a dark burnished green *Eumolpus*; a bronze-brown species of *Silphodes*, allied to *S. Philippinensis* of Westwood; a new species of *Dorcus*, and a *Lucanus* allied to *L. Saiga* of Olivier; a new species of *Bolboceras* (*B Koreensis*, Adams and White), with a black thorax, and black and brown elytra; an *Adoretus*, of a rusty-brown colour, allied to *A. ranunculus*; a new species of *Mononyx*, of a dull blackish-brown, which hides in the sandy soil, and when caught feigns death; and a *Scutigera*, found under stones, and which when disturbed runs with great celerity. Besides these may be added a species of *Scarites*, entirely of a shining coal-black colour, which is very active, running about all day among the heaps of sea-weed thrown up along the beach. When approached it burrows rapidly in the sand, bites very severely, and makes vigorous efforts to escape. It is a most predacious creature, feeding greedily on the *Talitri*, *Gammari*, and other small Crustacea that abound in these situations. I have watched them enter the holes in the sand, and on giving them insects of any description, they would seize them savagely with their powerful jaws, and rapidly tear them in pieces. I have found this same insect lying concealed in the burrows of a small *Ocypode* that perforates the sandy soil in all directions, and which most probably forms part of the prey of this carnivorous insect. Many other *Coleoptera* besides the *Scarites* appear to have the same habit of burrowing in the sand; as the *Hesperophilus arenarius*, and some species of *Bledius* and *Dyschirius*. At the back of the Isle of Wight I have observed a large beetle with similar habits.

Several handsomely marked varieties of *Stomatella rubra*, besides the *Stomatellæ auricula* and *sulcifera*, and *Stomatix phymotis* and *duplicata*, were found strewing the beach of some of the coral islands, mixed with a species of *Crepidula*; and in the deep water between some of the wall-sided basaltic islets a rich harvest of *Terebratulæ* including two large characteristic new species of a beautiful and delicate red-rose colour. The former shell occurred in great numbers, and was observed washed up along the coasts filling the holes of the rocks; thus proving that typhoons and violent tempests in their agitation of the sea penetrate to very considerable depths below the surface, requiring these delicate shells to be anchored for further security by a byssus to the stones at the bottom. Submarine agitations have been known to reach to a depth of 200 feet, and so violent in their operation as to break rocks in pieces. A single valve of a large and interesting new species of Cockle (*Cardium*

Bechei, Adams and Reeve) was obtained by the dredge from the same locality, and in the straits separating Korea from the island of Kiusu, one of the Japanese group, a specimen of the remarkable *Fusus pagoda*, together with several scarce *Nuculæ* and some *Murices*, among which was a magnificent new one I propose naming in honour of Sir William Burnett, were procured. The rocks of the Korean islands were covered with a large kind of *Monodonta* which boiled with a little salt, were excellent eating; adhering to the stones was a *Mytilus*, which, when masticated, was of a peppery taste; and the mud-flats in the neighbourhood of fishing-wears, were covered with the *Cardium Sinense*, and a species of *Bullæa*; while the rare *Lingula tumidula*, Reeve, was found buried a little below the surface.

The *Cryptostoma* generally inhabits very deep water. It is cautious and timid in the extreme, contracting its body on the slightest touch. When, however, it fancies itself secure and unobserved, it gradually expands its shapeless form, protrudes its long large foot, and explores the surface on which it crawls, with a small finger-like process, in the manner of a leech before fixing itself. It progresses with a tardigrade movement, sliding like a Limax, on its ventral disc, the short tentacles exserted, and the posterior lobes of the mantle dilated. It is closely allied to *Natica* in every particular.

The *Eburna* is leisurely in its movements, exserting its tentacula and crawling with a slow and measured pace. It is, however, quick and rapid, when alarmed, in perceiving the enemy, and immediately retracts the soft parts within the shell. Swainson states it has no operculum, which is not correct. The mantle of this species is of a dull, dirty pinkish white, covered with large irregular shaped, reddish-brown blotches, distributed in no regular order; the siphon is marbled with the same colour, but of a lighter shade; the tentacles are dull pinkish-white. Living *Eburnæ* are very common in the China sea. They generally live in a muddy botton, and in about fourteen fathoms of water. The Chinese fishermen along the coast frequently bring them up in their nets, together with *Dorippe*, *Dromia*, and other Crustaceans; and I have seen them carefully set apart in the stern of their craft, as if for the purpose of being eaten.

Among the islands of the Korean Archipelago, the coral-beds are very splendid, and appear, as you look down upon them, through the clear, transparent, water, to form beautiful flower-gardens of marine plants. The polypi which protrude their hydra-forms, are coloured green, blue, violet, and yellow, which gives the corals a very different appearance to the dry, calcareous masses seen in museums, and calls to mind the exclamation of St. Pierre: "Nos livres sur la nature n'en sont que le roman, et nos cabinets que le tombeau." Indeed few sights of nature can exceed, in beauty and interest, these submarine parterres, where, amid the protean forms of the branched corals, huge madrepores, brain-shaped, flat, or headed like gigantic mushrooms, are interspersed with sponges of the deepest red, and huge asterias of the richest blue. But as Spencer very properly observes,

"Much more eath to tell the stars on hy,
 Albe they endless seeme in estimation,
 Than to recount the seas posterity :
 So fertile be the floods in generation,
So huge their numbers, and so numberless their nation."

Among these numerous small islands of the Korean Archipelago, *Sponges* are very plentiful, and in some spots may be collected in almost any quantity. They are also easily studied here in a living state. Apathetic and immovable, Sponges may be said hardly to exist; nourished by permeating canals, which pervade in every direction their porose bodies, they have properties but no instincts, attributes but no sensations. Their living and gelatinous crusts show no vital energies, save the ceaseless vibration of innumerable cilia, that properly belong to animal existence. Mechanically the surrounding fluid moves in through myriads of pores and larger vents, and then they grow rooted and immovable, and gradually assume their specific forms and full dimensions. Soft and delicate, they love the deep still waters of the tropic seas, where, in obscure recesses, they propagate, and grow, and die. Among the islands I enumerated ten or twelve well marked species which are most likely new. Some were flat, and split into numerous riband-like branches, others were round and digitated, others filiform, elongated and cylindrical, while some were in the form of hollow tubes; others form delicate lace-like aggregate cells, others wide cancellated infundibuliform cups. Some again have broad scalloped rounded leaves, and others dense white branch-like foliations, some are hard and horny, some quite solid with calcareous spicula, and others loose, light, and very expansible.

Various singular species of the fleshy-lobed *Sarcophyta* and handsomely coloured varieties of *Tubastræa*, with numerous other showy-looking Corallines were common on all the beaches.

Leaving Hong-Kong on the 1st of April, we touched

at Batan on the 17th of May, were at Ibugos on the 19th, at Bayat on the 20th, sighted Botel Tobago on the 2nd of June, and on the 3rd landed and examined the small isolated island of Sama-Sana, of whose existence on the surface of our globe serious doubts had been entertained. On landing in the boats we noticed two large junks hauled up high and dry upon the beach, and on inquiry through our Chinese interpreter found that they had just brought emigrants from Chin-Chu and Amoy. On proceeding to their village, while the Captain was engaged in fixing the position of the island and taking the necessary observations, I found about two hundred people dressed in the manner of the lower orders of Chinese, with the features of Tartars or Cochin-Chinese, living in houses wretchedly dirty, and constructed in the manner of those of the poorer classes of Pa-tchung-san. With much politeness these poor islanders led me into one of their hovels and brought me Samschiew, rice, boiled lily-roots, dried mollusks (*Haliotis*), and roasted ground-nuts or pods of the *Arachis hypogea*. They had brought a beautiful valley in the vicinity of their hamlet into an excellent state of cultivation, growing rice, sweet potato (*Batatas edulis*), Indian corn and ground-nuts, with a little tobacco. They appeared to be much addicted to chewing the areca-nut, and betel-leaf, and were, moreover, almost continually smoking. The women were very ugly, even for members of the Mongolian race, but by no means shy or distant, as is generally the case in these countries. An old man at parting gravely placed upon my finger a ring made from a species of *Conus*, with the spire and produced part of the body-whorl ground down. In a ramble through the island I procured specimens of a beautiful *Polychrus*, (a species of Lizard,) and noticed the lovely green Sizé Moosee or *Tachysaurus Japonicus*, and a small brown species of *Zootica*. Frogs were numerous in the padi-fields, contrary to what might have been expected on so small an island. The land and fresh-water shells were similar to those of the Meïa-co-shimahs, namely a small brown snail, a *Paludina*, and two species of *Lymnæa*.

Herons, snipes, and plovers were numerous on the island. Among the trees the Banyan and *Ficus tinctoria* formed in many parts dense shady groves. In the course of my rambles I made a capture of a large Dynastes, several Cetoniæ, and a splendid new member of the Curculio family, a species of *Platyrhynchus* allied to *P. multipunctatus*, but differing from that insect in several particulars. As the species named by Schonherr, *P. Waltoni*, is synonymous with one previously described by Waterhouse and Chevlotat, I have named this Sama-Sana beetle *P. Waltonianus*, in honour of that gentleman who has devoted such minute attention to this branch of Entomology. The insect is dark, shining-black, covered with round opaque, powdery spots of a deep smalt-blue colour, and having the thorax and elytra sculptured. Found on the leaves of plants.

As our party were quietly regaling themselves with a cold collation, seated comfortably on the turfy side of a hummock near the sea, we were suddenly rocked and tumbled about in a very absurd manner by the intestinal commotion and up-heaving of an earthquake, the shock of which extended to the ship, and was distinctly felt on board.

A survey of the small island of Kumi, placed us once again among our ancient friends, the Meïa-co-shimites. Our welcome was as polite and ceremonious, the same attention was paid to our wants, and a similar active and a vigilant espionage was bestowed upon all our movements, resembling that we experienced at Pa-tchung-san. They erected rude huts as watch-houses near our tents, supplied us with mats, lent us horses, and accompanied us from village to village, in a similar manner. We found the scenery of the island in many parts very pretty and picturesque, and even in some places discovered scenes of considerable grandeur and sublimity. Along the coast we were frequently obliged to trust implicitly to the sagacity and sure-footedness of our tough little horses, which conducted us safely by many a "mauvais pas" along the edge of precipitous cliffs and overhanging rocks. The villages are most delightfully situated and often laid out with very considerable taste, the houses being neatly built, and prettily disposed among clumps of trees. In the centre of the island we were obliged to ascend on horseback a stone-road cut in a winding manner up the side of a hill, in order to obtain a favourable view of the island. About half-way up we found a beautiful clear spring shaded with trees, and in fording the tranquil pool formed by the trickling water, I noticed numbers of aquatic beetles of the genus *Cyclous* with shining, polished, pitch-black elytra, short, broad legs, formed like the flattened blades of paddles, disporting on the surface like so many gigantic whirlwigs, (*Gyrinus natator,*) those silvery-looking little insects which weave mystic mazes during the summer-time in the ponds of

Europe. Large flocks of handsome pigeons were committing depredations on the padi-fields; several elegant and showy-looking *Cetoniæ* (coleopterous insects) were flying about the grass on the summits of the hills, which were peopled moreover by thousands of those singular long-headed Orthoptera, the *Truxalis*, beautiful green *Phyllopteræ* with large, soft, leaf-like elytra, and an odd-looking *Tropidinotus*. In the evening, glow-worms were exceedingly numerous in all parts of the island. In the still, calm nights, the "diapason of the deep" lent its powers of pleasing, as the waves idly dashed against the rock-bound coast, and very soon lulled the small party, tired with their days rambling, to a sound sleep on the mats and grass laid for them on the ground.

On the 5th of August we were anchored in Nangasaki Bay, with the mountainous country covered with vegetation, surrounding us on all sides. The hills being prettily surmounted with trees, and their sides beautifully cultivated in terraces after the Chinese fashion, together with the batteries and tents for the troops on shore, and the surface of the bay swarming with imperial guard-boats, fishing craft, and pleasure boats, gave an air of great vivacity and novelty to the scene. The gentlemen of Japan were most polite and courteous in their manners, conducting themselves with refined and polished urbanity, and walking about with a solemn and respectful demeanour, putting to shame the ill-breeding of the seamen who ventured to laugh at them. When they meet one another, they close the hands, bring them together at the knees, and, bending the body, make a very graceful bow. Their curiosity and desire for information was very great.

Many among them spoke Dutch, and some a little French. They appeared to be very well acquainted with geography, and pointed out their three principal islands, (which they pronounce Kew-Sèw, Nipung, and Sikòk,) on the map with the greatest ease. Some of them seemed to be well conversant with guns and gunnery; others could even master a few words of English. When I offered an old gentleman who paid us a visit in the midshipman's berth a penknife, he said very distinctly, "I must not;" although no compunction of that nature was manifested when eatables and drinkables were in question. Those of more respectable appearance, and who were doubtless interpreters sent off as spies, were all furnished with writing materials. Their "Yahtati," or inkstands, were very compact, and similar in principal and nearly in form to the ancient Atramentaria found at Pompeii, and in use among the Greeks, with little covers to keep the dust from the ink. The Japanese, however, had the advantage over these, in being provided with a long hollow metallic handle, in which the pen was always kept in readiness. Many of these people had a debauched and debilitated look. Like the Loo-Chooans, they dress in long loose robes of various texture and colour, secured about their middle with a broad sash, in which among the upper orders two sabres are thrust.* The pattern of their robes is very various, blue being the chief and favourite colour; some however are light black, some buff colour, some chequered black and white, some striped, others flowered, many quite plain, some marked with characters on the back, others with various circles and mysterious hiero-

* See Frontispiece.

glyphic devices, each doubtless having a meaning as denoting the rank of the wearer, or his office; but to us they were quite unintelligible. Unlike the Loo-Chooans, however, over this flowing garment, which extends as low down as the ankles, the Japanese wear a large loose jacket, with very wide sleeves, which reaches as far as the knees. Like those of Loo-Choo, their feet are protected with sandals, neatly made of plaited rice-grass, and their socks either black, dark blue, or white, have a separate compartment for the great toe, like the Mandarins of Napa. Like these latter they go bare-headed, carry their short pipes in a neat case, and use paper pocket-handkerchiefs. Some of the soldiers wore tight pantaloons and gaiters.

In their gait, from the constant practice of wearing sandals, they are slouching and awkward. The head is shaved from the front to the nape of the neck, the hair on the sides is strained upwards, tied at the top, and the ends of the hairs glued together by grease or wax, forming what they call a "Kami," which is tied in two places with silver wire, and brought forward on the bald crown, thus differing somewhat from the "Kotuxa" of Loo-Choo, where the hair is secured in a knot. They shave the cheek and chin, differing also in this particular from the people of Loo-Choo. The boatmen and lower orders are nearly naked. They were treated with disdain by most of the higher classes, who would not allow them to come on board. These men are very active and strong, and of a much browner complexion than the better classes, many of whom are almost white. The deep, oblong, sunken eye of China is common among these men, although I have seen some with eyes nearly as full as those of Europeans.

They all evinced a great repugnance to having their scimitars withdrawn from their sheaths, and showed great aversion when questioned about the operation of ripping up the belly in cases of honourable suicide, but intimated that the short straight sword was the one employed, and the long curved one for fighting. The blades of these weapons were highly tempered, keen-edged, and beautifully wrought with figures. The sheaths, in numerous instances, were very splendid. Some were of black polished lacquer, with gold figures inlaid; others of shagreen, and others covered with various devices in silver; the guards were ornamented in an equally chaste and tasteful manner. They wear the sharp edge upwards, the reverse of most other nations. On the whole, they appear from all accounts to be more upright, honourable, and at the same time more jealous than the Chinese, more refined and civilised than the Koreans, and more warlike and intellectual than the Loo-Chooans. Many of the arts and sciences have arrived at considerable excellence among them, more particularly those of an imitative character; their manners are softened and polished to the utmost degree of refinement; and at the same, if Titsingh and others are to be believed, their morals are at a very low ebb indeed.

Although surrounded by the imperial guard-boats, which watched all our movements with a jealous vigilance, numbers of interesting shells were procured from a muddy bottom, at about eight fathoms water, by dredging under the stern and in the ship, both coming in and going out of the bay. Among these were species of *Nucula, Pandora, Myadora, Arca, Neæra, Anatina, Mya,* and *Cardium,* obtained in the living state; and *Balanus,*

Venus, Pullastra, Tellina, Pecten, Ostræa, Modiolus, and *Lima*, in a dead state. Among the univalves which were obtained in a living condition, were *Pleurotoma, Clavatula, Cancellaria, Terebra, Murex*, and *Nassa;* and dead species of *Cylichna, Natica, Mitra, Dolium, Bullæa, Terebellum, Turritella*, and *Dentalium*. Altogether the dredge furnished us with thirty-two genera, and numerous species of Mollusks, besides *Spatangus, Asterias, Leucosia, Matuta, Echinus*, and *Sipunculus*.

On our passage from Nangasaki to Loo-Choo, we sailed through a small archipelago comparatively unknown, and consisting of from fifteen to twenty conical islands, all of them evidently being the tops of a sunken chain of volcanic mountains, some of them still in an active state of eruption, vomiting forth smoke in large volumes, from terminal craters or fissures in the sides. These submarine mountains must be very steep and lofty, for quite close to the shore no bottom was found with two hundred fathoms of line. On one islet, named "Disaster," on account of the upsetting of the Captain's gig and loss of numerous valuable instruments, hundreds of the amphibious *Bulla viridis* of Rang, or *B. calyculata* of Sowerby, were discovered crawling on the surface of the rock, a little way removed from the dashing of the waves. On some few of these sterile meteoric islands goats were seen hanging from the flanks and browsing on the scanty herbage; and these, mixed with a few Sweet-potatoes, would seem to constitute the food of a few poor miserable wretches of the human species, who have most probably been banished to these inhospitable shores from Japan or Loo-Choo, and who here contrive to maintain a precarious existence on roots and goats'-flesh. They are not, however, sufficiently versed in geologic lore to understand on what ticklish ground they tread, or that they stand a chance of being one day either burnt or drowned.

The Mollusk that constructs the shell of *Bulla viridis*, Rang, would appear to form the type of a new genus, which may be thus characterised. *Smaragdinella*: body oval, and somewhat depressed; lateral lobes moderate, reflexed, covering a small portion of the sides of the shell, opened and produced in front, and rounded posteriorly where they are continuous with the foot; foot moderate, rounded before and behind; head-disc five-sided, narrow and notched behind, rather broader on each side in front, flattish above, with two small tubercular tentacles in front of the central eyes, which are round, black, sessile, and placed rather wide apart. Shell partly external and naked above, with the body whorl turned inwards, open, and forming a very peculiar, shallow, cup-shaped process, which renders it quite different from other *Bullidæ*.

The animal of *Bulla viridis* of Rang, or the *Bulla calyculata* of Sowerby, is figured in the Voyage of the Astrolabe (t. 26, f. 13.) In that figure are correctly represented the peculiar prolongation of the lateral lobes forwards, the square-shaped cephalic disc, and the two round sessile eyes; but in the animals I examined there were observed the rudiments of two tentacular processes, situated anterior to the eyes. The head-disc in this genus, as in other *Bullidæ*, occasionally assumes various forms according to the will of the animal, being either deeply indented in front with lateral sharp projecting angular processes, or rounded lobes, or very much produced in front, forming an elongated finger-shaped process, which it employs as an exploring organ. The lateral lobes in like manner may vary in their outline, tapering in front to form on either side a salient angle which curves outwards, or a portion of the thin margin, which partially overlaps the shell, is produced into a rounded lobe or process; the two lateral lobes are continuous behind, and may extend much more beyond the shell and posterior lobe than is represented in M. Rang's figure. The *Bulla smaragdina* of Lewkart, which is formed into a genus by Ehrenberg, under the name of *Cryptocephalus olivaceus* (Symbolæ physicæ Mollusc Tab. 1, f. 4), is totally distinct from *Smaragdinella viridis*. *Smaragdinella* is amphibious and entirely marine, crawling slowly on rocks immediately above the ripple of the sea. The animal of *Smarag. viridis* is dark olive-green, speckled and mottled with a yet darker shade; the margins of the foot, those of the lateral lobes, and of the head-disc are of a lighter green; and the eyes are black.

CHAPTER IX.

BORNEO.

Indian Butterfly-flower—Mangrove, Casuarina, and other trees—Bird-catching plant — Curious Tree-louse — Nidification of Pigeons—New Bulimus—Wasps' and Ants' nests—Borneon Mammifera—Haunts of Molluscous animals—Their Habits—Localities of certain fresh-water species—Habits of Crustaceans—Singular larvæ—Instincts and varied forms of Spiders—Visit Kabatuan—Muda Mohammed—The Dusuns—Molluscous animals.

IN the course of our survey of the north-west coast of Borneo, including Abai, the river of which is said to communicate with the waters of Kini Balu lake; Tampassook, the noted haunt of Illañon pirates; Kabatuan, which has the brother of Muda Hassim for Rajah; and Ambong, peopled chiefly by Bajows or sea-gipsies, we obtained several interesting forms, more particularly from that southern portion of the Chinese Sea, which washes this part of the Borneon coast.

Balambangan is a very flat and most unwholesome looking island, covered in a great part of its extent with Mangroves and Casuarinas, and in parts, where fresh-water pools occur, overrun with pitcher-plants (*Nepenthes destillatoria*). The *Phalænopsis amabilis* or Indian Butterfly plant, at the time of our visit, was in full flower.

This lovely epiphyte, which is considered one of the choicest and most splendid of the Orchidaceous family, grows in thick clustering masses, on the bark of the trees; and I have seen as many as twenty-five large white satiny blossoms on a single raceme, constituting a most gorgeous floral plume, and, contrasting with the dark-green foliage over which it hangs, forming one of the most lovely objects in the world of plants. Large tracts of the island are fringed with Casuarina trees of rather small dimensions, but I am unable to say of what species.

The *Casuarina equisetifolia* sufficiently indicates the peculiar appearance of the foliage of those showy-looking feathery trees that are usually seen stretching along many parts of the coast of Borneo, more particularly in the vicinity of the mouths of rivers where the ground lies low. These trees are dioecious, and produce small woody cones, which, together with their horsetail-like leaves, remind one of pine-trees, and may perhaps be considered the representatives of the *Coniferæ* in tropical regions.

Another tree, the name of which so repeatedly occurs in the pages of travellers, is the Mangrove, which renders hundreds of miles uninhabitable by man. There are two species of Mangrove common in Borneo: one of which, the *Rhizophora Gymnorhiza*, is a very tall and handsome tree, with leathery leaves growing in radiated tufts at the ends of the branches; and with very singular-shaped elongated fruit, which falls down into the mud, where it sticks with its sharp point buried, and thus becomes a young tree. I have seen many acres covered with these strange pointed young Mangroves, in every stage of development. The roots of this kind of *Rhizophora* appear above the ground, giving the specific name of *Gymnorhiza* to the tree; those of a single individual sometimes extend in a complicated series of loops and arches over a considerable space of ground, offering secure retreats for myriads of *Gelasimi*, jumping fish, mosquitoes, and other animals that love to frequent the low swampy banks of rivers. This species ordinarily affects fresh water; but near the sea, and often fringing the low islets that extend along the coast in many parts is another kind, the *Rhizophora Mangle*, which is a much lower tree, with smaller leaves and a fruit differently shaped, which by means of its twisted matted roots forms excellent break-waters, binding together the loose soil and shingle, and thus effectually preventing the encroachments of the sea among these low islands.

The *Aquilaria Agallocha* is one of the most common trees in the forests skirting the sea. It is a very large showy-looking tree, with the veins of the oval polished leaves running from the mid-rib to the margin, like those of some Endogens, so that there can be no difficulty in distinguishing it. The wood is frequently used by the Chinese, but is not very durable; it yields the Lignum Aloes of commerce, and has faint medicinal qualities.*
Another very common plant is the *Coculus cordifolius*, with its long filiform pendent stems, which hang suspended from the tops of the high forest-trees, producing a singular effect when they are numerous. The Malays employ some of the species of the genus *Coculus* in the

---

* The Agila wood, the produce of this tree, enters extensively into the composition of the Joss-sticks employed by the Chinese in their religious ceremonies.

cure of intermittent fever, and it is said with much benefit. The *Coculus Indicus* of commerce, the seeds of which are used to adulterate beer, belongs to quite a different genus, the *Anamirta*. I have frequently collected berries which leave almost an indelible yellow stain on the fingers, and have no doubt many valuable vegetable dyes yet remain to be discovered in Borneo. The men frequently, during watering and wooding, stained their hands with a yellow sap, perhaps that of the *Terminalia Chebula*. The smooth, black, shining nuts of the *Semecarpus Anacardium*, yield a juice which produces an indelible stain, and forms much better marking ink than the caustic usually employed for that purpose.

At Pulo Tiga, Sir Edward Belcher discovered a species of *Pisonia*, a plant remarkable for having the perianth surrounding the fruit covered with hooks and viscid glands, and the inflorescence being in loose pannicles and covering the tops of large bushes, birds frequently become involved among the branches, and while feeding on the fruit get caught by the sharp recurved hooks, assisted by the viscid secretion which acts like birdlime. Many old forest-trees in Borneo, where the soil is superficial, unable to sustain the weight of their wide-spread leafy crowns, and deprived of that sheet-anchor the tap-root, throw out strong butresses from their sides in the shape of wing-shaped masses, which extend in various directions, and maintain the perpendicularity of the trunks. Crawling slowly on the leaves in the forest of Balambangan, is found a very remarkable form of *Acarides*, allied in many respects to the genus *Ixodes*. It is about half an inch in length; the back is covered with rounded elevations very symmetrically disposed, and nearly concealed by a mealy efflorescence, which when rubbed off, leaves the surface smooth and of a light red-brown; the under surface is smooth, and of a pale brown; the legs are very short, and the eyes are invisible. A remarkable form of Arachnidans, a species of *Macrocheles*, with a hard flat body, of a reddish-brown colour, with a straw-coloured head, is also to be met with on this island.

On the 21st of March, 1846, the day on which we received orders for England, I landed on a small islet between Banguey, or more properly Banggi, and Balambangan. The ground was partially clear among the trees, and studded with a very elegant species of *Pandanus*, on the crown-shaped bunches of the leaves of which, numbers of large blue Pigeons had built their nests, consisting of a mass of leaves and earth, rudely put together. Each nest contained two large, oval, milk-white eggs, and I observed that the young ones sometimes tumbled over the edge of the platform, which performed the office of cradle, and that the old birds did not seem to have the power or sagacity to pick them up again. I noticed the mother of one of these unfortunate outcasts, tenderly caressing and offering it food, while, in other parts, several callow nurslings were lying dead upon the ground. All day the adult birds remain concealed among the dense clouds of foliage, high up above their nests in the Pandanus trees, while their monotonous cooing serves as a lullaby to their little ones; but towards the cool of the evening, these Pigeons take their departure in large flocks, and proceed direct to the forests of Banguey, whence they return with their crops distended with green berries, and other fruits, among which I noticed young Guavas and the wild nutmeg.

Arboreal *Cyclostomata*, of elegant form, and covered with delicate markings, were observed crawling on the long Pandanus leaves; a small, flat, yellow *Helicina* was found adhering to their under surface; and a single specimen of *Nanina* was obtained. A tree, partially cut through at the base with axes, fell upon one of the carpenters wooding on the island, and besides depriving him at the time of sensation, inflicted a severe wound on the temple. What proved a misfortune to the man, however, presented to science a new and very beautiful species of *Bulimus*, which I discovered in considerable numbers, adhering to the foliage of the prostrate tree. This species, which has been named *Bulimus Adamsii* by Mr. Lovell Reeve, is of a pale yellow, with the base of the columellar lip of a violet colour, a chain of oval spots of the same colour winding round the convexity of the body whorl, and running between the convolutions of the spire as far as the apex; the shell is reversed, and the markings vary in almost every individual, some being nearly covered with spots, and others being entirely of a pale straw colour.

Naninæ are very lively animals, living high up among the foliage of the trees; they have the cloak produced in front and divided into two rounded lobes, and the posterior extremity of the foot truncated and provided with a remarkable gland. There are four tentacles, and the well developed eyes are placed at the extremities of the longest pair. Extending along the lower margin of the foot, is a singular border formed of deep vertical striæ; the posterior part of the foot is marked with straight lines directed backwards, while the anterior is finely tesselated as in the bodies of common snails. Under the name of *Vitrina*, Quoy (Voy. Astrol. t. 2, fig. 1, 2, 8, 5, 16,) has given several figures of this genus, which was established by Mr. Gray. The species observed by me was of a pinkish-white colour, and brownish-red towards the anterior part and end of the tail. The animal, like the shell, was very delicate and semipellucid. The shell was faint flesh colour, with a crimson stripe following the suture of the body whorl.

Attached sideways, by a slender peduncle, to the under surface of the long leaves of the Pandanus trees, with which as I have said the interior of this pretty little islet abounded, were numbers of wasps'-nests, belonging to a species of *Polistes*, and beautifully fashioned of a paper-like material. They consisted of several tiers of cells of the usual hexagonal form, with their mouths directed downwards and to one side, and increasing in number as they receded from the point of attachment, thus rendering the nests of a conical shape. In each cell reposed a fat white larva, somewhat doubled up, with its head downwards, and to one side. Some of the cells were covered with a lid and were full of honey, but whether the larvæ could get at it appeared to me somewhat problematical, unless their careful mothers fed them, like sparrows and pigeons do their little ones. I noticed two kinds of ants'-nests on the island, one species of the size of a man's hand adhering to the trunk of trees, resembled, when cut through, a section of the lungs; the other was composed of small withered bits of sticks and leaves, heaped up in the axils of branches, somewhat in the form of flattened cylinders and compressed cones.

As might naturally be expected from the circumstance of the island comprising the vast chain of the Oriental Archipelago lying within the tropics, the equinoctial line extending nearly through the centre, the animals peculiar to the entire group partake of a certain uniformity of character; many islands having, however, certain well marked varieties of animals peculiar to their own Fauna. Borneo, like the other islands, may be said to bear the same relation in its animal and vegetable productions to India, as the West Indian Islands do to America; but Borneo, occupying a more central position between the zoological regions of Hindostan and Malacca on the one hand, and of Australia on the other, has more large quadrupeds than New Guinea, but at the same time fewer forms which are peculiar to the Australian Fauna. The Dutch, however, have ascertained the existence of several species of those anomalous mammals, the Tree Kangaroos (*Dendrolegus*) in Borneo, the Pteromys will represent Petaurista, and I have seen a small Gerbil which might represent the Kangaroos on the one hand, and the *Gerbillus Indicus* on the part of Hindostan. Herds of Elephants are stated to tramp the vast unexplored forests of the promontory of Unsang, although during our visits to that part of the coast no traces of those huge Pachyderms were reported to have been seen; but as the Elephant has been found in Sumatra, and as the Indian Tapir exists in Borneo, the probability is that the Elephant may some day be discovered. The researches of Messrs. Diard, Korthals, and Müller, have ascertained the existence of a species of Rhinoceros, but it is uncertain whether it belongs to the two-horned species of Sumatra, or the one-horned species found in Java; the Leopard of Borneo appears to be the *Felis macrocelis*, although the existence of a much larger carnivorous quadruped may be inferred from the long sharp canine teeth worn in the ears of the Orang Sagai, and which appeared to me to have belonged to an animal nearly as large as the Royal Tiger, a variety of which, indeed, is found both in Java and Sumatra. The Dyaks, in explaining their mode of killing this tiger by surrounding him in great numbers, and then shooting him with sumpits or poisoned arrows, described him as being large and fierce, and living among the mountains. Mr. Brooke has ascertained the existence of three species of Orang Utans in Borneo; namely, the *Simia Wurmbii* or Mias Pappan, the *Simia Morio* or the Mias Kassar, and the Mias Rambi, which he states is either the *Simia Abelii*, or a fourth species; he observes, moreover, that "the existence of the Sumatran Orang in Borneo is by no means impossible." The Wou-Wou of Borneo is of a darker colour than the Javanese species, and has been named *Hylobates concolor* or *H. Harlanii*; it is represented in India by the **Great Gibbon** or *Hylobates albimanus*. Among other quadrumanous animals peculiar to this great island, may be mentioned the *Semnopithecus nasicus* or Proboscis Monkey, the *Semn. auratus* and *Semn. cristatus*, and the *Inuus nemestrinus*; Borneo swarms, however, with monkeys, among which doubtless are many undescribed species. The *Tarsius* or the *Didelphis macrotarsus* of Gmelin, is an inhabitant of this island, thereby connecting it to the Fauna of the Moluccas; and *Sciurus bicolor*, *S. nigrovittatus*, *S.*

exilis, and *S. melanotis*, together with several kinds of *Tupaias* are also found. At the northern extremity we observed large numbers of a great deer which came down to drink at the pools of brackish water that abound there, most probably identical with the *Cervus hippelaphus* of Cuvier, which is also found in India; the Antelopes of that continent are represented by the Pigmy Musk, (*Moschus Javanicus*,) a diminutive and graceful little animal, which bears the same relation to the poetry of Malayan Asia, as the Gazelle does to that of Persia and Arabia. The Bovine races which inhabit India, as the *Bos frontalis* or Gaour, and the Arni or wild Buffalo of Hindostan, are represented in Borneo by herds of wild cattle, which so far as I could make them out at Point Sampang Mengayu, where they are very numerous, have short curved horns, long legs, small dewlaps, and a straight back; the domestic Ox which I have also seen is perfectly different, and owes its descent most probably from the Zebu, as the wild one does from the Arni. That striking resemblances can be made between the Faunas, not of northern or central Asia, but of Hindostan and Malacca, is not to be very much wondered at, when we consider that the chain of the Great Indian Archipelago is nothing more than a long, curved, disjointed mass of land broken by volcanic force from the south-eastern portion of the Asiatic continent, and separated merely by the superficial waters of the China Sea. The breed of small and wolf-like dogs employed by the Dyaks in hunting the boar, are stated to occur in a wild state, thus representing the Dingo of Australia, and the *Canis rutilans*, or Wild-dog of the Mountains of Asia. Sumatra has a wild dog, the *Canis Sumatranus*, as has likewise Java, *Canis Javanicus;* the Borneon variety may in like manner be termed *Canis Borneoensis.* The *Viverra zibetha, Paradoxurus typus, Sus barbatus*, and the *Cercopithecus cynomolgus* may also be enumerated among the Mammalia of this vast island, and the list might easily be extended. The *Stenops tardigradus* is possibly represented in Asia by the Slow Lemur of Bengal; the *Sciurus bicolor* is also found in India, and the same may be said of the *Pteropi,* Ichneumons, and Bats. The war-dresses of the Sagai Dyaks consisted in numerous instances of the dried skins of large Felinæ, on the ears of many of which I observed tufts of hair like those of a lynx. At Kabatuan some of the women wore necklaces or amulets, formed of the scales of the Pangolin or *Manis pentadactyla,* which in India is represented by *Manis crassicaudata;* the *Helarctos Malayanus*, a small Bear, is found both in Borneo and on the Malayan Peninsula. One of these animals paid us a visit at the encampment at Sarāwak, but although hotly pursued and fired at, contrived to escape unscathed into the jungle; on another occasion, I found myself face to face with an individual of the same species, which on seeing me, trotted leisurely away.

At the village of Kabatuan, I noticed a very fine specimen of the red-necked Ichneumon (*Herpestes semitorquatus*); it was quite tame in the house of one of the principal Pangerans, but although I affected to admire it exceedingly, the old gentleman did not seem inclined to part with it; and on the mountain of Serambo, the Dyaks brought us a living specimen of a beautiful little squirrel no larger than a Dormouse, the *Sciurus exilis;* it was perfectly mild and docile, but soon pined away and died.

In many parts of Borneo, Celebes, or indeed any of the islands of the Oriental Archipelago, if you wander along a portion of the coast, where from a steep and stony beach beset with rocks, a level sand-flat extends beyond for a long distance, and is bounded seaward by a barrier of coral, against which the ocean dashes with violence, and forms breakers which leap tumultuously over and fill numerous small ponds on the inner side,—if you wander along this, and observe with the curious eye of a Naturalist, you will notice various generic forms of Mollusks engaged as follows, and in something like the following order: Herbivorous Mollusks, that live upon the *Fuci* and *Algæ* covering the rocks and stones, come first; *Purpura* and *Littorina*, pretty brisk at certain times, and busy grazing as the day closes in on their sea-weed pastures on the exposed rocks, in company with Nerites with painted backs, marked and figured with every variety of pattern; while *Chiton, Murex, Doris,* and *Rissoa*, more timid and retiring, or more dull of disposition, hide under or adhere to the surface of the stones, Nature having so closely assimilated their forms, in many instances, to the stones, and their colours to the cryptogamic plants that surround them, as to make them invisible to the eyes of their enemies. To these individuals which enjoy the blessings of limited locomotion, may be added those more inert members of the great Molluscous family, *Siphonaria, Patella* and *Vermetus;* those Crustacean forms *Conia* and *Balanus*, which are fixed upon the exposed rock-masses; and *Policipes, Mytilus, Ostræa* and *Byssoarca*, which are stuck fast in the crevices, or safely anchored in clefts and anfractuosities. Succeeding these, on the level sandflat, you will notice *Natica* and the glossy Olives, partially covered by their mantles, leisurely forming burrows in the moist soft bed on which they spend their lives; gaily-coloured Volutes, and apathetic Mitres, with cloaks begrimed with dirt, crawling about with a slow deliberate motion, wherever there remains a little water; and when that is gone, and they can no longer enjoy themselves, they sink into the yielding sand, generally, if possible, choosing places where it is mixed with mud. Then come *Buccinum*, the large-footed *Bullia*, and *Nassa*, with its bifid, turned-up tail, considerably more lively than their last mentioned neighbours, of greater latitude in their progressive movements, and which form long sinuous tracks as they traverse on their foot-like bellies the loose saturated sand; *Natica* and *Oliva* excavate the surface more deeply still, and move in burrows underneath the soil; while *Venus*, *Solen*, and the light-shelled *Mactra* perforate obliquely the loose and moistened sand. At dead low water, among huge stony madrepores and branching corals that serve to form the barrier-reef and break-water to protect those Mollusks that live inside and love calm water, may be found embedded in their substance *Lithodomus* and *Pholas*, *Magilus* and *Leptoconchus*, snugly lodged in their calcareous dwellings, secure from every foe; *Haliotis* will be found clinging to loose stones, or crawling over and under them, exposed ever to the raging, roaring surf; amid the rocky beds, *Tridacna* rests secure in her stony house; *Cypræa* cowering in the deep nooks, holes, and corners, creeps forth cautiously and with care, frequently hiding under stones so rough and large, that one wonders her beautiful porcellaneous shell is not more often scratched and broken, or her tender mantle torn and bruised. Here also *Stomatia* loves to reside, crawling with deliberate pace among the branching coral trees; but polished *Stomatella* prefers the dead banks of coral débris within the reef, hunting in company with *Parmophorus*. Outside the reef, the hand-dredge will furnish you with *Marginella*, *Fusus*, *Pleurotoma*, *Phorus*, *Clavatula*, *Strombus*, *Triphoris*, and *Rostellaria*, the first three genera affecting, however, much shallower water than the others. In very deep water, *Terebratula* and *Cylichna*, *Nucula* and *Neæra*, will be met with, and reward industrious dredging with new and singular forms. In very deep, still water the shells are noticed to be very thin and delicate. We obtained a *Fusus* off the Cape in 135 fathoms and from a soft, muddy, and sandy bottom, with a very thin, light, fragile shell, and a brown epidermis, covered with hair-like appendages; and a new species of *Tricotropis* was dredged also in deep water and from a muddy bottom, in the bay of Nangasaki, Kiusu, Japan.

Although I have examined hundreds of *Cypræa tigris* in a living state, I never saw those changes of colour in the mantle of the animal noticed by Mr. Stutchberry, junior, who moreover states, that they crawl about usually exposed to the sun; while the result of my experience would lead me to believe, that they almost invariably lurk in holes of rocks or under loose stones, and among branching coral. The species of *Cypræa* vary considerably in colour, thus the animal of *Cypræa carneola* is of a beautiful red colour, with the foot and mantle covered with numerous opaque, oval, white spots; that of *C. talpa* is of a pale brownish-black, with minute whitish specks; that of *C. caput-serpentis* is of a rich green-brown; and in *C. lynx* the mantle is covered with numerous tufts of various forms, nodulous, trifid, or ending in two short processes; that of *C. Mauritania* has conical tubercles; of *C. erosa*, numerous rather long branching arborescent appendages; of *C. moneta* with but few, and those chiefly around the free upper edge of the mantle; while in some, these processes are altogether wanting. In *Cypræa annulus* the siphon is of a dirty-white colour, the tentacles orange, the eyes black, the mantle brown, covered with small dark spots, the foot white, with black reticulated markings. In *Cypræa errones* the mantle is light brown, perfectly smooth, and covered with dark brown reticulations; the foot is brown, with minute white spots; the peduncle of the eye is of a brilliant white; the head is brown; the base of the tentacles is a dull white; the tentacles beyond the eyes, light brown. In Quoy's figure (Voy. Astrol. t. 48, f. 18) of *Cypræa Isabella*, the edge of the mantle is simply lobed, and the remainder of the surface naked and void of appendages. In the animal of *C. errones* the edge of the cloak forms a continuous slightly-waved line, and the surface covering the shell is perfectly smooth, and adorned only with the delicate anastomosing lines mentioned above.

The young of *Cypræa*, when first they issue from the ovum, are provided with two membranous alar expansions, like some of the Pteropods, and a delicate hyaline, simple, spiral, flattened, ear-shaped shell, which fully confirms the observation of Professor E. Forbes, who observes, speaking of the Gasteropoda generally, that "they all commence life under the same simple form, both of shell and animal;

namely, a very simple spiral helicoid shell, and an animal furnished with two ciliated wings or lobes, by which it can swim freely through the fluid in which it is contained."* This forms the nucleus of the Cowry shell, which afterwards grows and undergoes several changes in form, gradually becoming more and more complicated until the outer lip is inverted and marked with numerous sulci. The converse of this, however, would appear to take place in other Gasteropoda, as shown in the development of Dolabella, Aplysia, and others, where the shell at first turbinated and nautiloid in shape, afterwards becomes an internal, flattened, horny plate. On placing the young Cowries in a watch-glass of sea-water, they may be seen to whirl about like the Hyalæa and Cleodora, and, like Atlanta, to adhere when fatigued to foreign bodies, not indeed by any sucking disc, but by means of the dilated expansion of their mantle. In the course of growth these fleshy expansions become entirely absorbed, and do not ultimately constitute the lobes of the mantle which embrace and partially cover the shell in the adult. It would constitute an interesting enquiry to observe the transitions in the figure of the animal and shell throughout the entire series of Molluscous groups, as I am convinced that many phases exhibited in their metamorphoses would throw new light not only on the identity of species, but on the reality of the existence of certain genera.

Rostellaria has all the habits of the *Strombidæ*, progressing by means of its powerful and elastic foot which it places under the shell in a bent position, when suddenly, by a muscular effort, it straightens that organ, and

---

* Edin. Phil. Journal, xxxvi. p. 326.

rolls and leaps over and over. It is, however, far more timid and suspicious than *Strombus*, which has a bold disdosition. On the low sandy beach, near the mouth of the Lundu River, in Borneo, dead shells of *Rostellaria rectirohsis* are numerous, but generally in a very imperfect condition. At the small fishing village of Samahrtan I inspected a large heap of these shells, which the Malays had brought together for the purpose of turning them into lime. On enquiring of these poor fishermen whether it were possible to obtain them in a living state, we were informed that they never procured them in their nets, but that they lived in deep water at a considerable distance from the shore. The animal of *Rostellaria fissa* does not differ from that of Strombus, and is of a dull brown colour, varied with lighter brown. It is, however, one of the most lively among Mollusks, jumping several inches, and throwing itself about with the most astonishing activity. It has none of the extreme timidity of the former mentioned species.

The perfect development of the large, fine, pedunculated eyes of *Strombus*, together with its very elongated, powerful, muscular body and foot, and claw-shaped stout, jagged, horny operculum, constitute it one of the most active and intelligent of Mollusks. It is, in fact, a most sprightly and energetic animal, and often served to amuse me by its extraordinary leaps and endeavours to escape, planting firmly its powerful narrow operculum against any resisting surface, insinuating it under the edge of its shell, and by a vigorous effort throwing itself forwards, carrying its great heavy shell with it, and rolling along in a series of jumps in a most singular and grotesque manner.

Among new and interesting forms of those Molluscous animals which are denied any calcareous defence in the form of a shell, and the breathing organs of which are consequently exposed, hence procuring them their name, *Nudibranchiata*, may be mentioned two new species of *Dendronotus*, one of which (*D. stellifer*, Adams and Reeve,) is of a pale flesh colour, marked with undulating vertical vermilion lines, freely anastomosing towards the foot, and the veil overhanging the head provided with a star-shaped tentacular appendage on either side. The other species of this curiously-shaped genus (*D. tenellus*, Adams and Reeve,) adheres like the former to floating Fuci; crawls pretty briskly, and swims, when detached, by lateral inflexions of the body. Among the *Dorididæ*, the *Polycera cornigera*, (Adams and Reeve,) is one of the most beautiful of the family, the body being of a pale straw colour, beautifully marked with bright vermilion, which covers entirely the dorsal portion, and descends in numerous vandykes towards the foot; there is a row of bright ultramarine spots on the anterior tubercle, and another row of the same colour extending across the top of the head. A species of the genus *Hexabranchus* of Ehrenberg, which I have named *H. sanguinolentus*, is also of the most lovely colours, but yet is made to yield the palm to the type of a new genus, which may be termed *Heptabranchus*, and which I have dedicated, by permission, to Sir William Burnett, the Medical Director-General of Hospitals and Fleets. The nearest approach to this peculiar form of Dorididæ (*Heptabranchus Burnettii*,) appears to be the animal named *Doris Sandwichienne* of the "Voyage de la Bonite;"* but in that Mollusk the mantle

* Tom. 25, f. 1, 2.

entirely covers the foot, whereas in this type the foot extends beyond the mantle and behind it in the manner of a *Goniodoris*. In the above-mentioned figures of the French Naturalists, there are eight distinct branchial tufts, but in this animal there are but seven, arranged in a semicircular manner around the projecting tubular fecal orifice, so that in these singular Mollusks, the number of tufts that constitute the branchiæ seems to vary; in the beautiful *Hexabranchus prætextus* of Ehrenberg, (Symb. Phys. Mollusc. t. 1, f. 1, 2,) the branchial tufts are six in number, and emerge from six distinct apertures around the anal orifice, which, as in *Heptabranchus*, is prominent and tubular.

Tropical *Assimineas* seldom or never live entirely in the water; they love to frequent the soft muddy banks of shallow ponds in shady places, or to crawl among the roots of high grass on the low swampy banks of rivers. The *Telescopium* lives among the Mangrove-roots in brackish swamps, where, in some parts of the day, the water entirely recedes and leaves the mud bare. Miles of muddy ground beyond the range of the sea at high-water mark, and kept moistened by dull trickling rivulets, are planted with thousands of the large black *Telescopium*, with their acuminated spires sticking out of the soil, while the body and head of the animal are busily engaged in seeking for food beneath the surface. The *Terebralia* of Swainson loves the water more than the *Telescopium*, and lives nearer the sea in shallow ponds, and still, warm pools, among the tangled Mangrove-roots in the society of the *Quoyia*, or *Leucostoma* of Swainson. The *Nematura* inhabits very shallow water in still and half stagnant ponds, adhering generally to the under surface of dead and decaying leaves that float suspended in the water near the margin, but sometimes I have found them crawling very slowly on the soft muddy banks, forming slender tracks, as *Nassæ* do, in crawling over the moist sand-flats near the sea. Generally speaking the *Auricula Judæ* inhabits dark, damp woods, choosing the vicinity of water, but I have, however, found them by hundreds crawling over the moist mud of the Mangrove swamps. They are blind, and appear to be most active in the evening. At Monado, in Celebes, a species of *Assiminea* covers the perpendicular banks of the river; the mud-flats left exposed during low tide are covered with thousands of *Neritinas* and *Clithons*: *Melanias*, of the long-spired division live in the mud in shallow places with the water just covering them; while Pirenas inhabit the bed of the river in rather deeper water. Some Neritinas found by me in this island, live among the foliage of tall trees, that overhang ponds and rivulets; others cling to the roots of Nepa palms and various trees near the margin; others crawl on the stones in the water; many live in deeper water, half-buried in the mud; a few in brackish water, and others again in water perfectly salt.

Off Tampassook, several *Ixas* were obtained by the dredge. They inhabit very deep water, are feeble and inactive, and were it not for the dense solid carapace, armed with strong lateral processes with sharpened points, would be very defenceless animals. Two new species of this rare and beautiful genus have been added by us to Zoology. A new species of *Parthenope*, with large eyes and the carapace ornamented with tuberculated ridges was obtained. This genus has precisely the same habits as *Lambrus, Cryptopodia*, and others, simulating death when alarmed, and retracting its members under the carapace. A new genus the *Ceratocarcinus* (Adams and White) was obtained off Balambangan in twelve fathoms of water, having the same helpless appearance and inactivity of habits, as *Parthenope* and *Lambrus*. The species (*C. longimanus*, A. and W.) is of a blood-red colour with five light bands across the carapace. The *Cosmonotus* (Adams and White), another new genus, was obtained near Unsang, on the east coast among the clear sandy pools within the reef-barrier. It has the same habits as *Hippa* and *Remipes*. The species (*C. Grayii*, A. and W.) is of a brick-dust red colour and scarlet, minutely speckled, with white legs and chelæ. The *Notopus dorsipes* has the same habits, and the *Albunea*, like the *Hippa*, seems also to prefer the still water just within coral reefs, or the small deep pools you find on steep rocky shores. Here they swim rather rapidly in straight lines from stone to stone, or from brink to brink, when they usually rest or remain quite stationary. They seem to crawl badly, but dart, like some spiders, on their prey from among the weeds, or

"Under rocks their food in jointed armour watch."

The *Zebrida*, a new genus of Mr. White and myself, was dredged in about six fathoms from the mouth of the Pantai river, on the coast of Borneo. It is a torpid, though elegant little Crustacean, having all the apathetic peculiarities of the *Lambrus* and *Parthenope*. The species

(*Z. Adamsii,* White) is of a light pink-colour with dark red-brown longitudinal stripes. It is perfeetly smooth, polished, and hairless. *Lissocarcinus* and *Gonatonotus,* two other new Genera, besides numerous new species, were likewise obtained along this coast.

The Chitons, in the tropics, appear to be more vivacious than those found further north. If turned over on their backs they will gradually bend their calcareous jointed bodies in every direction, contracting and dilating their ventral disk until they assume their natural position. Their progressive motion is scarcely perceptible however, the principal object apparently being again to fix themselves to the surface of the rocks which Nature has given them to inhabit. Their food consists of Fuci and other Algæ, with which the rocks and stones are covered, and their excrement is solid, and formed like that of an insect iu the larva state.

Among coral masses on this north-west coast of Borneo, a large and handsomely-marked species of *Vermetus* was found, the head of which is elongated, flattened, tapering behind, broader in front where it is divided between the tentacles into two lobes; the tentacles are compressed vertically, conical in form, with the small sessile black eyes situated at their outer bases; the mantle, with a thickened rim, forms a wide loose tubular sheath around the sub-cylindrical body; the foot is circular, but without exhibiting any of those tentacular appendages usually observed in this genus, the margin being simply thickened; the operculum is large, circular, flat, and horny, with concentric elements; and, when the animal is retracted, entirely closes the aperture of the shell. The slight development of the foot indicates the sedentary nature of the animal, whose shell is firmly embedded among the madrepores. The mantle which, in the ordinary condition, is closely applied against the walls of the shell, is covered, like the entire surface of the body, with white reticulated markings upon a rich deep chesnut-brown; while the thickened fleshy rim surrounding the foot is of a delicate pink colour.

In the woods of Tampassook, the larva of a butterfly forms a curious spherical nest out of the pinnules of a species of fern. It bends down the leaflets, and fixes them ingeniously by a glutinous thread; the grub, at the time of its incarceration, feeding on the verdant walls of the cavity. I have found another larva which inhabits the pod of a species of leguminous plant, and which, having consumed its contents, forms a cocoon in the empty siliqua. Another remarkable larva, belonging to an *Oiketicus*, or *Psyche*, of the Lepidopterous family, *Arctiidæ*, forms a very remarkable case or tent out of small dry pieces of sticks and leaves, and being thus protected, crawls about the surface of the foliage, consuming the parenchymatous tissue. One of these was marbled pale yellow and black on the head and first three segments; the rest of the body straw-coloured, with two rows of small black dots on each side above the spiracles. The case was lined with a soft, loose, cottony down, composed of minutely comminuted vegetable fibre.

The animal of M. Lovèn's genus, *Cylichna*, crawls very slowly, moving by an almost imperceptible series of undulations of the foot; it has a peculiar habit of extending the head, when a somewhat slender rounded peduncle, resembling a neck, comes into view. By this means the animal is enabled to move its head about in any direction with ease and facility; the front part of the foot is short and truncate, not elongated and dilated in front, as in *Bulla aplustre* and some others, and behind it is furnished with two flattened lateral conical processes or tubercles, a peculiarity which I have not observed in any other *Bulla;* the lateral lobes appear to be entirely wanting, and the posterior lobe is concealed within the shell, which, as in *Bulla columna*, is altogether external.

The forms of *Arachnida* are as wonderful and as varied in Borneo as in other parts of the world, but their study is exceedingly difficult, and their bodies not easily preserved. In the forests, you will often perceive large species, suspended high by a single thread to the leaves and branches of the trees, of fantastically-formed *Acrosomata*, with their flattened, painted backs, and strange spiny protuberances. I discovered at Saráwak a very beautiful new species, which I have named *Acrosoma trivirgulata*. It is in form very near *Gasteracantha transversa, gemmata*, and *fornicata* (Koch, Tab. 113, fig. 259, 260, and 261,) but it is black, with three broad, transverse, yellow bands on the abdomen, with numerous faint annuli, and three bright yellow spots on the posterior part. The thighs are banded with yellowish-green, and the under surface is black, with bright oval yellow spots. Like many others, it was found suspended by a thread from a lofty tree, and, when taken, contracted its members and simulated death. The nests of these spiders are as extraordinary in form as the bodies of the spiders themselves, which, in numerous instances, they very much resemble.

The section of *Epeira* with lobed abdomens, named *Argyropes*, build beautiful webs in every part of the forest. Some of them are very handsome spiders, shining with gold and silver, and ornamented with elegant patterns of crimson and yellow. A species of *Phalangium*, with long legs of exceeding tenuity, may be frequently seen hanging by its feet to the under surface of leaves, and vibrating its body so rapidly, as to be at times undistinguishable to the eye. *Nephilæ* of enormous size spread their large nets very low in shady thickets, so that a man in penetrating the forest will become entangled and more annoyed by a spider's web than he will readily allow. It is a fact constantly brought before the notice of the observer, that those species of spiders that live on the bark of trees are mottled grey and brown, and those which you find upon the ground are altogether black or dingy-coloured; while those living among flowers have beautifully variegated bodies. How admirably, in these examples, is shown the fitness of things, maintained even between organisms usually deemed so abject, and the domains they owe to ever-careful Nature! It matters not much whether we say the place determines the nature of the animal, or whether the animal is adapted to the place, although perhaps it is more pleasing to an observer of nature to trace the harmonies and adaptations to an Intelligent Foresight, like the good St. Pierre, than to make them merely the necessary results of a physical arrangement of the earth's surface, like the ingenious author of the "Vestiges of the Natural History of Creation."

Not very far from Tampassook, while we were surveying a small bay, numbers of canoes came alongside for the first time during our examination of this part of the coast, and offered fowls, yams, and sweet-potatoes, in exchange for empty wine bottles, which they seemed to covet in an especial manner. These people were principally Malays, very poor, very dirty, and very ill-looking; they assured us, however, that they were good men and not pirates, and that their ruler or chief was a brother of Muda Hassim and of the unfortunate Budduruddin, and in the evening, a Pangeran arrived from the town, which he called Kabatuan, situated up a river of that name, informing the Captain that the Rajah was sick, and required medical assistance. I accordingly, with the permission of Sir Edward, took a seat in the Pangeran's canoe, and proceeded to visit the village. As we left the ship, I noticed that all the Malays took off their krisses and placed them under a mat, a proceeding, possibly, to remind me of their friendly intentions. Escorted by numerous canoes, we rapidly ascended the river to the distance of about eight miles, at which point I found, on tasting it, that it continued perfectly salt. Large and strong stakes were here thrown across the river, and suddenly turning short round, the boats entered a narrow creek concealed in the left bank, where there was only room for the passage of a single canoe at a time. Proceeding along this for some little distance, we suddenly emerged, and entered another reach of the Kabatuan, and after paddling for some time, came to shallow slimy mud-flats, the whole of the natives here getting out, and sliding their long canoes over the mud at a quick walking pace. Once more launched upon the stream, which here appeared a very deep river, particularly on the right bank, I noticed a very large war-prahu, similar to those in use among the Illañons, full of armed men, evidently preparing for some predatory expedition; several sailing prahus were likewise at anchor; and under a kedjang-shed I observed a large newly-built sailing boat, probably of twenty tons burden. How these craft came into this part of the river is to me a mystery, as the natives seemed to have brought me by one of the secret passages leading to their haunt or hiding-place. The town is situated among low jungle in a morass, with the river winding about it at a little distance from the central mass of houses. As I landed, a Pangeran took me by the hand and escorted me to his house, where, seated on an elevated platform, I was offered a cup of toddy and a long cigar, formed of tobacco rolled up in a plantain leaf, which I smoked to the evident gratification of some hundred Dusuns, who probably had never before seen a European. From this I was led across swampy ground, walking on narrow planks and across slender bamboo bridges, to a neatly-built square-shaped isolated edifice, where I was introduced to the Rajah, who, shaking me by the hand, begged me to be seated in an arm-chair by his side. After ascertaining that his Highness was suffering merely from the effects of a slight debauch, I prescribed something warm and stomachic, which I had brought with me. Mr. Brooke, who on his first arrival at Sarāwak, had an interview with this brother of Muda Hassim, describes him as " a sulky-looking, ill-favoured savage, with a debauched appearance, and wanting in the intelligence of his brother, the Rajah." Muda Mahommed is a very large man, inclined to corpulence, with a sensual countenance, and what gave him a somewhat peculiar appearance, was the circumstance of his wearing no handkerchief round his head, and his hair being cut quite short. The "Hall of Audience," as usual in these cases, was crammed with numbers of old, ugly, crafty-looking Malays, all squatting on their hams, with their faces turned upon their Chief; but peeping curiously in at the open doors and windows were numerous Dusuns, a wild tribe that inhabit the mountains of the northern parts of the island. The Rajah informed me, with some emotion, of the cruel murder of the noble-minded Budduruddin, and expressed himself in strong terms concerning the character of Pangeran Usop, and concluded by hoping that Sir Edward Belcher would proceed at once to Brunai, avenge the death of his brother, and destroy the city. He asked me, moreover, if I did not remember his younger brother to whom he presented me, and I recognised him as having formed one of the suite of Muda Hassim. Reposing in picturesque attitudes upon the ground, or leaning on their shields, and conversing in little groups around this so-called palace, were some dozen Dusuns, a handsome and prepossessing race of aboriginal Dyaks, whose name implies, according to Mr. Brooke, that they are an agricultural people, having a peculiar dialect of their own. In person, the Dusuns are about the average stature of Malays and Dyaks, that is below the height of the generality of Europeans, and their forms appeared to me very symmetrical and well-proportioned, particularly when contrasted with the large-headed, bow-legged Malays, who seemed to regard them with supreme contempt, not permitting them to enter and join in their conference. The colour of their skin struck me as being very peculiar, being of a dark, blackish, dull brown, more resembling that of the natives of some parts of Hindostan than of Malays and Dyaks in general; their countenances have a very mild, agreeable, and open expression, quite different either from the sharp cunning peculiar to the tribes of Serebus and Sekarran, or the grotesque good humour of the wild, broad-faced Orang Sagai; their eyes are large, clear, and expressive; their noses straight and prominent, but having the alæ considerably developed; and their mouths well formed, and not too large; their teeth are filed straight, concave externally, and stained black. In those I saw, the hair was worn long behind, and flowing down the back, cut straight in front across the forehead, and confined by a single fillet of white bark-cloth. I did not observe that the bodies of any among them were tattooed. The most extraordinary peculiarity, however, about these *indigines*, was the circumstance of their thighs, and loins, in particular, being encircled by great numbers of thick, bright, polished, wire rings, which rattled as they moved, and gave them a very singular appearance. Similar rings depended from the lobes of their ears, and were worn around their necks. They carried large shields, formed of wood, and ornamented with tufts of hair, and were armed with sumpitan and parang.

CHAPTER X.

MAURITIUS TO ENGLAND.

Scenery and Vegetation of Mauritius—Æstivation of Tropical Mollusca—Great Indian Tortoise—Habits of the Dolabella—Singular species of Bullæa —St. Brandon Shoals—The Cocoa-nut—Aspect of the reef and islets — Sea-birds — Their habits and nidification — Instinct in Fish—Animal of Ancillaria—Pelagic skeleton Crustacea—Anomalous Zoæas —Cypridina Adamsii—Habits of Janthina——The Carinaria and Atlanta—The Hyalæa and Cleodora—The habits and development of the Argonaut—Insects at Sea—Concluding Remarks.

MAURITIUS, so famous for its mountain of Peter Bott, so immortalised by the sweet tale of Paul and Virginia, and so interesting to Zoologists in being the probable birth-place of that monstrous extinct pigeon, the Dodo, is certainly a very beautiful island, abounding in scenery of the most varied and delightful description, any attempt to expatiate upon which, after St. Pierre's glowing pictures, would be presumptuous. To fully enjoy his exquisite little narrative, one should make a sentimental pilgrimage, and wander from the Shaddock Grove to the river of Fan-palms, from Cape Misfortune to the Alley of Bamboos, and from the Pass of Saint Geran to the bay of the Tomb, and what one misses in sentiment, might be gained in contemplating the sweet scenery of the island. No wonder such a charming spot should have changed names and masters so often, with such advantages in climate, situation, and productiveness. It has been called Swan Island by the Portuguese, Mauritius by the Dutch, and Isle of France by "La Grande Nation," for each has held it in rotation, and now the British Lion's paw is on it. In the general character of its vegetation, Mauritius is somewhat similar to that of the Cape in the number of succulent plants, Cactuses, Spurges, Aloes, House-leeks, Fig-marigolds, &c. Many plants from Europe, Africa, Madagascar, and India are acclimated, and flourish well. Among others I noticed the *Cycas circinalis, Chrysanthemum Indicum*, and the *Argemone Mexicana*, which notwithstanding its name, is very common, and when in flower, its large yellow petals and glaucous prickly leaves have a very pretty appearance. Shady groves of Mango and dense masses of *Mimosa* are met with, in short, nearly every beautiful tree of the tropics. While staying at Port Louis, I accompanied Sir Edward Belcher and Sir David Barclay some miles into the interior, and spent a very delightful day at Sir David's country house, a pleasant villa situated half-way up a mountain, and surrounded with beautiful grounds. Numbers of flowers, natives both of India and Europe, flourished luxuriantly in the garden; the dry, prickly-leaved Euphorbia of Madagascar, with the succulent-leaved Mesembryanthemums of the African coast; the sweet Rose of Persia, with the wild flowers peculiar to the island. The Heliotrope in dense masses, and the sweet-scented Verbena in hedges, were contrasted with Mimosas, Cassias, and Palm-trees. A stream of clear water from the mountains ran through a channel, and filled tanks in various parts where numerous Physas, Succineas, and Water-beetles were observed. In the wilderness at the back of the villa, fine oaks formed natural summer-houses, and groups of large trees, natives of the Mauritius, were mingled with the Gourd and Coffee-tree. In the holes of tree trunks, and under the decayed mass of leaves which strewed the ground, we found numbers of a large *Achatina* in a state of hibernation. The large *Achatina* of the Mauritius, during æstivation, forms a strong, dense white epiphragma during the dry season, and conceals itself either in holes of decayed trees or under the surface of the soil; the *Megalomastoma* of Mindoro closes its shell with its round horny operculum, and congregates in numbers in fissures of trees some distance from the ground; the *Cerithium truncatum*, in Singapore and Borneo, suspends itself by glutinous threads to dead sticks on the margins of rivers; the *Caracolla* of the Philippines, hides under loose bark, where it adheres very closely; the *Cyclostomata* and *Scarabi* bury themselves under the stratum of dead leaves with which the ground is always covered; the *Assimineæ, Melaniæ,* and *Ampullariæ,* conceal themselves in the soft mud of ponds and rivers; the *Nematura* adheres firmly to floating sticks, and to the under surface of leaves in stagnant pools; the snails glue themselves together, as they do in England, and congregate in holes of rotten trunks; the *Bulimi* adhere firmly to smooth branches and boles of trees; and the *Helicinæ* to the under surface of leaves generally in an elevated situation. The *Potomis* and *Telescopium* bury themselves in the muddy Mangrove swamps, many *Neritinæ* do the same thing, and I have noticed in the island of Basilan a dark-brown species of *Conohelix*, which conceals itself also in the soft mud, several inches below the surface, among the roots of the *Rhizophora Mangle* above high-water mark.

Man is not the only animal which has wandered by chance or inclination from the old to the new world. The great black Indian Tortoise, originally a native of Madagascar and the Mauritius, is identical with that species whose habits have been so admirably alluded to by Mr. Charles Darwin, who describes it as inhabiting the low islands of the Galapagos Archipelago. It is likewise found in California, and I believe has been met with in other parts of the west coast of South America. A gigantic specimen of this Tortoise made a voyage to England in the 'Samarang,' but unfortunately died shortly after its arrival, in consequence, probably, of injuries received during a gale in the Bay of Biscay.

The *Dolabellæ* seem to love the still and rather shallow water of creeks near the sea, where they congregate under large stones, and in deeper water remain fixed by their ventral disks to the surfaces and sides of submerged rocks, in a collapsed and motionless state. They prefer a gravelly or stony bottom, and at the rising of the tide I have seen them crawl pretty briskly towards the shore, when they proceed to the small shallow pools to feed upon the sea-weed that abounds there. Having instructed the boat's crew where to find the animal, and its appearance, they waded up to their waists and soon returned with considerable numbers of very large specimens which were all deposited in a pool together, so that I had ample opportunities of drawing and observing them.

In a remarkable form of *Bullæa,* found on the shores of this island, the anterior lobe or cephalic disk is entirely destitute of eyes or tentacular appendages; it is thin, broad, flattened, dilated in front, on the same plane as the foot, and continuous on either side with the lateral lobes; posteriorly where it joins the posterior lobe, it is deeply indented, as in most *Bullidæ.* The lateral lobes, large, extended, and fitted for natation, partially overlap the posterior lobe, are on the same plane with the foot, continuous in front with the indistinct head, and end behind in a broad, truncated border, which is notched in the centre. The posterior lobe which lodges the shell, and contains the viscera, is rounded above, partly enveloped by the lateral lobes, and slightly notched behind.

L'île Saint-Brande, situated to the north-east of Rodriguez, called the Saint-Brandon Shoals by the English, and Cargados Garajos by the Portuguese, has derived a few cocoa-nut trees from the latter island, which in its turn obtained them from the Mauritius, according to St. Pierre, who relates that when the philosopher François Seguat and his unfortunate companions, formed in 1690 the first inhabitants of that little island, there were no cocoa-nut trees on their arrival; but as if Providence had invited them to remain there and cultivate it, the useful and agreeable present of several germinating cocoa-nuts was thrown ashore by the waves. He observes, moreover, that these two islands although situated in the course of a current, which, during the year, runs alternately, six months towards one and six months towards the other, had not communicated all the plants peculiar to each. In the course of time all the small, scattered islets of this extensive shoal will become united, and constitute one large island covered with cocoa-nut trees. Well then, may we exclaim with Mr. Crawfurd when speaking of that vegetable blessing, the cocoa-nut: "How wonderful to discover this useful plant silently propagated over many thousand leagues, among hundreds of barbarous tribes of dissimilar languages, whose very names and situations are unknown to each other!" How extremely fortunate is the curious fact that the cocoa-nut should grow the easiest, and thrive the most luxuriantly, always near the sea coast, and with what pains has Nature, to ensure a safe passage to the tender embryo, encased it in a strong thick husk that will remain uninjured when dashed upon the shore by the billows!

The general aspect of these small islets, thus formed out of a huge reef in the middle of the ocean, is by no means inviting. It is a wild and barren scene. The soil is sand, and ornamented only by a few stunted shrubs; the sullen ocean roars in the distance, and breaks over the barren reef, and upon the beaches of the islands, in vast rolling surges, while screaming all around, flocks of snow-white tern, and long-winged gulls hover over the water, or cover the bare ground as they sit brooding over their eggs.

On some of the low islets you could not walk without crushing the marbled eggs, or treading on the callow young, of Tern, Petrels, and Noddies. One species of *Puffinus*, allied to *P. fuliginosa*, sleeps, by day, in burrows formed by its feet in the sand, at the bottom of which it deposits a milk-white egg, as large as a duck's. It frequents the centre of the islands, and howls most dismally all night long, making a mournful noise, like the cooings of doves, mingled with the wailings of the Chacal. A beautiful *Sterna*, black above and white beneath, also lays a mottled egg in the middle of the islands, about two feet apart, on the bare ground. The female sits on the egg and defends it stoutly. The young are spotted white and brown, and run like little Partridges.

Another large, dark, ash-coloured species frequents the vicinity of the sea, and lays a large, oval, white egg, among the loose stones, near the shore. The young are sometimes white, sometimes grey, and often black.

Another *Sterna* of smaller size, dark ash-coloured, with a lighter coloured head, builds in the middle of the islands, among the low bushes, constructing a rude kind of nest of straw and leaves, forming a sort of platform. It deposits one mottled egg, the size of a Pigeon's. The young are grey or whitish. A small white species lays a single egg (mottled and marbled,) close to the water's edge, on a flat stone, quite exposed and unprotected. The young are snowy-white, though occasionally greyish. With all this incubation going on around, I could not help thinking of Milton's description of a somewhat similar scene, where he alludes to the birds in his "Paradise Lost,"

> "Hatching their numerous brood from th' egg, that soon,
> Bursting with kindly rupture, forth disclos'd
> Their callow young, but feathered soon, and fledge,
> They summ'd their pens, and soaring th' air sublime,
> With clang despised the ground, under a cloud
> In prospect."

The Saint Brandon Shoals, abound with fish of every description, which afforded a rich treat to the ship's company, who caught them in large numbers, alongside.

Among others, I noticed Pomfret, Rock-cod, a species of *Gadus*, of a splendid red, covered with round ultramarine spots; the handsome *Diploprion bifasciatum*, a small species of Tunny, a *Pelamis* with transverse green bands, several kinds of Sharks, the *Serranus hexagonatus*, and a splendid *Serranus* of a chrome yellow, with broad blackish bands. Snappers, marked with blue and yellow, and with silvery bodies, and several species of *Pelamis, Poropsis, Lethrinus, Chætodon, Balistes, Chrysophris,* and *Mugil.*

Saint Pierre, after alluding to the cunning of certain flat fish which bury their large fins in the sand, and show only their cheating side when the tide has receded, and left them to await patiently its flowing, and thus elude the notice of the fishermen, makes the following remark with much glee: " C'est ce que je leur ai vu faire plus d'une fois, encore plus émerveillé de la ruse de ces poissons, que de celle des pêcheurs." The large Ray, which was captured on the Saint Brandon Shoals after a hard struggle, was of a bluish sand colour, and its back studded with white tubercles, thus resembling very much in appearance the bottom of the sandy coral patch on which it lived; and a Skate pursued by a boat's crew over a muddy flat in very shallow water at Basilan, was of a dirty yellow brown, precisely the same colour as the place it was accustomed to inhabit. I have noticed that among low coral reefs where *Pleuronectes* are frequently found, their tails are often ornamented with rather vivid colours, and their upper sides marked with somewhat striking patterns, whereas those that are half buried, as for instance in Manilla Bay, are as dull and dingy, as the surface in which they are found.

The nature of the animal of *Ancillaria* appears to be not very well understood. M. Rang observes: "Animal furnished with a lobe of the mantle covering the shell, in other respects unknown." (Manuel de Mollusques, p. 227.) Mr. Gray, founding his opinion on the figures of M. Quoy, observes: "The shell is nearly sunk in the very large expanded foot of the animal, which is deeply cut in on each side in front. The siphon alone is exserted." It appeared to me, however, when examining these animals, numerous living specimens of which were dredged by us on the east coast of Africa, that the lateral lobes or processes which partially envelope the shell, are precisely analogous to those of the *Bulla*, and are as much entitled to be called the mantle, as are the loose expanded lateral folds which cross upon the back of the *Aplysia*. These alar expansions of the mantle are enormously dilated, the right one is generally longer than the left posteriorly, and both curl upwards and inwards during the ordinary progression of the animal, and folding themselves on the shell, almost entirely conceal it from view. At the anterior part, they are in close juxta-position, in the middle they slightly overlap each other, and posteriorly they are rounded and open, and projecting beyond the spire, form a loose, open sac. Anteriorly, the foot is produced, as in *Natica* and *Bulla*, forming a cephalic disc, which however is divided by a deep furrow or groove into two triangular lobes, and separated from the lateral portions of the foot by deep lateral clefts or fissures; behind, the foot is slightly cleft or bilobate, and below, it is furnished with a furrow in the median line, and is smooth, wide, and provided with a slimy, mucous secretion, another peculiarity in which it resembles *Bulla*. I have no doubt, moreover, that occasionally the lateral membranous expansions are horizontally extended, and that the animal is enabled to swim in the same manner, as I have mentioned, as peculiar to some of the *Bulla* tribe. The *Ancillariæ* crawl with a sliding motion, and with considerable celerity. As they glide briskly along, the tubular cylindrical siphon only is visible. It is directed backwards and upwards, and sometimes is laid flat on the back of the animal; while the two triangular lobes placed anterior to the foot, are extended laterally, and in front moving about and exploring the ground like tentacles, and no doubt serving the same purpose. It is rather surprising that such an active Mollusk as the *Ancillaria*, should have been apparently deprived by Nature of sight, no eyes being visible to my observation in the specimens I kept alive. The species which were dredged by us from a sandy bottom, and in about fourteen fathoms water, were of a dirty-white colour, with dull, brown, elongated, oval blotches, rather sparsely and irregularly distributed. In the enormous size of the foot, and its being prolonged anteriorly and transversely lobed in front, and in the shell being partly concealed in the body of the animal, *Ancillaria* resembles *Natica*.

Among the pelagic skeleton Crabs may be ranked the genera *Erichthus* and *Alima*, curious transparent shrimp-like creatures, with spiny shields and elongated tails. I have detected, among the number of those we obtained, many new species. They are erratic and restless little animals, and swarm on the surface of the Atlantic, when the water is calm and tranquil. The *Phronima*, another genus allied to them, is very frequently found inside the hollow, transparent bodies of the *Beroe* and other Medusæ, but whether the *Phronima* employs these *Acalephæ* as canoes to sail about in, or whether it lives parasitic on their bodies, or feeds on the animalcules contained in them, I am unable to determine. The *Rhabdosoma armatum* (Adams and White) had been hitherto found only in the sea between Amboyna and Van Dieman's land. The head of this extraordinary Crustacean is terminated by a snout or beak nearly as long as the body, and the tail is furnished with three stylets as long as the muzzle, which, added to its elongated form and enormous eyes, makes it look like some imaginary fabrication, rather than a normal production of Nature. It swims by suddenly straightening its stick-like body when in a bent position, and moves either backwards or forwards. It is sluggish in its motions compared with other *Hyperiadæ*. Another genus is allied to *Vibilia* (Milne Edwards,) but has a more slender conformation, and wants the thickened and cylindrical superior antennæ; the four last segments of the body, moreover, are more elongated, and differ from the rest. The *Phyllosomata*, with their foliaceous, transparent carapaces, and diaphanous members, and of which we have observed one or two new species, move about like the ghosts of Stomapods. They are apathetic and sluggish, notwithstanding their eyes being well-developed, and their organization pretty complex, and in calm weather may be taken with a net in large numbers floating on the surface of the sea. Despite the fifteen species enumerated by Edwards, those described by M. Guèrin in the Voyage de la Coquille and Mag. de Zool. for 1833, and those that exist in the British Museum, there still remains much to be known before a perfect monograph of the *Phyllostomatidæ* can be formed.

Notwithstanding that Crustaceology abounds in forms sufficiently bizarre, those very singular paradoxes, the *Zoeæ*, exceed them all in curious and fantastic shapes. One form, which I have provisionally christened *Zoea-boops*, would serve as an excellent model for a grotesque monster in a pantomime: in fact, they all more resemble phantasms than the ordinary organizations we are in the habit of contemplating. I have noticed and figured several varieties, and from the constant recurrence of regular types among them, I should be inclined to doubt the accuracy of Dr. Thompson's opinion, that these whimsical-looking beings are merely the larvæ of different kinds of Crabs; and this more particularly, as the Zoeæ are generally found in the high seas, where few of the larger Crustacea are ever discovered, were it not for the investigations of Rathké on the development of the *Astacus fluviatilis*, and the additional testimony of Capt. Du Cane and M. Joly, who have obtained similar results. I can with certainty affirm that *Megalopa* is no true genus, as 1 have observed specimens in every stage of growth between the common type of *Megalopa* and that of ordinary Brachyarous Crustacea. Among Entomostracous Crustaceans, small animals with natatory feet terminating in two branches, and belonging to that division named *Cyproides*, the bodies of which are enclosed in a conchiform carapace, which causes them occasionally to be mistaken for bivalve Mollusca, were several individuals of the genus *Cypridina*, distinguished by having two elongated eyes situated in the median line, about the middle of their carapace. These rare and interesting little animals have been ascertained by Dr. Baird, who has studied profoundly this little known and difficult branch of Zoology, to be specifically distinct, and he has done me the honour to dedicate them to me under the name of *Cypridina Adamsii;* they are the third and largest species known.

The eyes of *Ianthina* are very minute, and terminal at the end of a peduncle, the animal, in this respect, and in having a long extensile proboscis and divided foot, resembles a Strombus. In the act of swimming, the dilated natatory appendages of the mantle are kept fully expanded, but I never observed them used in the same manner as the alar expansions of the *Hyalæa*, although, doubtless, in their progression through the water, their use is very great. The vesicular float adhering to the posterior flattened division of the foot, which is considered by some to be an extraordinary form of operculum, has the egg-sacs attached by short peduncles to the surface, and the female *Ianthina* appears to have the power of detaching that portion of the float to which the nidamental sacs are fixed, which then remains suspended on the surface of the water, where, exposed to the influence of heat and light, the ova undergo their ultimate development. Although we found these beautiful Mollusks cast up by thousands on the shores of the Meïa-co-shimahs, I never observed them make the slightest effort to crawl, but have frequently noticed them adhering together in masses, attached by the anterior part of the foot, which acts as a sucker. In company with the thousands of *Ianthina* swimming on the surface of the South Atlantic, were innumerable little fish of the genera *Gonostoma*, *Ichthyococcus*, and *Scopelus*, some of which were of singular forms, and, in general, of a steel colour. Among the pelagic heteropodous Mollusks, which we found, in crossing the South Atlantic ocean, were vast numbers of *Atlantæ*, and numerous *Carinariæ*. They are crepuscular animals, like the *Pteropods*, and are furnished with hyaline shells, of the greatest delicacy and beauty. The *Atlanta*, with an elegant, glassy, spiral, carinated shell, globose in one species, and flattened in the other, is quite a sprightly little Mollusk, probing every object within its reach by means of its elongated trunk, twisting its body about, and swimming in every direction, by the lateral movements of its vertical, dilated foot. I have frequently seen them descend to the bottom of the glass vessel in which they were kept, fix themselves there in the manner of a leech, by their sucking disc, and carefully examine the nature of their prison-house, by protruding the front portion of the foot in every direction. The shell of the globose species (*Helicophlegma Keraudrenii* of D'Orbigny,) is nearly membranous, and becomes opaque and shrivelled on exposure to the air; the compressed species (*Atlanta Peronii* of Lesueur,) has a firmer and more vitreous shell. Lamanon, one of the Naturalists who accompanied La Pérouse, considered the *Atlanta* to represent the shells of those extinct fossil shells the Ammonites, to which, however, it has but a faint resemblance. Although it is perfectly true that pelagic Mollusks generally swim on their backs, in a reversed position, as *Ianthina*, *Firola*, *Carinaria*, and *Atlanta*, yet, in figuring them, the analogy of the parts is better represented by placing them in the position most common to animals of this class. Thus the species of *Scyllæa, Doris*, &c., are never represented in a reversed position; nor are snails that lead an arboreal existence. The vertical expanded part of the body of *Carinaria* and *Atlanta* is sometimes erroneously regarded as a fin; and in the figures of Rang, Blainville, and De la Chiage, which are in an inverted position, this idea would, in the eyes of the uninitiated, be confirmed. Although I have myself frequently seen them swimming in this reversed position after capture, they frequently progress feebly with the shell uppermost. When fresh and just taken, I have seen both the *Carinariæ* and *Atlantæ* swim with their bodies in every position on their sides, on their backs, and with the foot downwards. The *Carinariæ* are swift and rapid in their movements, and dart forwards by a continuous effort, moving their foot and caudal appendage from side to side, as a powerful natatory organ, and do not progress by sudden jerks, like the *Atlanta* and *Hyalæa*. In these particulars, my observations are conformable with the statements of M. Rang. The true analogue of the foot of Gasteropods in *Atlanta* and *Carinaria* is the sucking disc placed at the posterior part of the vertically-flattened appendage of the body, but its use is circumscribed to that of enabling the animal to anchor itself temporarily to floating bodies when fatigued, therein offering an analogy to the gasteropodous genera of *Notarchus* and *Scyllæa*, which cling, in the same manner, with the back downwards, to floating sea-weed. The shell of the *Carinaria*, like that of the *Testacella* and *Cryptostoma*, covers only a small portion of the body of the animal, defending the more delicate organs; and in this we see a wise provision for permitting these pelagic Mollusks to move freely about, without being encumbered with a dense, heavy skeleton. M. Rang offers, as a generic character, the constant presence of asperities on the mantle; but I think this will hardly serve, as I have figured a species from the South Atlantic, which I believe to be new, which is perfectly smooth, and totally devoid of any processes on the mantle.

The mantle of *Cleodora*, like that of *Hyalæa*, is very much dilated, and forms two swimming appendages, and the intermediate lobe is semicircular; but there are no elongated lateral expansions similar to those that emerge from the slits in the side of *Hyalæa*. In many figures of these animals, the swimming lobes are represented as varying in form in different species, but from my observations, I should say that the lobes, vandykes, and foldings of the margin, are purely accidental contractions, and that commonly the margins are entire. The animal of *Cleodora Byzantium* has, when alive, the two swimming expansions very much elongated laterally, rather slender and rounded at their free extremities. In *C. cuspidata*, they are shorter and rounded. The *Hylææ*, no doubt, like the *Amphibia* among the reptiles, respire by the entire cutaneous surface, which is so soft and permeable; although, it is true, they have distinct breathing organs, disposed in the form of an oval ring, between two layers of the mantle on the dorsal region, which are open, to receive currents of water transmitted by the lateral apertures of the shell. The long, loose, lateral, pallial prolongations, which these testaceous Pteropods protrude from the lateral fissures of the shell, do not appear to be of much use in guiding or propelling, which functions are performed by the wide alar expansions. They may assist, however, in extending the surface of the mantle for the purpose of aëration.

On our passage home, I had numerous opportunities of observing the animals of *Argonauta tuberculosa*, and *A. hians*, in the living state, both species having been captured by us in large numbers by means of a trawl as they came to the surface of the South Atlantic, in calm weather, at the decline of day, in company with *Carinaria, Hyalæa, Firola*, and *Cleodora*. My observations all tend to prove, as might have been expected, the accuracy of Madame Power and M. Rang, and the fanciful nature of the statements of Pliny, Poli, and the poets. It is quite true that the female Argonaut can readily disengage herself from the shell, when the velamentous arms become collapsed, and float apparently useless on each side of the animal, and it is equally certain that she has not the ability or perhaps the sagacity, to enter her nest again, and resume the guardianship of her eggs. On the contrary, she herself, if kept in confinement, after darting and wounding herself against the sides of the vessel she is confined in, soon becomes languid, and very shortly dies. Numbers of male Argonauts were taken by us, at the same time, without any shells, and this being the season of ovoposition, may account for the females, in such a number of instances, being found embracing their shell-nests. As a convincing proof that the thin shell of the Argonaut is employed by the female as a safe receptacle in which to deposit her eggs, I dissected a specimen of *Argonauta tuberculosa*, which was firmly embracing the shell, which contained a large mass of eggs occupying the discoidal portion of the chamber, and the posterior portion of the roof.* The eggs very numerous, ovoid, pale-yellow, and semipellucid, are all united together by a delicate, glutinous, transparent, filamentous web which is attached to each ovum by a slender, tapering peduncle fixed to one extremity. The entire egg-mass is suspended to the body-whorl of the spire, at its anterior part, by means of a pencil of delicate glutinous threads, which retain it in a proper position.

On my return to England, I had an opportunity of examining the figures which Poli has given us in his magnificent work, "Testacea utriusque Siciliæ," where he has represented the egg-mass, though not *in situ*, but unravelled.† He observes regarding this body: "Ovorum congeries eboris nitorem æmulantium, partim jam ab ovario emissa, ac racemorum instar composita, cymbæ puppi involutæ adhærebat.‡" Professor Owen, in his Lectures on Invertebrate Animals, mentions the same fact; he observes that "in the Argonaut, the minute ova are appended by long filamentary stalks to the cavity of the involuted spire of the shell, where they are hatched.**

The posterior, globular part of the body of the female is in close opposition to the mass of ova, and thus, like a strange aquatic *Mygale*, or other spider, does this remarkable Cephalopod carry about her eggs in a light

---

* This calcareous nest of the Argonaut, so ingeniously formed by the instinct of the mother for the purpose of protecting her eggs from injury, thus resembles, in some measure, those nidimental capsules secreted by many marine Gasteropods for the preservation of the immature embryos.

† Tab. xli. f. 2.

‡ p. 10.

** Lect. on Comp. Anat. of Inv. An. p. 360.

calcareous nest, which she firmly retains possession of by means of the broad, expanded, delicate membranes of the posterior pair of tentacles. When disturbed or captured, however, she loosens her hold, and leaving her cradle to its fate, swims about independent of her shell. There is not, indeed, the slightest vestige of any muscular attachment. In the specimen from which I made the drawings which will be given in the "Zoology of the Samarang," the ovary was distended with ova, but in a much less advanced stage of development than those deposited in the shelly nidus. Some of these latter were sufficiently matured to enable me to trace, under the microscope, the early indications of the being of the Argonaut, and although I have not followed the process very far, it is sufficient to ascertain the similarity, in a great measure, with the changes observed by Poli in the same genus, with whose remarks I have compared my own: the only difference, of any importance, appears to be, that Poli has regarded as the shell what I have called the yolk-bag. At first, the ova are semi-opaque, pale-yellow, and apparently minutely speckled, which is owing to the granular yolk seen through the delicate shell of the egg; afterwards, they become clouded with light brown blotches, and three dark spots make their appearance, one for each eye, and one for the viscera; these spots, in the next stage, approach each other, and a faint outline of the future Argonaut is perceived in the form of a club-shaped embryo, rounded in front and tapering behind; the front part then becomes lobed, a black mark for the horny mandibles is perceived, and the eyes become large and prominent. The yolk-bag or vitellus, is next seen very distinctly, and the processes, extending from the head, are become more elongated. Here, however, I was obliged to stop, this being the most perfectly-developed embryo I could find among the ova. The eggs in contact with the front part of the discoidal portion of the shell, where the egg-mass is attached by the glutinous threads, are the most forward in their development, while those in the posterior part of the chamber, are much less matured. Poli's account of the development of the ova is as follows: "Ova quæ in primis eburneo candore nitebant, tenui veluti nubecula perfundebantur; mox bina puncta subrubentia hinc et illinc sese conspicienda præbuerunt in regione oculorum eaque deinceps protuberantia evadebant. His perfectis, aliud punctum eodem colore perfusum prope ovi fastigium oculos supereminens apparuit: quod quidem oris embrionem satis luculenter ostendebat."*

There is considerable difference between the animals of *Argonauta tuberculosa* and *A. hians*. In the *A. tuberculosa* the sac-like mantle is more ovoid and elongated; the head is narrower; the infundibulum is broader, shorter, and furnished, at the upper and anterior extremity, with two conical prolongations; the eyes are considerably larger, and slightly more prominent; the tentacular arms are much shorter in comparison, and of greater width, more particularly at their basal portions. The suckers are much larger, more prominent, and placed closer together. This species varies also considerably in colour from *A. hians*. The extremities of the brachia are marbled with deep redbrown; and, in the other parts, are covered with large

---

* Test. utriusq. Siciliæ, &c., p. 10.

irregular, oval, reddish blotches, each margined with a dark colour. The circumference of the suckers is marked with brown spots. The upper surface of the infundibulum is covered with pale pink, rather scattered, and irregular quadrate blotches, margined with a dark red-brown. The mantle, on the dorsal surface, is densely sprinkled with round and square spots of a chesnut-brown and crimson, of different sizes. The velamenta are minutely punctulated with crimson and red brown, and have a more bluish tinge than those of *A. hians*. The under surface is mottled and punctulated with dark chocolate on the arms, and on the body, is marked with small, irregular, dark, red-brown spots. In *Argonauta hians*, the body is more globose, and broader from side to side, the head is much wider, and the tentacles are narrower and more elongated. The suckers are less elevated, smaller in comparison, and situated at a greater distance from each other. The mantle is covered with round spots and longitudinal linear markings, of a bright crimson colour. The entire animal wants the brown, dark appearance produced by the markings of *A. tuberculosa*, and is of a lighter tinge and more delicate appearance.

The following Epigram of Callimachus on a Nautilus which addresses Venus, on having been deposited by Selene as a votive offering of maidenhood in her temple, though often alluded to by writers on Natural History, has not, so far as I am aware, been hitherto rendered into English. My readers are indebted for the present version to my brother, Mr. Ernest Adams, who informs me that it was the custom of the Greek girls, on arriving at years of discretion, to consecrate to Venus the playthings of their childhood:

> "Once as a sailor-shell I sported o'er
> The azure wave: but now on Smyrna's shore,
> Cypris, I grace thy shrine—the darling toy
> Of fair Selene and her childhood's joy.
> If wandering winds breathed soft, my tiny sail
> Was duly spread to catch the summer gale:
> If golden calm upon the waters came
> My nimble feet were oars; and hence my name:*
> I cast myself on Julis' shore, that thou
> Mightst glory, Cypris, in the maiden's vow.
> No radiant Halcyon now with azure crest
> Will seek my chambers for its sunny nest.
> Thank fair Selene, then, whose virtues grace
> The city of her proud Æolian race."

Becalmed off the African coast, some hundred miles from the land, large numbers of insects were perceived floating on the surface of the water, some *Acrydia* and *Locusts* being still alive. A large species of *Colymbetes* was taken quite perfect; but other singular forms, as *Coreus*, &c., were more or less injured by the action of the water. These were blown by the off-shore breeze, most probably from flat, sandy tracts, where there is but little shelter and few trees. More than one species of *Halobates* was seen swimming on the calm water, in the manner of *Gerris* and *Geometra*, by sudden jerks. This insect however appears, if not pelagic, to be at least altogether marine.

* Polypus—many-footed.

CONCLUDING REMARKS.

"When a traveller returneth home," says Bacon, "let him not leave the countries where he hath travelled altogether behind him." Acting up to this excellent advice, I have, in the preceding Journal, written at the time, and generally on the spot, thrown together notes on the habits of various animals, and a few ethnographical and physical remarks on the inhabitants of the countries visited during the expedition of the Samarang; and with these I have interspersed, here and there, desultory botanical observations, and short descriptions of natural scenery. Being but an amateur Naturalist, and not extensively acquainted with the bibliography of Zoological science, I have seldom ventured to give more than the name of the generic group to which the animals I have alluded to, respectively belong. The scientific results of the voyage will be brought before the public in the "Zoology of the Samarang," now preparing for publication.

The researches of various nations in the Indian Archipelago, and among the islands of the Chinese Seas, instituted by the wise liberality of European governments, or suggested by the pious zeal of philanthropic men, have been gradually revealing numerous interesting and important phenomena in the history of that comparatively unknown world. The wonderful and mysterious forms of animal and vegetable life that enliven those ocean-gardens, and the physical and social peculiarities of the various tribes that inhabit them, are daily becoming more familiar to the reading public. Our political connexion with the Chinese coast, has invested the numerous tribes, that throng the approaches to their ports, with an interest they never possessed before; and the recent cession of Labuan has, perhaps, laid the foundation of a British interest in those seas, that may materially interest the future destinies of our eastern possessions.

All over the world Creative Intelligence has thrown organic matter into living forms of such interest and beauty, that the "divina particula animi," which renders man

> "Lord of the wide world and wat'ry seas,
> Endu'd with intellectual sense and soul,"

cannot fail to observe them, and, having observed, to appreciate, and endeavour to make others appreciate them. Now, being engaged in the survey of seas hitherto but imperfectly explored, and in the examination of islands, many of them barely known beyond their existence on the charts, it is hardly to be wondered at, that our harvest has been plentiful and our researches crowned with success. And really, when among those chosen individuals, who are destined, "mid sands, and rocks, and storms, to cruise for pleasure," I observe any of their number pass unheeded by such golden opportunities as they might enjoy, I am apt to exclaim with Beattie's Minstrel,—

> "O, how canst thou renounce the boundless store
> Of charms which Nature to her votary yields!
> * * * * * *
> O, how canst thou renounce, and hope to be forgiven!"

Keen perceptions of the sublime and beautiful in nature, constitute in an intelligent mind one of the most pleasurable sources of human enjoyment; and I agree with what Pythagoras is reported to have said in his conversation with Leontius, that "as there is nothing more noble than to be a spectator without any personal interest, so, in this life, the contemplation and knowledge of nature are infinitely more honourable than any other application." My opportunities of ascertaining the existence, and defining the limits, of those centres of organization said to exist on the surface of the earth, and which researches into the geographical distribution of plants and animals tend to elucidate, have been very limited; indeed a Naturalist, in a ship, may be compared to a bird of passage, which, reposing here and there in the course of its flight, gathers a stray grain or so, and is off in a moment; nor must the remark of Bernardin de Saint-Pierre be lost sight of:—"La nature est infiniment étendue, et je suis un homme très-borné."*

With reference to the natural history of the Philippines, that sagacious and most indefatigable traveller, Hugh Cuming, Esq., has anticipated us in many points; and in the China Seas, the elaborate researches of De Haan and others, have left us little more to do than follow in their footsteps. A parting word in extenuation of the style I have adopted in the preceding Summary, and I respectfully take my leave. It is, I think, right, that in the present reading age, the Naturalist should impart to the

* The multifarious avocations of the Naturalist are thus pleasantly alluded to in a letter written by De Lamanon, one of the unfortunate Zoologists of the Expedition of La Pérouse: "I have fish to anatomize, quadrupeds to describe, insects to catch, shells to class, events to relate, mountains to measure, stones to collect, languages to study, experiments to make, a journal to write, and Nature to contemplate."

public some of the amenities of science, as well as those results of graver studies, which can necessarily be appreciated by but few. What a pleasant halo, for example, has Darwin thrown around the Linnæan system of Botanical arrangement, by bestowing on us his " Botanic Garden!" White of Selbourne, Waterton, and Mudie have bestowed the same bright charm on Ornithology, Johnson on Zoophytes, and Mantell on Geology. It savours of melancholy to admire beauty only in terminologies, and, as Alfred Tennyson observes,

> " See no divinity in grass,
> Life in dead stones, or spirit in air."

www.ingramcontent.com/pod-product-compliance
Lightning Source LLC
Chambersburg PA
CBHW082058230426
43670CB00017B/2887